POLAND

Irena and Jerzy Kostrowicki

POLAND

Landscape and Architecture

Arkady, Warsaw 1980

ISBN 83-213-2980-2

More than a thousand years ago, the Polish state came into being in the area between the Carpathian and Sudety (Sudeten) Mts. in the south and the Baltic Sea in the north and between the rivers Odra in the west and the Bug in the east, as the result of the unification of related West Slav tribes. A decisive part was played in this process by the Polanie (Polanes), who inhabited Wielkopolska (Polonia Maior). This powerful tribe gained power and imposed their rule on the others, giving their name to the state. The first historical ruler was Mieszko I, of the Polane Piast Dynasty. Mieszko was baptized into the Christian faith in 966, accepting Christianity through Bohemia from Rome, thus leading the Polish state into the sphere of influence of the Mediterranean culture prevailing in western Europe. This had a far-reaching influence on the culture and architecture of Poland. Mieszko's successor, Bolesław Chrobry (The Brave), the first crowned king of Poland, completed the work of his father, creating a strong state over an area of about 250,000 sq. km. into which he later incorporated for a short time the Czerwieńsk land in the east, Slovakia and Moravia in the south and Milsko (Milzenland) and Łużyce (Lusatia) in the west.

In the following centuries, due to the weakening of the central authorities resulting from division into duchies, the frontiers of the Polish state and also the territories inhabited by the Poles underwent changes. Despite the unification in the 14th century of most of the Polish lands and the strengthening of the state thanks to the wise policy of the last of the Piasts, King Casimir the Great, centuries of German expansion pushed the state frontiers eastwards in relation to the area originally occupied by the Polish tribes. The germanization that followed expansion also moved the ethnic boundary eastwards (thus changing both the state and national frontier). The Germans made the greatest inroads eastwards in the north, along the Baltic coast, where their conquests and germanization policy led to the submission not only of a large part of the Slavic Pomeranians, but also the Baltic Prussian tribes living to the east of them, who were later exterminated or germanized by the Order of the Teutonic Knights. They were replaced by German colonists and later by the Mazurians, who came from nearby Mazovia, most of whom also gradually underwent germanization. German expansion in the south was also considerable, along the Sudety Mts., the aim being to separate the fraternal nations of Poland and Bohemia. Although Silesia lost its ties with the Polish state early, being taken over first by the Luxemburg Dynasty, then by the Hapsburgs and later being incorporated into Prussia, the people of this region resisted germanization for a long time and in the eastern part never ceased to be Poles.

Wielkopolska, the cradle of Polish statehood, resisted German pressures for many centuries. Its western political and ethnic frontier only underwent slight changes until the 18th century, when the whole of Poland, weakened internally, was partitioned between the neighbouring powers of Prussia, Austria and Russia.

Poland's eastern frontier also underwent considerable changes. In the early Middle Ages, it largely coincided with the ethnic frontier between the West Slav Polish tribes and the East Slav Ruthenian tribes and the Baltic Prussians, Sudavians and Lithuanians. Poland's union with Lithuania enlarged the common Polish-Lithuanian state by considerable areas of Ruthenian territory. Under the rule of the Jagiellon Dynasty, the frontiers of this state extended far to the east beyond the rivers Dnieper and Dvina and its area increased to more than a million sq. km. This was the period of Poland's greatest political might, economic growth and cultural development. As the Polish element was the strongest in this state, the colonization of the eastern territories by Poles and the polonization of the Lithuanian and Ruthenian population inhabiting these areas extended Poland's ethnic boundaries to the east. Numerous Polish "islands" came into being in Lithuania and Ruthenia, mainly in the towns and surrounding areas. A large part of the Lithuanian and Ruthenian nobles and burghers were also polonized.

Polish expansion to the east was checked in the 17th century. In the middle of that century, during the wars with Sweden, Russia and Turkey, the process of pushing the Poles back from the areas they had occupied began. At the time of the partitions of Poland, the Polish state had an area of not much more than 700,000 sq. km.

In the period of more than a century of foreign rule, the partitioning powers further reduced the area inhabited by Poles. The germanization process in Silesia, Pomerania and East Prussia was intensified. The numerous Polish "islands" in the east submitted to russification. The growing national consciousness of the Ukrainians, Byelorussians and Lithuanians checked the polonization process and in some cases even diminished its range. At the same time, towards the end of the 19th century, the Polish population began to emigrate in search of work to western Germany, Belgium and France, and overseas to the United States, Canada and Brazil.

The Polish state which was reborn in 1918 united most of the lands inhabited by Polish population. However, more than one million Poles living in Silesia, the southern part of East Prussia and parts of Pomerania and Wielkopolska, which were still part of Germany, remained outside the frontiers of the Polish state. In the east, the Polish frontiers embraced – with the Polish "islands" – large areas mostly inhabited by Ukrainians and Byelorussians. In the period between the two world wars, the frontiers of Poland were very long and irregular. With an area of 388,000 sq. km. and 35 million inhabitants (1939), the Polish state had frontiers 5,500 km. long with only a 70 km. coastal strip, access to which was threated from the west and east by the Germans. Constituting territories which for more than a hundred years had been part of different political and economic organisms, with at least one third of the population consisting of national minorities, torn by class struggles and exploited by foreign capital, the inter-war Polish state was both economically and politically weak. However, it managed to achieve national integration of the population and the economic unification of the country.

The invasion of Poland by Nazi Germany in 1939 led to another fall of Polish statehood, this time only for a short period. The destruction and losses caused by the war were enormous. More than six million Polish citizens, that is, nearly 20% of the population, lost their lives in battle, in concentration camps, in the streets of towns and villages, or died prematurely due to the terrible conditions that prevailed during the Nazi occupation. A considerable part of the national property (38%) was lost. Numerous monuments of culture were destroyed by fire or plundered.

After the Second World War, the Polish state returned to the lands where it came into being at the very beginning of its history. Today it is situated between 49 degrees and 54.5 degrees latitude north and 14.07 degrees and 24.08 degrees longitude east. From the north to the south of Poland it is nearly 650 km. and from the west to the east – about 700 km. At present Poland occupies a compact area, septilateral in shape, of 312,683 sq. km., which is 2.7% of the area of Europe and 0.2% of the area of the lands of the globe. The length of the state frontiers is 3,538 km., of which 524 km. is sea coast. At the end of 1978, Poland's population was 35 million, which is 5.2% of the population of Europe and 0.8% of the world population.

Poland's position in the European continent – between Western Europe, influenced by the Atlantic Ocean, and continental Eastern Europe – means that the natural conditions are of a transitory nature. Poland's territory does not form a separate geographical unit, but the boundaries of several great geographical units run through it, which extend to the east, west and south of the Polish state frontiers. Across the eastern part of the country, there is, above all, the boundary line running from the northwest to the south-east, dividing the west European maritime climate zone from the east European continental climate. At the same time, another boundary running through Poland from west to east, divides the area of the great European Plain from the belt of low mountains and the central European Uplands as well as the Carpathian Mts. These boundaries divide Poland's territory into several smaller geographical units, which (except one) are also found in the neighbouring countries. In the north, in the area of the great European Plain, there are parallel belts, namely the coastal belt, the lakeland belt and the lowland belt without lakes, the western part of which belongs to the Central European Plain, and the eastern part to the East European Plain, which also includes the Polesie Lowland. In the south east, Polish territory includes a small part of the Volhynia Upland, constituting part of the great Pontic Plateau belonging to the forest-steppe zone of South-Eastern Europe. The low mountain belt and the Central European Uplands bordering in the south on the European Plain are represented in Poland's territory by the Sudety Mts. and their Foreland, belonging to the Bohemian Massif, and by the Małopolska Upland, which is the only larger geographic unit completely within Poland's frontiers. To the south of this Upland are the Subcarpathians, the foreland of the Carpathians, a young mountain chain. The northern slopes of the Western Carpathians, of the western part of the Eastern Carpathians and also of the highest and most beautiful of Poland's mountains – the Tatras – which belong to the Inner Carpathians, come within Poland's frontiers.

In these natural conditions, cultural, social and economic differences arose through the ages. At first they were due to the tribal differences, later due to the division of the land into duchies. Three main mother-regions can be distinguished, namely Wielkopolska, Małopolska and Silesia. The last mentioned region lost its ties with the Polish state quite early, in the 14th century. Mazowsze kept its political separateness till the 16th century. Podlasie, to the east of Mazowsze, was a bone of contention between the Poles and the Lithuanians until the Polish-Lithuanian union. In the north, Pomerania and the lands of the Baltic Prussians and Sudavians gradually submitted to German conquest and germanization and had weaker ties with Poland. Only Gdańsk Pomerania was re-united with Poland in the 15th century after a century and a half of foreign rule.

When the country was divided into duchies, there were ethnic and cultural differences, which decreased as the Polish nation became more and more a uniform whole. However, economic and social differences became greater with economic growth. Already in the 16th century there were evident differences between Wielkopolska, which was economically the best developed, with thriving towns and better organized landed estates belonging to the medium gentry, and Małopolska where the magnates' big landed estates dominated, and Mazowsze and Podlasie, not nearly so advanced in their development with a predominance of petty gentry.

These differences deepened during the period of partitions, when different parts of Poland became part of the three partitioning powers with different levels and growth rate of social and economic development. Of these states, Germany was the quickest to develop, especially after 1870, and this brought a corresponding growth in the Polish territory under Prussian rule. Galicia, a peripheral province of the monarchy of the Hapsburgs, showed a very weak economic development, had practically no industry and over-populated rural areas, but due to the more liberal policy of the Austrian government attained a high development of cultural life. The Polish Kingdom, which was part of the Russian Empire, showed an uneven rate of development, generally rather weak, as regards social and economic growth. As a result of this, the Polish state that was reborn in 1918 had a very varied level of development in different areas and great spatial differences. This was expressed by some scholars in a division of Poland into more and less advanced regions from the social, economic and cultural point of view, designated by the terms Poland A, B and C. Despite the great efforts made, the inter-war years did not bring the liquidation of these disproportions in development that had arisen during the centuries, and then the terrible destruction caused by the Second World War, as well as a change in frontiers, led to a further differentiation.

The first task of the post-war Polish state was to rebuild the country and rehabilitate the Western and Northern Territories. This work was accompanied by extensive reforms in the political system, social relations and economic life, which created good conditions for a dynamic development of the country. As a result of the radical agrarian reform, there were areas where almost all the big landed estates were divided up among the peasants and also areas where most of the landed estates were turned into state farms. The policy of accelerated industrialization of the country brought further spatial differentiation of Poland's territories due to the concentration of industry in certain areas, resulting in the development of big industrial urban agglomerations. Above all, the Upper Silesian agglomeration expanded greatly, concentrating most of the mines and a large part of Polish industry and becoming the main economic centre of Poland. Also the Warsaw agglomeration – the main centre of political and cultural life in Poland – developed rapidly. The agglomerations of Gdańsk-Gdynia and Szczecin developed largely due to their functions as ports. Industrial-urban agglomerations also grew up round the large provincial centres of Cracow, Wrocław and Poznań. New agglomerations are taking shape round Bydgoszcz and Toruń, in the Sudety Mts., the Holy Cross Mts., around Lublin, Bielsko-Biała, Częstochowa, Białystok and others.

In between these agglomerations, which are the main lever of Poland's economic growth, there are extensive rural areas which are undergoing big changes in connection with the social and economic development of the country.

There has been a growth, though at a different pace, of the number of rural non-agricultural population commuting to work in nearby industrial and urban centres or working in non-agricultural trades being developed in their place of residence. At the same time, there has been a decrease in the percentage and the density of agricultural population in relation to the area of agricultural land. Despite this, there has been a growth in the productivity and commercialization of agriculture, though in a varying degree, depending on natural conditions, historical past and the present agrarian structure with the resulting spatial differences. In areas that have suitable natural conditions, there has been a development of recreational centres. All these processes have been greatly accelerated since 1970.

It should be pointed out that this spatial differentiation of economic activity is not harmful, on the contrary, it can be a favourable factor on condition that it is based on the best possible utilization of the local natural, social and economic conditions and other resources and that it does not lead to excessive differences in the income of the population with the consequent social and cultural differences that could

appear. Such differences are diminishing in Poland. This is due to a number of factors. Basically, this results from the very principles of the new social and economic system and their implementation. Class differences are practically nonexistent, unemployment has been eliminated and the over-population of rural areas has been greatly relieved. The differences between town and countryside are also disappearing, everyone now has an equal start. As a result of these processes, differences in the economic and social position of different groups of the population are fast disappearing too. The fact that today's Poland is an ethnically uniform country is not without its significance.

Regional differences in the countryside are also disappearing. Only here and there does one find that the rural population has retained its distinct character as regards customs, building, costume and other elements of folk culture. Linguistic differences are also disappearing under the influence of education for all, the development of reading and the influence of mass media such as the radio, TV and the press. Traditional regional building is being replaced by new buildings that mostly lack style, but are more convenient to live in. The old rural buildings and household and farm equipment can mostly be seen now in Skansen type museums. Folk music and folk dances and also sometimes traditional regional rites are cultivated, by regional ensembles that perform them. Folk art, both hand-work and articles made by industrial methods, is sponsored by the state.

The towns are also undergoing changes. Although historical buildings and whole complexes are carefully preserved, renovated and in some cases wholly reconstructed where the war destroyed them, larger and larger areas are occupied by modern blocks of flats, which are much better equipped, but rather standard in design, and the service and administrative buildings accompanying them. In many towns, new central districts have been built. With the development of industry, there are more and more modern buildings put up by industrial methods. New arterial roads and communication facilities are also making their appearance.

Urban building is penetrating ever more to the rural areas in the form of industrial buildings and service pavilions and also blocks of flats in state and co-operative farms. Tourists are being catered for ever more frequently in the rural areas where motels and inns, holiday hotels and hostels are being built.

Today, as in the past, there are processes introducing uniformity and others making for differentiation of Poland's territory and landscape. As a result, Poland though not a big country provides plenty of variety, not only as regards its natural conditions but also as regards its historical, economic and cultural features. However, the boundaries of units determined by natural conditions, those based on common histori-

cal experience as well as by the modern economic and administrative units of today rarely coincide with each other.

The aim of this book being a comprehensive picture of Poland in its natural, historical, economic and cultural aspects by regions, the authors had to divide the country into units, not too numerous but showing as well as possible the differentiation of its territory in all these fields. Finally the division into units was based on the grouping together of natural units, taking into consideration either historical ties or economic considerations depending on which of these factors seemed more important. So, while not keeping strictly to the scientific principles of regionalization but having in mind the aim and subject matter of the book, six regions have been distinguished: I. The Carpathians and Subcarpathians, II. The Polish Uplands, III. The Sudety Mts. and Silesian Lowland, IV. The Wielkopolska Lowland, V. The Mazowsze and Podlasie Lowlands, VI. The Coastal and Lakeland Belt.

Each of these regions has been described in separate chapters, from the point of view of the spatial differentiation of its historical, social and economic features in general outline. This general outline is followed by illustrations chosen to show the typical landscapes, the most important historical buildings of the given region, with examples of modern architecture to represent the present day.

The Carpathians and Subcarpathians

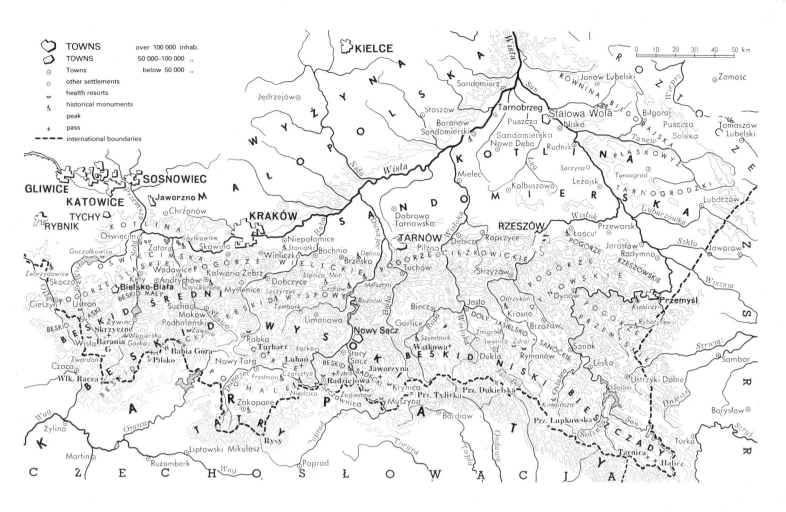

KIELCE

Jędrzejów

WYŻYNA MAŁOPOLSKA

Sandomierz
Staszów
Baranów Sandomierski
Wisła
Nida

Tarnobrzeg
Stalowa Wola
Puszcza
Nisko
Sandomierska
Nowa Deba
Rudnik
San

RÓWNINA BIŁGORAJSKA
Janów Lubelski
Biłgoraj
Zamość
Puszcza Solska
Tomaszów Lubelski
PŁASKOWYŻ
Tanew
Tarnogród
Wieprz
ROZT

GLIWICE
SOSNOWIEC
KATOWICE
TYCHY
RYBNIK
Jaworzno M
Chrzanów
Przemsza
KOTLINA
Oświęcim
Goczałkowice
Zebrzydowice
Skoczów
Cieszyn
Ustroń
Żywiec
POGÓRZE ŚLĄSKIE
BESKID ŚLĄSKI
Barania Górka
Wisła
Skrzyczne
Zwardoń
Czaca
Wlk. Racza
Żylina
Martin
Ružomberk

KRAKÓW
Skawina
Zator
Skawa
Szaflkowice
Wadowice
Kęty
Andrychów
Bielsko-Biała
BESKID MAŁY
BESKID ŚREDNI
Sucha
Maków
Podhalański
Węgierska
Babia Góra
Pilsko
Żołwko
Rabka
Nowy Targ
HALE
Zakopane
Niedzica
Rysy
TATRY
Orawa
Liptowski Mikulasz
Poprad
Wag

Niepołomice
Wieliczka
Bochnia
Brzesko
POGÓRZE WIELICKIE
Dobczyce
Myślenice
Lanckorona
Kalwaria Zebrz.
BESKID WYSPOWY
Tymbark
Limanowa
Łącko
Lubań
Turbacz
Czorsztyn
Frydman
Dunajec
Łapszanka
Szczawnica
Żegiestów
BESKID SĄDECKI
Radziejowa
Jaworzyna
Krynica
Muszyna
Raba
Staniątki
Lipnica Mur.
Czchów
Rożnów
Dunajec
Szczyrzyc
BESKID

Dąbrowa Tarnowska
TARNÓW
Pilzno
Tuchów
Biała
Mełsztyn
Ciężkowice
POGÓRZE CIĘŻKOWICKIE
Biecz
Gorlice
Ropa
Stary Sącz
Rytro
NOWY SĄCZ
Szymbark
Przeł. Tylicka
Bardiów

Dębica
Ropczyce
Sędziszów
RZESZÓW
Dębno
Jasło
Krosno
Brzozów
Dukla
Rymanów
Przeł. Dukielska
Jaśliska
Komańcza
Przeł. Łupkowska

Wisłok
Odrzykoń
Żmigród
Iwonicz Zdrój
DOŁY JASIELSKO-SANOCKIE
Sanok
Watkowa
Wisłoka
Jasiołka
BESKID NISKI
BIESZCZADY
Lesko
Solina
San
Ustrzyki Dolne
Terka
Tarnica
Halicz

POGÓRZE DYNOWSKIE
Dynów
POGÓRZE
Brzozów
POGÓRZE PRZEMYSKIE
Przeworsk
Łańcut
Jarosław
Radymno
Lubaczów
Lubaczówka
Szkło
Jaworów
Przemyśl
Krasiczyn
Rybotycze
Wisznia
PRZEMYSKIE
Strwiąż
Sambor
Borysław
Turka
Stryj
Strwiąż
Dniestr
R

CZECHOSŁOWACJA

Torysa
Topla
Ondawa
Poprad

The Carpathians and Subcarpathians are two natural units linking up with each other, and although they differ as regards natural features, climate, soil and plant life, they have the same geological past. As regards its history, this area was the southern part of Małopolska (Polonia Minor), rather retarded in its economic development, which was incorporated into Austria when Poland was partitioned in the 18th century. It was then known by the name Galicia. More than a hundred years under Austrian rule gave rise to certain internal similarities and differences in relation to the other parts of Poland in the spheres of economic development, culture and social relations.

The Carpathian range is an extension of the Alps, forming an arc curving northwards round from Bratislava on the Danube to the Iron Gate, also on the Danube, on the border between Rumania and Yugoslavia. The Łupków Pass divides the range into the Western and Eastern Carpathians. Depending on the age and origin of the rocks, we distinguish the Outer Carpathians – which are rounded and present rather monotonous forms, with successive strata of sandstone, schist and conglomerate rock called puddingstone – and the Inner Carpathians – with a much more differentiated geological structure and thus a varied, more rugged relief.

The most northerly part of the Carpathian arc comes within Poland's frontiers. It includes a large part of the Outer Carpathians, namely, the northern slopes of the Western Carpathians, otherwise known as the Beskids, and a small part of the Inner Carpathians – the Tatra Mts. and the Podhale region.

The Tatra Mts. are the highest and in spite of their small area (51 km. long and 17 km. wide) are the most varied and picturesque massif of the Carpathian range. The Liliowe Pass (alt. 1,952 m.) divides them into the lower, Western Tatras (alt. 2,100–2,200 m.), which are dome-shaped formations, mainly of crystalline schist, partly of limestone; and the higher, Eastern Tatras (alt. 2,300–2,500 m.), mostly of granite, rugged and rocky. The highest peak, Gerlach (alt. 2,655 m.) is in Czechoslovakia. On the Polish side the highest peak is Rysy (alt. 2,499 m.). The crystalline massif of the Tatras is additionally varied by numerous hollows, hanging valleys and cirques formed by glaciers. The lakes and waterfalls in the Tatras are also of glacial origin. In the limestone parts of the Tatras there is a wealth of Karst forms, such as caves, sink-holes, chimneys and underground streams. The northern part of the Tatra massif, known as the Zakopane Tatras (alt. 1,300–1,500 m.) is formed of limestone and dolomites, which take fantastic shapes at the end of valleys, resembling gates or corridors.

To the north of the Tatras is the Podhale region, an old basin at an altitude of 600–900 m., filled with later sediments and fluvial deposits, a depression dividing the Tatras from the Beskids. The northern, lower part of the depression is called the Nowy Targ Basin. A narrow curved chain of limestone mountains runs through the Podhale region. The Pieniny Mts. form part of this chain. They are not high mountains, the biggest rising to an altitude of 983 m., namely Trzy Korony (Three Crowns), but they are very picturesque, with the beautiful Dunajec Gorge running through them. The swift flowing Dunajec is one of Poland's most beautiful mountain rivers and the deep, narrow gorge (to 300 m.) winds through unforgettable scenery. Here, erosion has carved out caves, pinnacles and crags, and many other unusual Karst formations.

The Outer Carpathians are of different structure. The numerous rivers with their abundant waters have cut through the soft flysch massifs, forming several chains of dome-shaped elevations, perches, humps, and isolated mountains, which are of various heights and shapes, divided by passes, river valleys and basins. The Beskids are composed of three main parts: the Middle Beskids, the High Beskids and the Low Beskids. The Middle Beskids, which are the most westerly of this group, are situated between the River Bečva in Czechoslovakia and the Raba valley. They include the Silesian Beskids, together with the Barania Góra group (Skrzyczne, alt. 1,257 m.) and the Little Beskids (alt. up to 930 m.), separated by the Soła valley. The High Beskids, as the name indicates, are the highest of the Beskid chains and massifs, grouped in two main limbs – the Żywiec and Sącz Beskids. They are divided by the large Sącz Basin, formed by the Dunajec and Poprad rivers, which join each other here. The Żywiec Beskids consist of three groups with the peaks: Wielka Racza (alt. 1,236 m.), Pilsko (alt. 1,557 m.) and Babia Góra (alt. 1,725 m.). The Sącz Beskids include the Gorce Mts. (Turbacz, alt. 1,311 m.) and the chains of Lubań (alt. 1,211 m.), Radziejowa (alt. 1,265 m.) and Jaworzyna (alt. 1,116 m.). The Tylicz Pass divides the High Beskids from the Low Beskids (alt. less than 1,000 m.), which run farther east to the Łupków Pass. These three parts form the main chain, the backbone of the Western Carpathians. To the north of the High Beskids are the lower and more scattered Insular Beskids.

To the east of the Łupków Pass are the Bieszczady Mts., part of the Eastern Carpathians, consisting of long, regularly spaced mountain ridges with steep slopes running parallel to each other and divided by wide depressions. These ridges rise to an altitude of more than 1,300 m. (Tarnica, 1,346 m. and Halicz, 1,335 m.).

The outer and lowest part of the Carpathians in the north are the Carpathian Foothills, with a distinct faulted verge dropping 100–170 m. to the Subcarpathian Basin. This is a region of wide, gently rolling hills rising to an altitude of 350 to 500 m., and stretching eastwards. Only in the extreme east are there hills rising to an altitude of 600 m. Numerous wide river valleys divide the Carpathian Foothills into parts. In the Western Carpathians they are, the Silesian, Wieliczka, Ciężkowice and Dynów Hills; in the Eastern Carpathians – the Przemyśl Hills, the foothills of the Bieszczady Mts. Between these hills and the Low Beskids is a long, shallow basin called the Jasło–Sanok Depression.

The climate in the Carpathians is greatly differentiated. The higher the altitude the greater the rainfalls and the lower the temperature, but local differences, particularly the physical features and exposure to the sun, make for a great variety of climatic conditions. Depending on the steepness, shape and exposure to the sun, the mountain sides get varying degrees of rainfall and warmth. In some weather conditions, cool air flows down to the bottom of valleys between mountains causing low temperatures and mist. This is the reason for the cold climate of the Nowy Targ Basin, where the temperature is lower than in Zakopane, which is situated much higher up. In other weather conditions, where there is protection from the winds, valleys that get a lot of sun are warmer than the higher ground above them. The most severe climate in the Carpathians and in the whole of Poland is in the Tatra Mountains. The summer is very short there, and after the long winter and spring, the autumn seems to come almost directly afterwards. There is a thick covering of snow for more than 200 days in the year. The mildest climate is in the Carpathian Foothills and in some of the mountain valleys.

The basins have better soil conditions than the mountain slopes. The soil in the basins mainly composed of materials washed down from the mountain sides, is of soft texture with a thick layer of humus, whereas on the mountain slopes the soil covering is shallow and poor. On steeper slopes, the soil is only held by the permanent vegetation cover, meadows and, above all, forests. If this vegetation is destroyed, soil erosion and denudation of the bedrock results.

Depending on the altitude the mountain forests are divided into three levels or floors called regels. The lower regel (in the Beskids 500–1000 m. above sea level, and in the Tatras 500–1250 m. above sea level) consists of mixed forests with rich undergrowth. The dominating varieties are beeches, firs and spruces, with an admixture of sycamores maples, larches, mountain elms and others. In the Low Beskids and the Bieszczady Mountains a considerable part of the lower regel forests are beech trees. Due to bad husbandry in the past, the lower regel forests in many places were turned into a monoculture of spruce trees. The upper regel level (up to 1400 m. above sea level) has a poor and monotonous tree cover. The spruce tree reigns supreme and the undergrowth consists of bilberries, mosses, ferns and various kinds of mountain plants. The highest mountain pine level (1400–1800 m. above sea level) only occurs in the Tatra Mountains and the High Beskids on Mount Babia Góra and Mount Pilsko. Here the dominating variety is the dwarf mountain pine, which grows thickly at this level and, at the point where the upper sub-alpine forest meets it, there are also some stone pines. The undergrowth consists of numerous alpine plants, such as Clematis alpina, Rosa pendulina, Aconitum callibotryon, Doronicum Clusii, Ribes petraeum and Ribes alpinum, Archangelica officinalis, Gentianae, and also ferns, bilberries, grasses, etc.

The fauna of the regel forests does not differ much from that of the lowland forests. This mountain level is the habitat of wild boar, deer, woodgrouse, hazel grouse and – rarely these days – of the lynx and the wild cat. In the Bieszczady Mountains there are wolves and bears. At the upper regel level some specific mountain birds appear, namely, Micropus apus, Turdus saxatilis, Nucifraga caryocatactes, Picoides tridactylus, and at the mountain pine level – Phoenicurus ochruros, Prunella collaris and Anthus spinoletta.

Along the banks of the mountain rivers and streams at the regel level there are grey alder woods with ash trees, spruce, willows, bird cherry, hops and sometimes Myricaria germanica. This is the home of the water ouzel, mountain newt and salamander. In the streams there are trout and also salmon and bulltrout in the spawning season, though the last two are rarely seen these days. Amid the forests at all three mountain levels where the subsoil holds water there are mountain peat bogs and here one finds dwarf spruce trees, first birch trees and bushy willows, also sometimes the dwarf mountain pine. There are extensive peat fields with the dwarf mountain pine in the Podhale region.

Everywhere there are large areas of mountain meadows, growing where trees were felled and the open spaces afterwards used for grazing grounds. Among the plants growing in the meadow grass there are numerous alpine species. The meadows in the Tatras are a beautiful sight in spring, covered with a thick carpet of crocuses in bloom. The mountain pastures in the Bieszczady Mountains, with their abundant grasses, are also a well known beauty spot. The plant life in the meadows of the Pieniny Mountains, where the soil is rich in lime, is particularly interesting, these being a "haven" for Tertiary flora destroyed elsewhere by glaciers.

Above the dwarf pine level in the Tatras and on Mt. Babia Góra there are no trees. This is the alpina level with the characteristic low-growing herbaceous plants. They include: Saxifragae, Sesleriae, Mulgedium alpinum, Rhodiola rosea, Aconitum callibotryon, Dryas octopetalus mountain avens and alpine poppies. The highest level, only occurring in the Tatras, consists of rocky crags; in some places there are clumps of plants that can stand the severe climate and soil conditions. These are, above all, various lichens and liverworts and low-growing grasses and herbs. The alpine level and the rocky crags are the habitat of the chamois, Carpathian vole and pallitory manetel, as well as limited insect fauna specific to these parts.

Today, many rare species of mountain flora and fauna are under protection. In order to preserve whole complexes of mountain scenery and natural life, reserves and national parks have been created in the Carpathians. The Tatra National Park protects the only mountain area of an alpine character in Poland. The Pieniny National Park is to protect the exceptionally picturesque scenery of limestone mountains and the rare plants that grow there. The Babia Góra National Park is to protect the primeval Carpathian forests. A National Park has also been created in the Bieszczady Mountains and covers the most primeval forests and mountain meadows. The uplift of the Carpathian range caused the subsidence of its northern foreland, which in the middle Tertiary Period was occupied by what is known as the Pontic Sea. This depression was gradually filled up with thick layers of loam, sand and gravel brought there by mountain rivers and streams. After the sea had dried up, there remained in various places deposits of salt, gypsum and limestone. The Subcarpathian Basin, formed in this way, was then covered with deposits from the earliest glaciation (boulder-clay and sand) which the winds formed into ridges of dunes in some places, depositing masses of fine-textured loess along the Carpathian verge. The mountain rivers entering the valleys deposited coarse-textured sediments forming alluvial cones. They pushed gradually towards the northern edge of the basin along the bed of the Vistula, which covers a considerable area of the northern part of the basin with fluvial deposits.

The Subcarpathian Basins area gently rolling, flat area, 150–200 m. above sea level, intersected by rivers. The Cracow gorge divides the area into two parts: the smaller Oświęcim Basin to the west and the larger Sandomierz Basin to the east. These basins, protected on all sides, are among the warmest parts of Poland, with a long, warm summer, mild winter and with enough rainfall to make it a good farming area (600–800 mm.). Light sandy and gravelly soils predominate, largely podsolized. The more fertile podsolized clayey soils are found on layers of boulder clay of glacial origin and Tertiary loams. The valleys of the Vistula, Wisłoka and San are covered with alluvial soils and this land is used mainly as meadows. All along the Carpathian verge there are fertile loess soils, partly podsolized. At one time this land was covered with dry pine and oak woods, turning into sparse oak woods of a forest-steppe kind farther east. Where these woods once grew, between Przeworsk and Przemyśl, there is now chernozem soil, the most fertile of the whole Subcarpathian Basin.

The natural conditions of the Carpathians and the surrounding country, which were not conducive to human husbandry, were the reason why human settlement was relatively late here. The earliest settlements were along the Vistula and the lower reaches of its tributaries, and in the loess zone at the foot of the Carpathians. Next settlers came to the other parts of the Subcarpathian Basins and the last of all to be settled were the Carpathians themselves. Man gradually began to penetrate into the Carpathians, settling along the river and mountain valleys. The progress of colonization is marked by a chain of strongholds. The oldest route of expanding settlement was along the valley of the River Dunajec, through the Sącz Basin leading deep into the mountains on their southern side towards Hungary. Later settlements were set up in the Jasło–Sanok Depression, then in the Żywiec and Nowy Targ Basin. In the east, Ruthenian colonization developed. Settlement in the Carpathians began to develop more rapidly in the 11th to 13th century A.D. These processes, checked during the Tatar invasions and the internal troubles of the state in the 13th century, began to develop again in the following century in connection with colonization based on German law. Urban rights were also granted to many former fortified settlements, market centres and centres of cult. New towns also grew up, above all, along the Carpathian verge, in connection with the new trade route leading from Cracow to Lwów. Another factor enlivening urban settlement was the widescale extraction of salt from the salt mines in Wieliczka and Bochnia. Many Subcarpathian towns were engaged in the salt trade, distributing this commodity all over Poland and also exporting it to Hungary and Ruthenia. Colonization of the northern part of the Sandomierz Basin developed more slowly, and it was a long time before people began to settle in the huge Sandomierz forest, situated in the fork of the Vistula and San rivers.

As in the Subcarpathian Belt many centres in the Carpathians were granted urban rights in the 13th and particularly the 14th century. Here too, new towns grew up, mainly in connection with the inflow of settlers from Germany. Deeper in the mountains, in the Spisz region and neighbouring uninhabited areas, German colonists settled in the villages. Gradually these settlers were polonised. Traces of German colonization have remained in the polonized names of some towns and villages (i.e. Lanckorona and Szymbark). A certain influence on the development of settlement in the Carpathians was exerted by mine prospecting. It is known, for instance, that in the 16th and 17th centuries small quantities of copper, silver and even gold were found in Podhale.

As agricultural settlement developed, the farmers moved ever higher up the mountains. In the 14th century they settled on the gentler slopes of the Beskids, up to an altitude of about 400 m. In the 13th and 14th centuries, Valachian shepherds began to settle in Poland, moving along the main ridge of the Carpathians. This population, after mixing with the local population, came under Ruthenian influences in the eastern part of the Carpathians and Polish influences in the western part. Traces of Valachian settlement and their cultural influences can be seen in the specific anthropological type of the Polish highlanders, particularly those inhabiting the Tatras, in their folklore: costumes resembling those of the Balkan highlanders, the characteristic type of timber building, their specific folk art, music and dances, as well as local place names and words of Valachian origin in the highlanders dialect.

The period of Poland's might in the 15th and 16th centuries brought a further development of these regions. On the trade routes leading towards Hungary, towns grew up and became wealthy. A proof of their prosperity are the beautiful town halls, churches and monasteries. Having accumulated wealth from the salt mines, their Ukrainian estates and trade with corn, the powerful magnate families and gentry left a heritage of magnificent residences. To guard the frontiers with Hungary and Ruthenia and also to keep their subjects in order, they built many fortified castles to watch over the mountain passes and valleys. Numerous monasteries were founded, churches were built by the wealthy and powerful, as well as small parish churches, mostly timber, often made of larch wood. The ones that have survived till our times are fine examples of old timber building, demonstrating the high level of craftsmenship of the local carpenters, based on their native traditions. Many of them have rich polychrome ornamentation and carvings in their interiors, which are fine specimens of folk art.

The highland population, who loved freedom, did not allow themselves to be completely harnessed in the yoke of serfdom. Their answer to increased exploitation was rebellion, or they took to the mountains where they joined the legendary highland robbers of the Tatras. The belligerent highlanders also fought against foreign invaders. Their battles against the Swedes in the 17th century are well known, and in 1846, the highlanders of the Chochołów Valley organized an uprising against Austrian rule.

The economic crisis that occurred in Poland in the second half of the 17th century and the first half of the 18th century resulting from the wars that had harrassed the country for dozens of years, also influenced the situation in the Subcarpathians. There was a slump in handicrafts and trade, people left the towns and the population got poorer and poorer. At the time of the "Swedish deluge" (1655) many towns and villages in the northern part of the Subcarpathians suffered the ravages of war. Podhale suffered acutely from the invasion of Rakoczy's troops in 1656–1657. When Poland's political, military and economic weakness become a threat to her sovereignty, the Carpathians and Subcarpathians were among the first victims. After the first partition of the country (1772) they came under Austrian rule as part of the province known as Galicia. The new authorities did not take much interest in this area, treating it for a long time as the object of possible political bargaining.

Cut off from the other Polish lands by a political frontier, Galicia, situated on the periphery of the Hapsburg monarchy and separated by high mountains from the main economic centres of Austria, did not have favourable conditions for development, even after it was granted autonomy to govern itself in 1867. A certain economic enlivement came with the building of railway lines by the Austrian authorities for strategic reasons. The second half of the 19th century saw the building of the main Cracow–Przemyśl–Lwów line, running along the Carpathian verge, and also the main line known as the Transversal Line running parallel to it in the south, and linking up the mountain basins. With the exception of Cieszyn Silesia, industrial development was very weak in the Carpathians and Subcarpathians. Bielsko grew into quite an important centre of the textile industry and a wagon factory was built in Sanok. The only branch of industry that showed a really dynamic development in the second part of the 19th century was oil extraction from a wide belt of oil beds extending from Limanowa in the west, through Gorlice, Jasło, Krosno, Sanok and Ustrzyki Dolne and eastwards across the present-day frontiers of the state. Interest was shown in extracting crude oil as a result of the invention of the oil lamp by the Pole Ignacy Łukasiewicz in 1853. The quickly growing demand for crude oil led to the drilling of oil wills and construction of refineries by Polish enterprises. It was not long, however, before the Galician oil industry was controlled by foreign capital. The oil beds were exploited wastefully and most of the crude oil extracted was transported abroad for refining.

The poor economic development of the country and the lack of opportunities for the rapidly growing rural population to move to the towns and work in industry, led to agrarian overpopulation as well as the continous subdivision of farms, despite the considerable emigration of rural population overseas. Because of this lack of land, the peasants cultivated every scrap of land that could be ploughed, extending the areas of cultivated land and settlements higher up to the mountain slopes. Many hamlets grew up at a higher level than the existing villages. These in turn grew and merged with each other and, together with the old, large villages formed big Carpathian villages of

today, which go on and on for kilometres. Despite the heavy labours of the farmers the yields from this ground were poor. In addition, the destruction of the permanent vegetation on the steep slopes and excessive grazing accelerated erosion processes and the thin layer of soil was washed down the mountain sides. The denuded ridges and slopes were unable to hold the water from rainfalls and snow and it flowed down into the rivers. The river beds could not contain all this excess water. In order to prevent the ever more frequent floods efforts were undertaken in the years between the two world wars to protect the forests on the mountain ridges and work was started on regulating the mountain streams and building water reservoirs. Up to the outbreak of the Second World War the only project to be completed was the dam in Porąbka on the River Soła and work was well advanced on the construction of a dam at Rożnów on the Dunajec.

The frontiers of the Polish state that was reborn in 1918 embraced the Carpathians and Subcarpathians as a region of retarded development, very small peasant farms, and with a great surplus of agricultural labour and a poorly developed industry, mainly oil and textiles. Very little changed up to the middle of the Thirties. Industry was still developing at snail-pace, the only important undertakings being the building of a nitrogen works at Mościce, near Tarnów and the commencement of the exploitation of natural gas in the oil-bearing region between Jasło and Krosno. It was only in the last years before the Second World War that more investments were made in this area. In 1937, the construction was started of the Central Industrial District with a centre in the fork of the Vistula and San rivers. The industrial district was located there for military, demographic and economic reasons. Many projects were undertaken in the Central Industrial District. Among the most important ones in the Subcarpathians were power stations: the hydro-electric power generating station at Rożnów, the industrial power station at Stalowa Wola and the expansion of the power generating plant at the Nitrogen Works in Mościce. At the same time the network of high tension transmission lines and the regional grid were developed and so was the system of gas piping. The construction of a big steel works was started at Stalowa Wola. In Rzeszów, a factory producing aircraft engines, machine tools and headlamps was built. An arms factory was built in Sanok, a chemical synthesis plant in Dębica and a chemical works at Pustków. The production of aircraft was started at Mielec and of cellulose in Niedomice. The further development of the Central Industrial District was stopped by the outbreak of war.

During the German Occupation a large part of the Carpathians and Subcarpathians came within what was then called the General Gouvernement, with Cracow as its capital. The area to the west of the Skawa river was incorporated into the Reich as part of Silesia. In 1940, at Oświęcim, the Nazis organized a mass extermination camp (Auschwitz) in which more than four million people lost their lives. The prisoners were used as a labour force to build a big chemical works at Dwory, near Oświęcim. It was destroyed in 1945 by the retreating Nazi occupying forces, as were many of the installations in the Central Industrial District. Front line fighting went on for quite a long time along the Vistula and Wisłoka rivers causing a lot of destruction in this area. Just after the war, fighting went on against Ukrainian nationalists in the south-eastern part of the Carpathians and Subcarpathians. As a result of the fighting and the resettlement of Ukrainian population in the USSR, some parts of the Bieszczady Mountains and the Low Beskids were greatly depopulated.

After the war, the Carpathians and Subcarpathians went through a period of great changes. The agrarian reform brought the division of the big landed estates among the peasants. There was still not enough land for all the peasants in the over-populated Carpathian villages, but new opportunities emerged. Hundreds of thousands of peasants were given farms in the regained Western Territories, many people moved to industrial centres and towns in other parts of the country, and many found employment outside agriculture in their own region, which was the result, above all, of the development of local industry. The industrial plants destroyed during the war were rebuilt and expanded and many new ones were put up. The geological prospecting carried out after the war revealed rich deposits of sulphur near Tarnobrzeg and of natural gas in the area round Lubaczów, Przemyśl, Jarosław, Mielec, Dąbrowa Tarnowska and Bochnia. New deposits of domestic salt were discovered between Wieliczka and Bochnia.

Natural gas, sulphur and domestic salt are important raw materials for the chemical industry, which is one of the most developed branches of industry in the Carpathians and Subcarpathians. The old chemical industry centres at Tarnów, Dębica and Pustków have been expanded. The chemical plant at Dwory, near Oświęcim, has been rebuilt. At Machów, near Tarnobrzeg, a big sulphur processing plant has been built. Production of articles made of plastics is developing in Jasło. The electrical engineering industry has a large number of factories in the area. Means of transport are produced in Mielec (aircraft for agriculture), in Sanok (buses, minibuses, trailers) and in Bielsko-Biała (small cars and gliders). A large plant producing building machines has been built at the Steel Works in Stalowa Wola, another producing textile machines in Bielsko-Biała, and others producing mining machines in Gorlice and Oświęcim. Engines are being produced in Andrychów, Mielec, Nowa Dęba, near Tarnobrzeg and in Bielsko-Biała, and machine tools in Tarnów and Andrychów. The popular refrigerators produced in Rzeszów and the sewing machines made in Przemyśl are well known on the market. There is a large repair works for railway rolling stock in Nowy Sącz and in nearby Biegonice the production of carbon electrodes is developing well.

The iron and steel industry is represented by the Steel Works and Rolling Mill at Stalowa Wola and the first Polish aluminium plant, built after the Second World War at Skawina. The mineral industry is represented, above all, by the glass works at Jasło, Krosno and Jarosław. Kalwaria Zebrzydowska is a well known centre producing furniture and in Przemyśl the produc-

tion of fibre-board is developing. The paper mills in Niedomice and Żywiec are being expanded. Bielsko and Biała, merged into one urban organism, comprise a traditionally important centre producing woollen textiles and in Andrychów a large cotton mill has been built. The over-populated Podhale region has gained a footwear factory in Nowy Targ, which together with the fur industry there (also in Żywiec and Bielsko-Biała) provides employment in which the traditional skills of the highlanders can be put to good use. There are large centres of the food industry in Rzeszów, Tarnów, Dębica, Nowy Sącz, and also in Brzesko-Okocim and Żywiec, which are well known old brewery centres.

The development of industry has brought changes in the social structure of the villages. There has been a big increase in employment in industry and other non-agricultural trades. There is also a large group of peasant-workers, employed by industry but living on their own farms in the countryside. They invest the money they earn in their farmsteads, more comfortable homes with better equipment and furnishings. So everywhere where the influence of industry makes itself felt one sees new houses springing up. On the other hand, the fine old traditional rural buildings are gradually disappearing.

The methods of running farms and the lines of production chosen by the farmers are also undergoing changes. Farms are still very small, but there is no longer a surplus of manpower in the villages. Agricultural production is increasing and its structure is changing. Oats, once sown over large areas by every highland farmer, have now been largely replaced by wheat, particularly in the mountain basins. Clover is being grown more and more along the whole length of the Carpathians, and this has been conducive to cattle breeding instead of the former extensive sheep grazing. Sheep are now only reared on the higher mountain pastures. The increase in cattle breeding has improved the manure situation of the highland farms, which in turn ensures better yields. Where the conditions are favourable, particularly in the Subcarpathian loess belt, the cultivation of sugar beet is being expanded. The sugar beet is processed in the only sugar refinery in the area, at Przeworsk. In many places, particularly in the Sącz Basin, fruit growing is developing, ensuring supplies to the market and to the wine and fruit processing factories in that area.

Forestry plays an important role in the economy of the Carpathian region, supplying large quantities of timber, mainly spruce for the production of cellulose, and beech wood, highly valued as a raw material for carpentry and for the chemical industry. The forests also ensure a rich supply of bilberries, other forest fruits and mushrooms.

This economic enlivenment, the development of tourism and holiday resorts, as well as the increased mobility of the local population caused by people travelling to work has increased the demand for means of communication. There has been a great development of the network of better, hard surfaced roads in the Carpathians and Subcarpathians, which facilitates bus transport. A number of railway lines have been electrified. Power is supplied by the power and heat generating plants of the Upper Silesian Basin and local power stations. The number of hydro-electrict generating plants has increased; there are now seven of them, at Solina and Myczkowce on the San river, at Rożnów and Czchów on the Dunajec river, at Tresna and Porąbka on the Soła and lastly, the recently built pumped storage power plant inside Mt Żar on the Soła. With the exception of the last mentioned, all these power stations were built by dams and reservoirs, which play an important part in regulating the water level and preventing floods. The artificial lakes formed by the dams have also become popular leisure and water sports centres.

The network of towns in the Carpathians and Subcarpathians is quite well developed. The western part of the area is influenced by nearby Cracow and the Upper Silesian agglomeration. The main centre of the eastern part of the region is Rzeszów. It has grown from a small provincial town with 27,000 inhabitants before the war into a big voivodship centre with a population of 115,000. It is an industrial town with a well developed network of shops and services and a lively cultural life. It has two schools of higher learning attended by more than 8,000 students. The range of its influence goes beyond the bounds of the present day voivodship.

In addition to Rzeszów, there are six more voivodship towns in the area, which have only recently acquired this status – in 1975. Some of them had been large centres for a long time already, the others have only recently developed. Apart from their administrative functions, they also – to a greater or lesser extent – have production enterprises and provide services to the population.

Przemyśl (population over 59,000) is situated near the frontier with the USSR. It is a developed industrial and service centre and is also an important railway junction. Together with the stations Medyka and Żurawica, it forms a complex known as "the dry port" through which a large part of Polish-Soviet trade exchange passes. Tarnów, which in the course of less than 30 years has increased its population from 34,000 to more than 100,000, has developed mainly due to its industry, but it also has important cultural functions based on old traditions dating back to the 16th century. The development of Tarnobrzeg is unprecedented. In 1950 it only had 4,000 inhabitants. At present it has a population of 34,000. This lightning growth is due to the development of the sulphur industry. Bielsko-Biała (population 156,000), the biggest town of the Carpathians and Subcarpathians, situated at the most westerly point of the area, is above all an important industrial centre. It also fulfils trade and cultural functions, but of limited scope, not in proportion to the size of the town, this being due to the nearness of the very much larger centres of Cracow and Katowice. The industrial and cultural importance of Nowy Sącz (over 60,000 inhabitants) is growing rapidly. Krosno is the biggest oil industry centre in Poland and also has three glass works.

In addition to the above mentioned voivodship towns, there are many smaller towns in the Carpathians and Subcarpathians providing services of varying range to the surrounding rural areas. The development of some of them is connected with industry. Within the former Central Industrial District the following are important centres: Stalowa Wola (population over 50,000), Mielec, Dębica, Jasło, which is a centre of the oil and glass industries, Sanok, which apart from functions in the field of industry and trade, also conducts lively cultural activity. The largest museum of icons is in Sanok.

In the west, one of the most important towns is Oświęcim (pop. 43,000), a large centre of the chemical industry. Other large towns in the Silesian Beskids are: Żywiec, with a well developed industry and network of shops, where the wild and inaccessible surrounding country was once the haunt of mountain robbers in the 17th and 18th centuries, and Cieszyn, one of the oldest towns of southern Poland, today a frontier town, the eastern part of which – with the historical Old Town – belongs to Poland, and the remaining part to Czechoslovakia.

The main centre of the Podhale region is Nowy Targ, an industrial town and railway junction which also plays an important role as a tourist centre.

The most dense network of urban centres is found in the Oświęcim Basin and in the belt stretching along the verge of the Carpathians from Cieszyn to Przemyśl. To the north and south of that belt, the urban network gets more sparse, although to the south, wherever natural features permit it, for instance, in the mountain basins and along the rivers, there are more urban centres. On the other hand, to the north in the Sandomierz Basin, urban settlements are irregularly and sparsely distributed despite the flat countryside.

The network of villages is dense all over the Carpathians and Subcarpathians. The dominant type are long chain villages following the mountain valleys and streams. At right angles to the axis of the villages narrow fields stretch outwards, mostly rising up the slopes. As the population of the villages increased, the fields were divided crosswise and this was followed by the setting up of new hamlets higher up the slopes. Along the upper Vistula and lower San very large irregularly built villages usually with twisting streets are often found. In many places in the Carpathians old traditions and customs have been kept alive and the people still wear their regional folk costumes. The very versatile folklore of the Tatra highlanders has been preserved in all the villages of Podhale. Among the villages of the Silesian Beskids, the most vital centres of folklore are Koniaków, Istebna and Jaworzyna. The inhabitants of Zawoja and Zubrzyca Górna, beautiful highland villages picturesquely situated at the foot of Mount Babia Góra, also cultivate their regional traditions and folk art. Preserved magnates residences mark the centres of the former large estates. Among the finest of these are: Baranów (not far from Tarnobrzeg) a castle in Renaissance style, which has been converted partly into a museum and partly into a luxurious holiday hotel; Łańcut, near Rzeszów, a beautiful early Baroque palace; Krasiczyn castle, near Przemyśl, which is one of the most valuable examples of late Renaissance architecture in this country. The castle at Wiśnicz not far from Bochnia is very beautiful and the castles at Żywiec and Sucha are well worth seeing, as are many others in the area.

The quick development of industry and towns, the penetration of urban culture to the villages and the improved standard of living of the population has led to an increased demand for recreational facilities. Numerous mineral springs (at Krynica, Szczawnica, Rabka, Rymanów, Iwonicz and other places) have let to the development of spas. There are still a lot of untapped mineral springs, which augur the further development of spa resorts in this area. The healthy mountain climate, beautiful scenery, the specific style of the highland building and historical monuments of culture are attractions drawing more and more tourists and holiday-makers to the Carpathians. This has resulted in a rapid development of holiday centres with an increasing number of holiday homes and various kinds of accomodation for tourists. Winter sports centres are also being developed. Zakopane, once a quiet little village at the foot of the Tatras, was unknown till the middle of the 19th century and since then has turned into the "winter capital" of Poland. The surrounding Podhale villages also cater for holiday-makers and tourists, though on a smaller scale, and so do numerous places in the Silesian, Żywiec and Sącz Beskids and in the Pieniny Mts. For tourists who like wild scenery the Bieszczady Mountains are an excellent place to go for a holiday, in contrast to the Podhale region and the Beskids, well prepared to receive guests, but crowded with people taking a cure, with tourists and holiday-makers. The Bieszczady Mountains with forest covered slopes and meadows are sparsely populated, and it is precisely the wide open spaces that are the main attraction of this mountain group. This is where one can find nature still untouched and the peace and quiet so badly needed by man in this industrial age.

A panoramic view of the Tatra Mts. showing their alpine character. Although much smaller and lower than the Alps, the Tatras resemble them with their beauty, the variety of shapes and forms of their rocks, steep slopes and rugged peaks rising majestically over the surrounding countryside (5). The highest, most precipitous and rocky part of the Tatras are the Eastern Tatras, also known as the High Tatras, the main core of which is granite. There are magnificent valleys and mountain meadows, towering peaks and mighty mountain massifs in the High Tatras. At the foot of the precipitous, perpendicular or almost perpendicular rock faces there are piles of scree, and in the gullies, broken rock material.

In the main Tatra ridge is the Rysy group of peaks (4). The Czechoslovak-Polish frontier, which runs along this ridge deflects sharply to the north here, in the direction of Podhale. Of the three Rysy peaks, the highest (2,502 m.) central one is on the Czechoslovak side of the frontier, the next highest (2,499 m.) is on the boundary line and is the highest peak of the Polish Tatras. The view from this peak is considered the most beautiful in the Tatras. On a fine day one can see from here all the most important peaks and mountain ridges, the Tatra valleys and lakes, and also the intermontane basins round the Tatras, which emphasize the height of this mountain perch.

4
5

The largest and most beautiful mountain lake in Poland (covering an area of 34,5 ha) is Morskie Oko (Eye of the Sea) at an altitude of 1,393 m. (6). The name of the lake is derived from an old legend telling of its underground link with the sea. The highlanders also call it The Lake of the Fish because its crystal clear waters are the habitat of trout. Round the shores of the lake there are dwarf mountain pines and above them, clumps of spruce, rowan trees and also the beautiful mountain stone pines. Morskie Oko is both a cirque and moraine lake. Its waters fill a glacial hollow (cirque), closed by a terminal moraine on which a shelter has been built for tourists as a base for climbing expeditions. Numerous trails lead from the shelter to the nearest peaks and mountain passes and further on to the Rysy group, to the Dolina Pięciu Stawów (Valley of the Five Lakes) and also back to Zakopane. The lake is surrounded on three sides by steeply rising ridges with the peaks: Opalony Wierch, Miedziane, Wołowy and Mięguszowiecki (3), Żabie and Mnich, which are all excellent objects for climbers.

Mięguszowiecki Peak (alt. 2,438) rises more than 1,000 m. above the waters of the lake. The sharply pointed Mnich Peak (alt. 2,068) is only accessible to the most experienced climbers.

The extensive Dolina Pięciu Stawów Polskich (Valley of the Five Polish Lakes) (7) is an example of a valley carved out of crystalline rock by a glacier. The valley is U-shaped with numerous ground, lateral and end moraines, hanging valleys and lakes closed in by moraines and rock bars. The valley is closed in on the south-east by the Miedziane and Opalony peaks, on the south-west by the main Tatra ridge, and on the north-west by a high chain of peaks divided by high mountain passes. The most beautiful tourist trail of the Tatras, called the Eagles' Path, leads over the latter, encompassing the peaks of Kozi Wierch, Buczynowe Turnie, Krzyżne, Wołoszyn. There are several small lakes and five larger ones in the valley, hence its name. The biggest of them is Wielki Staw (Great Lake) covering an area of 34 ha. It is also the deepest lake in the Tatras (79,3 m.). The stream Roztoka, which flows out of it forms the Siklawa Waterfall, the highest in Poland (70 m). The highest of the lakes is Zadni Staw (The Hindmost Lake) at an altitude of 1,890 m. surrounded by steep slopes covered with scree. Czarny Staw (Black Lake) at the foot of Liptowskie Mury, Przedni Staw (Foremost Lake) at the foot of Opalony, and Mały Staw (Little Lake), between the Foremost Lake and the Great Lake, are all very picturesque. Many tourist trails leading to Zakopane, to Morskie Oko Lake and Roztoka, to the peaks of Kozi Wierch and Krzyżne, the Gładka and Szpiglasowa Passes, all run through the Valley. This is very good terrain for climbing expeditions of varying degrees of difficulty. It is also good skiing terrain in the winter.

The Western Tatras (8), built mainly of crystalline schists and limestone, are more rounded with gentler slopes. The glaciers did not play such a big part in modelling the Western Tatras as in shaping the High Tatras, but water erosion and weathering played a greater role. There are no lakes there, but there are many Karst forms. The vegetation is more luxuriant there and the meadows more lush.

7

8

Dolina Strążyska (Strążyska Valley) (9) formed by the mountain stream Strążyski is one of the most beautiful valleys in the vicinity of Zakopane. The marked trail to Mt. Giewont leads through it. The rock face of Mt. Giewont rises 600 m. above the higher parts of the Strążyska Valley. From Mt. Giewont one can see the deep groove which gives the ridge the appearance of the profile of a recumbent man. There is a legend attached to this about a sleeping knight.

Dolina Chochołowska (The Chochołów Valley) is the most westerly valley in the Polish Tatras and one of the largest in the Western Tatras. It has numerous smaller valleys branching off it. The peaks surrounding it are: Wielkie Zamczyska, Trzydniowiański Wierch, Kępa and Kominy Tylkowe. In two places it narrows sharply forming what look like rocky gateways. At one time iron ore was mined in the valley. In the upper part of the valley, in the Chochołów Dale, there is a big tourist hostel and shepherds huts – testifying to the former extensive grazing grounds for sheep and cattle that once existed here. The Dale is famous for the mass of crocuses that bloom there in the spring (10). In the winter, the Chochołów Valley is an attractive place for skiing.

9

10

30

Numerous species of high mountain plants are characteristic of the Tatras, such as are found in similar climatic conditions in other high mountains or in the far north. Some of the plants are characteristic of a granite substratum, such as: gentians, dwarf and glacial buttercups, small primroses (20), alpine campanula, spotted gentian, leopard's bane, and are thus found mostly in the High Tatras. Other plants, like the edelweiss (12), alpine buttercup (16), spring gentian, alpine violet and primrose (15), mountain aster, Tatra saxifrage (13) and the octopetalous mountain avens grow on the more fertile limestone substratum. There are also other plants for which the substratum is indifferent.

17

20

Some of these plants are only found at the alpine level growing low on the rocks, such as the Salix veticulata (17), the octopetalous mountain avens (11), Silene acaulis (14), Gentiana Clusii and Gentiana frigida (21), the small primrose (20), alpine violet. Others grow mainly on screes, for instance, the alpine poppy (18) and dwarf buttercup, in rock crevices, like the primrose, or in the moister gullies and places where snow lies longer, for instance the alpine buttercup (16) and Tatra saxifrage (13). Aconites, Tatra larkspur (22), Mulgedium alpinum, Ademostyles alliana, spotted gentian form a rich association of herbs at the borderline of the alpine meadows and mountain pine levels. Carlines (19), which grow in the Tatras and also lower, as far as the Polish Uplands, are often used as motifs in the regional folk art of the highlanders. All alpine plants are protected as rare species.

18

21

19

22

32

The fauna of the Tatras is also specific. Legal protection and human care help to preserve the rare species that are threatened with extinction. Rare and interesting species in the Tatras are the chamois (23), the marmot (24) and very rarely now, the bear and the golden eagle (25).

23

24   25

Hala Gąsienicowa (Gąsienica Alp) is a large mountain meadow on the borderline between the Western and Eastern Tatras, from which there is a magnificent view of the surrounding peaks. This old upland pasture with the shepherds huts that have been preserved to this day, is a very popular mountain holiday place and an excellent base for mountain climbing expeditions. On the upper forest line there is a tourists hostel called Murowaniec (27), beautifully designed to fit the landscape. In the winter, Hala Gąsienicowa is a favourite haunt of skiers, for a long and varied ski run crosses it, from the steep slopes of Mt. Kasprowy Wierch, through the forest (26) down to Zakopane. Tourism in the Tatras dates back to the second half of the 19th century. In 1873, the Tatra Society was founded. There is also a lively mountain climbing movement in Poland. Every year, many mountaineering enthusiasts (28) get plenty of thrills pitting their strength against the Tatran rock faces. Many of Poland's climbers gain experience in the Tatras before setting out on expeditions to the Caucasus Mts., the Andes or the Himalayas. The Voluntary Mountain Rescue Service is always on call to ensure the safety of those who go climbing in the mountains.

26

27   28

The cable car railway built in 1934 (29), which carries passengers from the station in Kuźnice, Zakopane, to the top of Kasprowy Wierch (alt. 1,988 m.), one of the peaks of the central ridge of the Tatras, makes it easier to go for expeditions in the High Tatras and provides many passengers with the pleasure of unforgettable views. The cable cars move over the forests of Bystra Valley to a change-cars station at Myślenickie Turnie, then up to the station on the Kasprowy Wierch peak. From there one gets a magnificent panoramic view of the High Tatras and the Western Tatras. Near the cable car exit is a meteorological station, which is situated at an altitude of 1959 m., the highest in Poland.

29

30

31

The "winter capital" of Poland – Zakopane – is situated at the foot of the northern slopes of the Tatras in a hollow called the Tatra Trough between Mts. Giewont and Gubałówka. From Mt. Gubałówka there is a beautiful view of Zakopane (30) with the Tatras in the background. Zakopane lies at an altitude of 800–1,000 m. It came into being as a village in the 16th century. In the middle of the 17th century there was an iron smelting centre at Kuźnice, the highest part of Zakopane. The first tourists came to Zakopane at the beginning of the 19th century, but its real development began after 1870. The climatic values of Zakopane were made known by Dr. Tytus Chałubiński. From then on more and more tourists began to go there, as well as holiday-makers and also people who sought a cure for their ailmonts. Zakopane also became the favourite haunt of the intellectual and artistic elite of Cracow and Warsaw. The main street, Krupówki (31), where social life and commerce are concentrated, is now a busy street such as one might see in many a large city.

As Zakopane developed the building style changed. Next to the old timber houses and farmsteads of the highlanders, villas were built which kept to the traditional highland style, for instance, the "Pod jedlami" Villa (32) which was designed by Stanisław Witkiewicz, who initiated the Zakopane style. Then came modern buildings, which are departing from the old style more and more. In Zakopane there are many sanatoria, holiday centres, tourist hostels such as Dom Turysty (34) and hotels. One of the newest and biggest of these is the "Kasprowy" Hotel (33). Examples of the original highland architecture and art have been preserved in Zakopane. It also has some interesting museums. Valuable ethnographic and geological collections and examples of the flora and fauna of the Tatras can bee seen in the Tatran Museum. In 1972, the Karol Szymanowski Museum was opened in the Villa Atma, where this famous composer lived and worked. It was there that he composed "Harnasie", a ballet based on highland motifs.

32

33

The alpine meadows high up in the Tatras, which in Polish are called "Hale", have been used by shepherds for centuries for seasonal grazing (35). In the spring, under the supervision of flock-masters called "baca", the shepherd boys (juhas) used to drive the flocks of sheep belonging to their villages high up into the mountains. They lived in wooden huts and were helped in their work of looking after the sheep by white Podhale sheepdogs. The shepherds made cheeses on the spot from ewes milk, namely "bunc", "bryndza" and "oscypki" cheeses. The shepherds had their own customs and special utensils for collecting the milk and making it into cheese. This was once the main occupation of the highlanders living in the large Podhale Basin, but today they are mostly engaged in farming. The pasture area has also been reduced since grazing was prohibited in the Tatra National Park. The spring and autumn "Redyk" (driving the sheep up into the mountains and bringing them down in the autumn) still take place, but in a changed form. Today the sheep are taken by train to the Low Beskids, the Bieszczady and Sudety Mts.

34

35

37

38

The highland folklore, preserved in the timber architecture, decorative art, regional costumes (36), music and dances, is beautiful and abundant. The men wear trousers of thick white woollen cloth embroidered with a characteristic motif called "parzenica", short woollen jackets called "cuha" sleeveless sheepskin waistcoats called "serdak", thick woollen cloth cloaks called "gunia" and round hats decorated with small shells. The older women still wear their flower-patterned skirts, bodices and beautiful kerchiefs. Attractive folk art objects are made in every highland village. The favourite motif carved by the highlanders is the carline and in their paintings on glass, the motif is the legendary highland robber Janosik. Carved furniture and ornaments adorn the homes of the highlanders. The old timber cottages of the highlanders have also been preserved, sometimes whole groups of them, as in the village of Chochołów (37), 17 km. west of Zakopane. There is also an interesting group of old timber buildings in Zubrzyca Górna, a village in the western part of Podhale called Orawa. The village elder's house, called "Moniak's House", built in 1784, now houses an ethnographic museum and Centre of Orawa Culture. Typical Orawa cottages (38) have also been brought to the museum from Jabłonka, an old inn from Podwilk, an oil mill and fulling mill and other Orawa buildings of the 18th and 19th century.

40

Rural sacral buildings of historical interest – old timber churches – are numerous, particularly in the northern part of Podhale. One of the most beautiful is the larch-wood church of St Michael the Archangel at Dębno (39), built in the second half of the 15th century, with a tower added later in 1601. It is partly shingle covered and the gable and pavilion roof is shingle covered too. The Dębno church is famed for its remarkable polychrome paintings and the triptych dating back to the beginning of the 16th century (40). Late Gothic sculptures have also been preserved there.

39 40

In the northern part of Podhale (41), the landscape is crossed by a belt of Jurassic limestone rocks, the prolongation of which are the Pieniny Mts. This area is predominantly agricultural. The long narrow strips of cultivated fields (43) rise far from the villages, which have grown up along the banks of the mountain streams. They are old chain-villages, evidence of settlement in the forests in the Middle Ages.

Not far from Czorsztyn, in the village of Kluszkowce, at the foot of the forestless andesite cone of Mt. Wżar (alt. 768 m.) a monument has been erected to the memory of those who lost their lives in the struggle to consolidate People's Poland (42).

41 42

43

45

The Pieniny Mts., a small mountain chain built of limestone with rugged crags, is famed for its wonderful scenery and luxuriant vegetation. The slopes of the Pieniny are covered with fir and beech forests with some larch and yew trees and mountain meadows with abundant grasses and flowers. On the warmer limestone rocks there are still relics of Tertiary vegetation, represented by the aromatic Zawadzki chrysanthemum. To protect the beautiful natural landscape of this mountain chain, the Pieniny National Park was founded in 1954. The highest and most varied part of the Pieniny Mts. is the Trzy Korony (Three Crowns) massif (45), the main peak of which is Okrąglica (alt. 982 m.) a magnificent viewpoint overlooking the Dunajec Gorge. The river flows through the Pieniny Mts. in a narrow, deep Gorge (46) curving in a deep arc with seven bends for nine kilometres. The Dunajec Gorge is considered to be one of the most beautiful in Europe and one of the tourist attractions there is floating the rapids on rafts made of several dugouts bound together, a thrilling and unforgettable experience. Mount Bystrzyk (47), rising over the right bank of the Dunajec on the border, belongs to the Little Pieniny Mts., a 12 kilometre ridge built of sandstone, marl and pudding-stone, with limestone rocks here and there.

Entrance to the Pieniny Mts. is guarded by two castles: Czorsztyn and Niedzica, former border strongholds along the trade route from Poland to Hungary and also the meeting places of diplomats from both countries. The Czorsztyn castle, a 13th century Polish stronghold, was enlarged by Casimir the Great in the 14th century. At the end of the 18th century it was destroyed by fire and since then it has remained in ruins. The Niedzica castle (44), on the opposite, right bank of the River Dunajec, was built by Hungarian magnates in the 14th century. It passed backwards and forwards between Hungarian and Polish lords and in the 16th century was for a time the headquarters of outlaw robber knights. After it was enlarged in the 17th century, it consisted of the upper Gothic castle which is in ruins today, and the lower castle rebuilt in Renaissance style. The lower castle today houses an Art Historians' Retreat for Creative Work.

47

46

To the north of the Pieniny Mts. are the Beskids. To the south-west, the boundary peak is Wielka Racza (1,236 m.) belonging to a mountain group which is part of the Żywiec Beskids. Among the forests of Wielka Racza there are beautiful, large clearings (48), which are excellent for skiing. The ski run down the western arm of the mountain to the Slovak side is regarded as one of the best in the Beskids.

The most westerly situated parts of the Silesian Beskids consist of the Czantoria Chain and the Barania Góra group. The Czantoria Chain (49) is lower and the slopes are gentler. The highest peak is Czantoria Wielka (alt. 997 m.). In the Barania Góra group, the main peak Skrzyczne rises to an altitude of 1,250 m., and Barania Góra itself has an altitude of 1,214 m. It is on the slopes of Barania Góra that the two springs Biała and Czarna Wisełka (50) have their source. The two streams link up to form the River Vistula.

48

The Barania Góra group is a very popular tourist and recreation area, visited in particular by the inhabitants of the nearby Upper Silesian Industrial District. The most well known resorts include Wisła, Brenna, Bystra, Szczyrk, Jaszowiec (52) and Ustroń (51). Many institutions have their holiday and recreation houses in these places. The well equipped sanatoria and holiday homes are often examples of original modern architecture introduced into the mountain scenery.

51

52

53

54 In the depression between the Silesian Beskids and the Żywiec Beskids there is a village called Koniaków, which is famed for the lace made there (53). The women of another village, Istebna, are also masters of this rare craft in Poland. In both of these villages one can see people in regional costumes any day. In many places in the Beskids there are abundant examples of highland folklore in the specific architecture, carvings, paintings, music, dances and colourful folk costumes (54).

Bielsko-Biała (55) came into being in 1951 with the merging of two separate towns – Bielsko and Biała – situated at the foot of the Silesian Beskids, and divided by the River Biała. In the times before Poland was partitioned, this river marked the frontier between Cieszyn Silesia, which belonged to the state of the Hapsburgs and the former Silesian Duchy of Oświęcim that was incorporated into Poland in the 15th century. In the 19th century, the River Biała was the frontier between Galicia and Austrian Silesia, and in the inter-war years it marked the boundary between the Silesian and Cracow voivodships. This division was the cause of considerable economic and social differences between Bielsko and Biała. This situation was only changed after the Second World War. Since they became one urban organism in 1951, Bielsko and Biała have become a large, rapidly growing centre of the textile and engineering industries. Since 1972, a factory producing the small Fiat 126p cars has been in operation there.

On the break of the River Soła through the Little Beskids, in the village of Porąbka, a dam and hydropower station has been built. It is one of the several projects of this type built on Carpathian rivers (56).

55

56

57

58   The highest mountains of the Beskids are in the Babia Góra group (57) with the rocky peak Diablak, covered with broken rock material, rising to an altitude of 1,725 m. The slopes of Babia Góra, up to about 1,400 m. are covered with rich Carpathian forests and, above this level, with dwarf pines and flowering meadows. To protect the original natural landscape, the Babia Góra National Park has been set up there. Lower, in the Little Beskids, there is an 18th century wooden church in Tokarnia (58), which is an interesting example of sacral folk architecture. Round the church are four chapels and a belfry. Inside it there are small altars and exhibits from prisoner-of-war camps in the Second World War.

At the foot of the Little Beskids, on the River Skawa, is Wadowice. As early as 1327 it was decribed as an "oppidum". It then belonged to the Silesian Piasts and was part of the Duchy of Zator. The Duchy, together with Wadowice, was purchased in 1494 by the Polish king John Olbracht. Nine years later the king granted it to Piotr Myszkowski. In 1802, the town bought its rights from the owner and in 1867 became a district centre. As early as the 16th century, Wadowice was known for its school, run by the burghers. However, the greatest fame was won by the town in 1978, when one of its sons, born and brought up there, became Pope John Paul II. The first written record concerning the present Pope is in the Christening Book at the old parish church, reconstructed in the 18th century in baroque style (59).

Amid the Wieliczka Foothills, the Wiśnicz Castle (60) rises majestically against the skyline. It was built on the route from Cracow to Hungary about 1500 by the powerful Kmita family, and enlarged in the 17th century by the Lubomirski family, the next owners, into a palatial residence and at the same time a powerful stronghold surrounded with defence walls with bastions of the new Italian type. The same kind of defence walls surrounded the town of Wiśnicz Nowy, below the castle, which was seriously damaged and plundered by the Swedes in the middle of the 17th century. After the big fire there at the end of the 19th century, Wiśnicz lost its significance and municipal rights. It was immortalized before the fire in the drawings of Jan Matejko, who often stayed there. A number of historical relics are still to be found in Wiśnicz, testifying to its glorious past.

59

60

The Rożnów Lake (61) – an artificial water reservoir (16 sq. km.) in the northern part of the Sącz Basin, was created by damming the waters of the Dunajec. The construction of the dam and hydro-electric plant at Rożnów, started before the Second World War, was one of the biggest investments of the Central Industrial District. The Rożnów Lake is a power reservoir, a safeguard against floods and at the same time an original accent in the landscape. The excellent conditions for holidays and water sports have led to the building of attractive tourist and recreation homes on the shores of the lake.

The capital of the Sącz region is Nowy Sącz (62). Founded in the 13th century as a fortified town, it grew wealthy from trade with Hungary. In the 14th and 15th centuries important assemblies and political conferences were held there. The town was granted many privileges, among others, the right to strike its own coins. It declined in the times of the partitions; in the interwar years it was a favourite haunt of artists and scientists. Today it is a rapidly developing industrial town, a cultural centre and the capital of a new voivodship. Despite the numerous fires in its history, Nowy Sącz still has many historical buildings, dating back to the Middle Ages. There are also many historical buildings in the older town of Stary Sącz (63), the origin of which can be traced back to the turn of the 10th century. It also belonged to the system of fortified towns on the "Hungarian" route. Having accumulated wealth from trade in corn and wines, it was one of the most prosperous Carpathian towns in the 14th to 16 th centuries and an important cultural centre. This historical town today lies on the fringe of a large fruit growing region, the centre of which is Łącko. The apple orchards alone in the region number about 50,000 trees. The plum brandy made in Łącko is widely renowned for its flavour.

61

62

63

64

66

65

67

There are many health resorts and spas in the Sącz Beskids. In the picturesque Grajcarek Valley between the Sącz Beskids and the Pieniny Mts. is Szczawnica, once a Carpathian village which became a well known spa in the second half of the 19th century when valuable alkaline-saline springs were discovered there. After the Second World War, the development of socialized medical care, both curative and prophylactic, made spa cures available to all. Many treatment centres and holiday homes have been built, among which there is a new physiotherapeutic centre (65) worthy of note.

Another well known health resort is Żegiestów (64) picturesquely situated on the southern slopes of the Poprad valley. It has abundant springs of acidulous waters containing sodium, lithium and manganese. The beautiful surrounding countryside and the mild climate, the long hours of sunshine and bathing in the Poprad, not to mention the fishing has made Żegiestów a very popular holiday resort.

However, the most popular resort of all is Krynica, the biggest spa in the Beskids, called "the pearl of Poland's spas". There are many mineral springs there, among which the Zuber spring is one of the most abundant acidulous-alkaline sources in Europe. The curative properties of the Krynica waters were already known at the end of the 18th century. The rapid development of the spa began in the second half of the 19th century and is still going on today. Apart from the old timber architecture (66), there are ever more numerous modern sanatoria and holiday homes (67).

In the eastern part of the Sącz Beskids, in the Low Beskids and the Bieszczady Mts., apart from Polish, Catholic villages there were also many villages inhabited by the Łemki and Bojki – highlanders belonging to the Greek-Catholic Uniate Church – originating from the Valachian settlers in the Middle Ages who spoke several dialects of the Ukrainian language. Their small churches, many of which – particularly in the region inhabited by the Łemki – are similar in construction and decoration to the wooden churches in the neighbouring Catholic villages, still stand in some places. An example of these is the shingle-covered church in Powroźnik (68), which is between Krynica and Muszyna. Built in 1643, it is one of the oldest and most beautiful Greek-Catholic churches in Poland. Among the fairly numerous preserved wooden Catholic churches in the area, special mention is due to the 16th century church in Sękowa (69), not far from Gorlice, of quoin construction, shingle covered with a timbered columnar tower.

68

69

70

To the north of the Low Beskids, on the borderline of the Jasło–Sanok Depression, there is the old town of Biecz (70) on the bank of the River Ropa. At the very beginning of our era a trade route existed here, along which Roman influences penetrated. The first written mention of Biecz dates back to 1023. In the 14th to 16th centuries it was a thriving trade centre on the "Hungarian" route, with well developed handicrafts and a lively cultural life. In the 17th century Biecz went into a period of decline, harrassed by fires and plagues, and was finally ravaged by the Swedes. The town revived somewhat at the end of the 19th century in connection with the development of the oil industry in the surrounding area. Today it is a centre of trade and culture, servicing the neighbouring rural area.

The Jasło–Sanok Depression, stretching between the Low Beskids and the Przemyśl Foothills is the oldest, and so far the most important Polish oil industry district. In the middle of the 19th century, an apothecary from Gorlice, Ignacy Łukasiewicz, elaborated a method of extracting crude oil and distilling oil and invented the first oil lamp in the world. Thanks to his inventions, Gorlice became the cradle of the oil industry (71). Shortly afterwards oil extraction was started in the vicinity of Krosno and Jasło. The first oil-well was sunk by I. Łukasiewicz at Bóbrka, near Krosno as early as 1854. In 1862, the first drilling rig was built there. The first oil refinery was built not far from Bóbrka at Chorkówka. An oil-well 18 metres deep and Łukasiewicz's workshop with boiler house and horse-gear, which have been preserved, became the nucleus of the first oil industry museum in the world.

71

72

The town of Sanok (72) is also connected with the oil industry although many people associate it with the production of buses. Sanok is situated on the extreme east of the Jasło–Sanok Depression in the Sanok Basin. Records from the year 1150 describe it as a fortified town. It gained municipal status in 1366. Having been granted trade privileges it developed well from trade with Hungary. During the Swedish wars it was seriously damaged and plundered. There was an economic enlivenment at the end of the 19th century in connection with the building of a railway line linking Sanok with Jasło and Drohobycz, the discovery of oil near the town and the expansion of its engineering works producing drilling equipment, boilers and wagons, which had developed from a small workshop producing boilers founded in 1832.

On the borderline between the Jasło–Sanok Depression and the Bieszczady Mts. the town of Lesko grew up. This small town was an important rade centre and stronghold in the 15th to 17th centuries. The powerful Kmita family built a fortified castle there in the 16th century, which stands to this day, having been partly rebuilt. Its late Gothic church, the remains of defence walls, two buildings which once served as inns and the synagogue (built at the turn of the 16th century) are all from the 16th century.

Jews settled in Poland as from the 13th century; they enjoyed considerable religious freedom and within their kahals (communes) had complete autonomy. During the Second World War, the Nazis not only systematically conducted an extermination policy towards the Jewish population but also destroyed their places of worship, not even sparing those of historical interest. The synagogue in Lesko (73) is therefore one of the very few extant buildings of this kind in Poland.

After the construction of the dam and hydro-electric power station on the River San, near Lesko, in the Sixties, a picturesquely situated lake was created among the hills, namely, the Solina lake, with an attractive tourist and water sports centre (74). Modern holiday homes, camping sites, etc. have been growing up on the shores of the lake since it was created.

74

75

58

The Bieszczady Mts. are the western limb of the Eastern Carpathians, consisting of long parallel mountain ridges divided by wide depressions. The highest peaks in the Polish part of the Bieszczady Mts. are Tarnica (alt. 1,346 m.) and the neighbouring peaks of Krzemień and Halicz (2), both rising to an altitude of 1,335 m. They are in the area embraced by the Bieszczady National Park.

The Bieszczady Mts. depopulated after the war during the fighting against the Ukrainian nationalists and due to the resettlement of part of the population to the USSR, are one of the most sparsely populated areas of Poland today. To make the area more accessible, the Bieszczady Loop Road (76) – winding attractively among the mountains – has been built. The top, open parts of the Bieszczady Mts. grown with tall grasses, abundant flowers and alder shrubs, are called "połoninas". The best known of them are the Caryńska and Wetlińska połoninas (77), used for a long time as grazing places for sheep. They are surrounded by beech forests (81), which grow up to an altitude of 1,000 m. The steep mountain slopes, grown with the dark regel forests, are cut through here and there by mountain streams, which flow into the San. The scenery, the unique monuments of nature, and the attractions of these rather primitive pioneer conditions are drawing more and more tourists to the Bieszczady Mts. But man is still only a guest here, moving along marked routes and rarely venturing deep into the wild country. Some go for hiking holidays with tents, but most people stay at the settlements at the foot of the high mountains and make excursions from there. The main excursion bases are Ustrzyki Górne, Cisna and Komańcza, where there is a Greek-Catholic church of historical interest (built in 1805), see (75).

75

76

77

There are plenty of wild animals in the forests of the Bieszczady Mts., among them deer and wild boars. There are even some European bison, recently brought there. But in the wild parts there are wolves (78), lynx (79) and bears (80). There are also venomous snakes in the area, but the Aesculap snake, not found elsewhere in Poland, is not dangerous.

78   79

80

After the destruction and depopulation of the Bieszczady Mts. caused by the war, this area was developed according to new principles. Exploitation of the forests and pasture-breeding of cattle was developed on a large scale by state farms. Sheep from Podhale are brought to the Bieszczady pastures for summer grazing.

The ancient custom of shepherds moving from place to place with their flocks has been given new forms (82) and wider scope, taking advantage also of abandoned farm lands, which began to be overgrown with grey alders after the war.

In the Dynów Foothills, as in the whole area of the Carpathians and Subcarpathians, agriculture is very fragmentated. Small farms and long narrow fields create a characteristic kind of landscape (83). Horses and manual labour are still the main driving power here. At a lower level than Solina, there is another dam at Myczkowce. Nearby, the River San cuts through the hills known as "Rusztowe" (Gridiron), rising in a sheer rock face 60–80 m. above the river (85).

82

83

84

On the banks of the San, near Przemyśl, there is a magnificent late Renaissance castle at Krasiczyn, the former residence of the Krasicki family, built in the years 1592–1614 by the Italian architect Galoazzo Appiani. It was partly rebuilt in the 19th century (85).

Przemyśl, one of the most beautifully situated towns in Poland (86) is on the banks of the River San where it flows from the hills into the Subcarpathian Basins. It was referred to in chronicles as a stronghold on the Polish-Ruthenian border as early as 981. It changed hands a number of times, finally to become a crown property after Halicz Ruthenia was incorporated into Poland in 1344. Situated on a trade route leading from Central Europe to the Black Sea, it grew into a big centre of trade and handicrafts. Under Austrian rule it was turned into a powerful fortress town, under siege in the First World War. Today it is rapidly developing as an important industrial centre and junction and since 1975 it has been a voivodship capital. There are numerous buildings of historical interest in the town: the partially preserved 14th century castle, the Gothic cathedral (1460–1571), later rebuilt in Baroque style, the Canon's House and former Cathedral school (16th cent.) and churches and monasteries from the 16th and 17th centuries, including the Baroque church of the Carmelites built in 1630, which in the years 1784–1945 was a Greek-Catholic church.

The first mention of Jarosław in chronicles was in 1152. In the 14th century it finally came under Polish rule. It was granted municipal status in 1375, as an important centre at the crossing of the trade routes from Silesia and the Baltic to the Black Sea. In 1387, Władysław I Jagiełło gave the town and the surrounding property of Jaśko of Tarnów to the founder of the Tarnowski family. Changing hands several times, Jarosław remained a privately owned town until 1846. The peak period of its development was in the 15th to 17th centuries and it is from this period that the preserved historical buildings originate, namely: Renaissance and Baroque churches and monasteries dating back to the 16th to 18th century, a Greek-Catholic church dating back to 1746, parts of the old defence walls and a beautiful market place with a Town Hall, which was first in Gothic style, then reconstructed in Baroque style, as well as some interesting 16th century houses, among which the house of the merchant family of Orsetti (87) is worthy of note. Under the Old Town, there are several levels of cellars and dungeons, which are a great tourist attraction.

87

88

89

The early Baroque castle at Łańcut was built in the years 1629–1641 by the architect Maciej Trapola. He was commissioned to build it by Stanisław Lubomirski, who wanted it to be a stronghold; and in fact it did withstand the attacks of the Swedes in 1657. The castle was enlarged and altered several times and at the end of the 18th century it was one of the most magnificent magnates residences in Poland (88). The decoration of the facade and the rich interiors of the palace (89) were the work of many well known artists, both Polish and foreign. Valuable art collections were taken from the palace at the end of the Second World War by the owner Count A. Potocki. At present the palace houses a museum with collections of paintings, sculptures, old porcelian, Gobelin tapestries, and period furniture. A separate section of the museum is the collection of carriages and coaches from the 18th to 20th centuries, to be seen in the old coach house in the magnificent park surrounding the palace.

90

91 Rzeszów on the River Wisłok was a border stronghold on the Polish-Ruthenian frontier. In 1344, it was incorporated into Poland and in 1354 it was granted municipal status. It was destroyed and looted many times by the Tatars, Swedes, Rakoczy's troops and the Saxons, so its development was slow. In the inter-war period it was a small town that was just beginning to develop in connection with the construction of the Central Industrial District. However, its real development only came in People's Poland. Rzeszów, now capital of the voivodship of the same name, an important industrial and cultural centre, has turned into a large, modern town (90). The buildings of historical interest include the 15th century parish church, churches and monasteries of the Bernardine and Piarist monks dating back to the 17th century, the 17th century castle of the Ligęza family, which later belonged to the Lubomirskis (91), the late Baroque palace of the Lubomirski family (18th cent.) and two reconstructed synagogues from the 17th and 18th centuries.

Where the hills and the Sandomierz Basin meet, on the banks of the River Biała not far from the place where it flows into the Dunajec, stands Tarnów, mentioned in chronicles as early as 1105 as a settlement belonging to the Benedictine Abbey in Tyniec. In 1330, the Cracow castellan Specimir, ancestor of the Melsztyński and Tarnowski families, was granted the privilege of founding a town, which he built according to the classic mediaeval layout, that is still evident today, with a square market place and a rectangular network of streets. Near the town was a fortified castle surrounded by defence walls. Owing to its situation in a place where important trade routes met, Tarnów developed well till the time of the Swedish wars. There are still numerous historical buildings from those times, among them the 14th century Gothic Town Hall, remodelled in the 16th century in Renaissance style (92), the Gothic cathedral built in the 15th century, the 16th century burghers houses round the market place and parts of the old city walls. Tarnów experienced a moderate growth rate in the second half·of the 19th century, but it was only the building of the Nitrogen Works (93) at Mościce (now a district of the town) in the years 1927–1929 and the development of industry after the Second World War that brought a real acceleration in its development. As new housing estates grew up, modern architecture came to the town, also evident in sacral building, an example of which is a new church (94).

The magnificent 17th century organ (95) in the Bernardine church in Leżajsk, completely built by Polish artisans, is one of the oldest in Poland. Leżajsk, situated in the Sandomierz Basin on the River San, gained municipal status in 1397. At the beginning of the 17th century, a notorious private war was waged in Leżajsk and vicinity between the „starost" Łukasz Opaliński and the Lord of Łańcut Stanisław Stadnicki, who, owing to his violent temper and ruthless treatment of the peasants, was known as the Devil of Łańcut. During this war with Opaliński, he attacked the town, looted it and burnt the church down. Shortly afterwards he was killed in a battle with the king's army. Opaliński then founded the Bernardine monastery there. Ravaged during the Swedish wars. Leżajsk could not recover from its decline for a long time. At the turn of the 19th century the production of woollen cloth began to develop there. Today the town is a service centre for a small rural area.

92

93

94

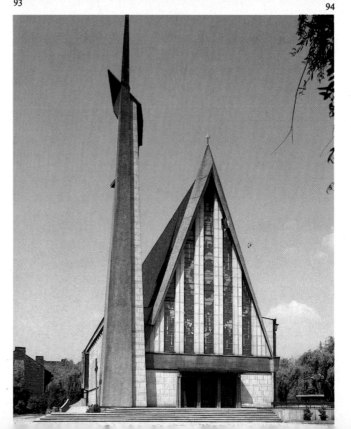

In March 1937, work began on the construction of a large steel works amid the Sandomierz forests on the site of the former village of Pławno. Two years later, the first steel was produced. The new settlement was given the name Stalowa Wola (Steel Will) and is to this day a centre producing high quality steel and recently also road machines (96). This was the biggest investment made in the Central Industrial District. The location of this industrial district in the central-south part of the country and the concentration of the factories and works in a "triangle of security" in the fork of the Vistula and San Rivers, dictated by strategic reasons, was at the same time intended to help the growth of a region that was economically neglected and overpopulated. Most of the industrial works in the Central Industrial District were built from state funds. Some of them had already started production before the outbreak of the Second World War, but the majority were only started up in People's Poland. The engineering works in Mielec (97) is producing special planes for agriculture, most of which are exported.

In 1953, near Tarnobrzeg, sulphur desposits were discovered, which turned out to be among the biggest in the world (98). Extraction was started in 1958, and in 1960 a big plant for processing the sulphur started production. The influence of industry has made the little town of Tarnobrzeg into a modern town which, since 1975, is the capital of a new voivodship.

96

97

98

99

Baranów Sandomierski, an old fortified town
between Tarnobrzeg and Mielec, won fame as
a centre of the Reformation Movement. In the 16th
century, its owners, the Leszczyński family, who were
Calvinists, turned the church into Protestant church,
and in 1628 they opened a printing house, which
issued many valuable works. Later the town became
the property of the Lubomirski family. One of them,
Karol, a zealous Catholic, destroyed all te evidences
of the worship of the other faith. The town then
declined. Today, Baranów is known for the
magnificent residence of the Leszczyński family,
a masterpiece of Renaissance architecture (99). It
was built in the years 1591–1606 by the Italian
architect Santi Gucci and was modelled on the design
of the Royal Wawel Castle in Cracow, with towers on
the corners, a decorative high parapet wall and an
arcaded courtyard (100). After the Second World
War, the castle was restored, the funds for this being
provided by the Sulphur Works. Among other things,
the castle now houses a Museum of Sulphur.

100

The village of Zalipie, near Dąbrowa Tarnowska is a well known centre of folk art. The traditional folk painting, which practically died out in the 19th century, was revived in Zalipie in the inter-war years. On the initiative of one of the village women, Felicja Curyłowa, all the village housewives began painting the quoins of their cottages (101) and adorning the interiors with plant motifs. After Curyłowa's death (1974) a museum room was arranged in her cottage exhibiting folk art (102).

101

102

Salt mining in Wieliczka goes back to at least the 9th century. The first documents concerning the salt mine date back to 1044. The enlargement of the mine is associated with the name of Kinga, the wife of Prince Bolesław the Chaste (1226–1279). The mine belonged to the royal family, but it was leased to magnates. After the partitions of Poland it became the property of the Austrian government and in 1918 – of the Polish government. Today, salt is still extracted in parts of the mine (103), and part of it has been turned into a museum, famous for the beautiful underground corridors and chambers, the most charming being two chapels with altars and sculptures in salt and the fabulous Crystal Grotto. Some of the chambers have recently been used for curative purposes.

To the west of the Sandomierz Basin is the Oświęcim Basin, where the Vistula flows along a wide valley (104). This area, abounding in waters and with large marshy stretches, was already known in the Middle Ages for its fish ponds, which are numerous. There are not many forests in the area, and those that have survived are predominantly of pine and oak trees. There is an interesting bird sanctuary of night herons in the marshy meadows near Zator, the only one in Poland.

103

104

Oświęcim, an important junction and industrial centre, is situated almost in the centre of the Oświęcim Basin. It has an interesting and tragic history. As an important stronghold, it was marked on a map made by an Arabian scholar al Idrisi as early as 1150. In 1179, separated from the Cracow principality it became the property of the Silesian Prince of Raciborz, and as from 1317, it was the capital of a separate duchy, which in 1456 was purchased by the Polish king Casimir IV Jagiellon and later (1564) incorporated into the Cracow voivodship. In the times of the Reformation, the town was the scene of violent religious struggles. After the first partition of Poland, it was incorporated into Austria. In the years before the Second World War it was a small industrial and trading town. During the Nazi occupation, a huge concentrations camp was set up there, one of the most terrible death camps (German name Auschwitz), in which more than four million people of 28 nationalities, lost their lives, Poles and Jews constituting the great majority of prisoners. In memory of their martyrdom, the whole area of the camp has been turned into a museum (105). The horror and sufferings of the martyred prisoners is shown by the exhibits that have been preserved there. A monument has been built (106) to commemorate those who died there.

The Polish Uplands

1

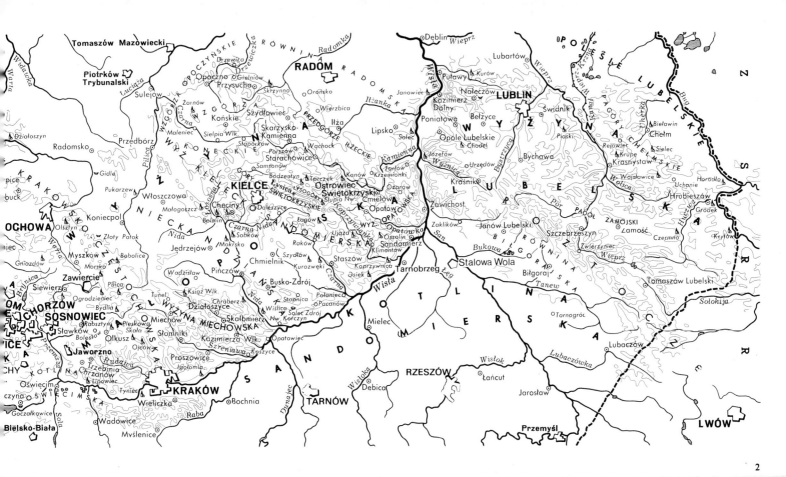

2

The Polish Uplands extend from the upper reaches of the River Odra to the upper reaches of the River Bug. They consist of various rock formations dating from the ancient Upper Cambrian period to the Quaternary, which vary as to type and resistance. The elevations run from the north-west to the south-east, that is, contrary to the whole system of uplands. This is because all its elements, formed and folded in various geological epochs, were compressed into one system when the Carpathians were folding in the Tertiary Period. The Vistula cuts through this system, dividing it into two limbs – the Małopolska Upland and the Lublin Upland.

In the past a considerable area of the Polish Uplands constituted the northern part of Małopolska (Polonia minor) and only the Silesian Upland came within the historical boundaries of Silesia. The Małopolska Upland consists of units of different ages and origin that have undergone considerable destruction and have a variety of elevations and forms. The oldest parts, the Holy Cross Mountains and the Silesian Upland, were uplifted in the Paleozoic era (by the Hercynian Orogenesis), like the Massif Central in France, the Harz Mts., the Bohemian Massif and the Sudety Mts. From the Sudety Mts. then being formed (they were then much higher than today) masses of rocky material were washed down into mountain valleys and depressions among the foothills, covering the luxuriant tropical flora that grew there. The area of the present Silesian Upland was just such a depression in the Upper Carboniferous epoch. As a result of these processes alternating layers of sandstone, conglomerate and slate, as much as several thousand metres thick, were formed, with coal deposits sandwiched in between them. The parts of the Silesian Upland and Subcarpathian Basin that have coal deposits form the Upper Silesian Coal Basin, one of the biggest in the world as regards size and abundance of coal. It covers an area of 5,400 sq.km., of which 4,450 sq.km. comes within Poland's frontiers, and its rich deposits are estimated at 65,000 million tons of coal (down to a depth of 1,000 m.). In later geological epochs the Silesian Upland was covered by a sea, at the bottom of which sandstone and conglomerate deposits formed and after these came layers of shelly limestone, which in many places turned into dolomites called "ore-bearing" because of the zinc and lead ores they contained, with an admixture of silver, cadmium and thallium. In the Quaternary epoch this area was covered by the oldest (Mindel) glaciation, traces of which are present in the form of glacial deposits (mainly sands) among the older rock formations in the depressions, and in connection with this sand dunes are commonly found in the area. The largest area of loose sands is the Błędów Desert (30 sq.km.) which is something quite unique in Europe.

As regards surface relief, the Silesian Upland is an undulating country with widely scattered isolated hills, ridges and flat elevations. But where there are dolomites and shelly limestones the landscape is more varied. The altitude of the Upland is slightly varied around 300 m. above sea level, but in several places it rises to 400 m. In the north and northwest, the Silesian Upland gradually descends to the Silesian lowland, in the south it drops towards the Oświęcim Basin and in the east and north-east it ends at the sharp rise (up to 150 m.) marking the verge of the Cracow–Częstochowa Upland.

The Cracow–Częstochowa Upland is a long belt stretching from Cracow, through Częstochowa to Wieluń. It is mainly composed of hard Jurassic rock together with a belt of soft Middle Jurassic clayey rocks containing deposits of iron ore. In the southern part, Triassic, Permian and older formations from Carboniferous to Devonian emerge from the Jurassic rocks, among them domes of effusive rocks, namely, diabases, porphyres and melaphyres. A characteristic feature of the Cracow–Częstochowa Upland are the isolated limestone rocks, "inselbergs", the highest of which rise to more than 500 m. above sea level (Ogrodzieniec, Ojców). The Upland is cut through by deep valleys with steep rocky sides and the whole area abounds in Karst forms, the best examples of which can be seen in the Prądnik Valley near Ojców. In the south, this Upland gradually descends to the Vistula Valley, slightly overstepping it near Cracow. In the north the Jurassic formations disappear beneath the glacial deposits of the Polish Plain and in the east beneath the soft cretaceous sandstone and marls and the loess layers of the Miechów Upland.

The Miechów Upland (300–400 m. above sea level) has the characteristic features of loess areas, large gently sloping humps divided by ravines. In the east it comes down into the triangular Nida Basin (200–300 m. above sea level), formed of cretaceous rocks, in the south covered with Miocene Sea deposite (limestone gypsum and loam) and in the north by thick layers of glacial sands. Some interesting gypsum Karst phenomena can be seen near Busko. In some places the gypsum has disintegrated into limestone and sulphur, deposits of which occur near Cracow, Szydłów, Staszów, Koprzywnica and Tarnobrzeg.

To the east of the Nida Basin is the Kielce–Sandomierz Upland, with an old Paleozoic massif of complicated structure and its Mesozoic frame. The whole of this formation was rejuvenated during the Alpine orogenesis. The Holy Cross Mountains and the Sandomierz Upland form part of the Kielce–Sandomierz Upland area. The Holy Cross Mountains consist of a number of parallel ridges extending from the River Pilica to the vicinity of Opatów. They rise from a common foundation at an altitude of 270 m. These ridges owe their elevation to the greater resistance of their rocks. The depressions between them were formed in places where the rocks were less resistant. The Łysogóry Range is the highest (592–611 m. above sea level). In the north-west it joins the Masłów Range and in the south-east – the Jeleniowskie Range. This main range is formed from hard Cambrian rocks (quartzites and sandstones) which in places, due to weathering, disintegrated into Goulder fields. They are found, above all, on the tops of Mts. Łysica (alt. 611 m.) and Łysa Góra (alt. 593 m.) which are the highest of the Łysogóry Range. The Dymińsko-Orłowińskie Range (alt. 370–450 m.) situated to the south is built from similar rocks, but is more dismembered, comprising a series of smaller and isolated ridges. To the north of the Łysogóry Range is the rather lower Klonów Range (Mt.

Bukowa alt. 465 m.) built of red Devonian sandstone. To the south-west of the Dymińsko-Orłowińskie Range is the Chęciny Range (Mt. Zelejowa alt. 367 m.), which consist of several sharp ridges of Devonian limestone, which in some places has turned into dolomite. The results of similar transformations also appear in the Holy Cross Mts. in the form of deposits of pyrites, iron ores (hematite, siderite), copper and lead. Barites are also found there. The Końskie Hills form the north-western part of the Holy Cross Mts. They are built of sandstone, slate and Triassic and Jurass limestones, among which deposits of iron ore, lignite and ceramic clay are found.

East of Holy Cross Mts. is the Sandomierz Upland, the foundation of which are Cambrian and Devonian formations, covered in some places by deposits from the Miocene Sea and later by a loess cover up to 30 m. thick. Near Sandomierz, Cambrian schists emerges from the loess cover. The high shoulder of the Upland extending to the Vistula Valley is called the Pieprzowe Mts.

The Małopolska Upland is a water node from which numerous rivers flow, although their waters are not very abundant.

Some of them flow direct into the Odra, and others through the intermediary of the River Warta. However, most of them flow into the Vistula and its left-bank tributary – the Pilica.

To the east of the Vistula, which flows through a deep valley (60 – 70 m. deep) cutting through the Polish Uplands, is the Lublin Upland, formed of thick layers of soft cretaceous rocks covered with loess. The Upland descends in a northerly direction from 320 to 220 m. above sea level and then drops steeply 20–40 metres from an abrupt verge towards the Mazovian and Podlasie plain. To the east this verge gradually disappears merging into the Chełm Hills, a transitional area, low and flat with isolated cretaceous hills. Rivers have formed the Lublin Upland into a number of slightly undulating elevations and hills with gentle slopes divided by shallow ravines. The surroundings of Kazimierz Dolny and Kraśnik provide the only variation in landscape with their deep gullies carved by water (to a depth of 150 m.).

The Lublin Upland is joined to the Podole Upland by a narrow ridge (15 to 20 km. wide) known as Roztocze. It rises 250 to 390 m. above sea level and is mainly of Miocene formations on a cretaceous foundation, covered with loess in the western part. Its flat surface, cut through by ravines formed by streams, ends in a sudden drop of 70 m. to the Sandomierz Basin. On the South-East a small part of the Volhynia Upland comes within Poland's frontiers.

The climate of the Polish Uplands is comparatively warm, but on the higher parts winter lasts longer and the growing season is shorter. Rainfalls are more abundant, generally more than 600 mm. and as much as 800 mm. annually in some places. The coldest climate is in the Holy Cross Mts. the warmest in the Nida Basin, the driest in the Sandomierz Upland and the eastern part of the Lublin Upland. Further east, the climate becomes more continental.

Owing to the great diversity of geological structure, the water conditions and vegetation, the Polish Uplands have the most varied soil conditions. In the Holy Cross Mountains there are acid clayey soils formed on the Cambrian or Devonian sandstone bedrock covered with beech or beech-fir forests. A large part of the Końskie Hills have dry, acid, sandy soils formed on sandstone covered with pine woods. On the foundation of various carbonate rocks (limestone, marl) rendzina soils of varying fertility have been formed. The Jurassic rendzina soils of the Cracow–Częstochowa Upland are practically sterile. Devonian rendzina soils of medium fertility are found on the southern parts of the Holy Cross Mts. The most fertile rendzina soils are those with a high humus content formed on the soft cretaceous marls and limestones covering a considerable area of the Nida Basin and the Lublin Upland. There are also other rendzina soils formed on gypsum, fertile, but difficult to cultivate. They are found above all, along the left bank of the River Nida. Fertile loess soils formed on areas with a loess deposits, and in places where grassy vegetation was once predominant there are the chernozem soils rich in humus. The most fertile are the chernozem soils in the vicinity of Proszowice, Sandomierz and Hrubieszów. Various podsolized soils, not generally very fertile, were formed on the postglacial formations covered with coniferous forests of the Nida Basin and the western part of the Kielce–Sandomierz Upland.

In the past the Polish Uplands were mostly covered with forests. The higher parts of the Holy Cross Mts. and some of the moister slopes of the Silesian and Cracow–Częstochowa uplands, and the Roztocze Ridge had fir and fir-beech forests, where oak, maple, mountain elm, sycamore, lime and spruce trees also grew, resembling the mountain forests of the lower regel level. The remains of these forests have survived in the Holy Cross Mts. (the famous Fir Forest now in the Holy Cross National Park). In the lower areas, not so moist, with clayey or sandy-clayey soils there were mixed forests with a predominance of pine trees and with a large percentage of fir, beech and oak tress. They have survived over considerable areas of the lower parts of the Holy Cross Mts. In this zone Polish larch woods grew quite frequently, the few remains of which are now under protection in special reserves (for instance, Góra Chełmska, near Nowa Słupia). On the sandy soils there were various kinds of pine forests, which still cover large areas of the Silesian Upland and Końskie Hills today. In damper places there are bog pine and alder forests. On the other hand, the sparse oak woods and the oak and hornbeam gronds that once grew on the fertile loess soils and cretaceous rendzinas are now a rarity. To the east of the Cracow–Częstochowa Upland, one sometimes still comes across small thickets of xerothermic vegetation, which have survived on the slopes of limestone, gypsum or loess hills, particularly those facing south. They are dense thickets composed of dwarf oaks, hornbeams, linden trees, as well as numerous bushes and many herbaceous plants. There are also some swards of xerothermic herbaceous plants resembling steppe vegetation.

The natural conditions of the Polish Uplands, conducive to human husbandry, led to very early settlement in this area. It was here, in the caves of Ojców and in the vicinity of Cracow and Zawiercie, that the oldest traces of Palaeolithic man in Poland (200,000 – 80,000 years back) were discovered. The discoveries from the Neolithic Age (4000 – 1800 B.C.) are: a flint mine found at Krzemionki Opatowskie, near Ostrowiec Świętokrzyski (Holy Cross Mts.) the biggest known in Europe with 700 to 1,000 shafts, and stone masons workshops near Ćmielów. The tools produced there, mainly axes, were distributed to distant places such as the Basins of the Vistula, Warta, Odra, and even the Elbe and the Niemen. In numerous Neolithic sites in the Prądnik Valley, and the Miechów, Sandomierz and Lublin uplands, finds have been made indicating human activity in the fields of land cultivation and animal breeding.

Agriculture results in a settled kind of life, and left the first traces of human settlements in the form of dug-outs. In the middle of the Bronze Age, the Polish Uplands came under the influence of the Lusatian culture (1250–400 B.C.). Agriculture developed, new tools were made of copper and bronze, and later of iron (from about 700 B.C.), first imported from the south and later (about 200 B.C.) produced on the spot. Bog iron ore with a low iron content was commonly used for smelting and in the Holy Cross Mts. probably also the soft Devonian hematites. In addition to the smelting furnaces, there were also smithies producing such agricultural implements as scythes, sickles and coulters. There are numerous traces of potters' kilns. Roman coins found in the area are a proof of extensive trading.

Traces have been found of fortified settlements built by the local population to defend themselves from the Huns, the Awars and other nomadic tribes from the east at the time of the Great Migration. It was probably these invasions that inclined some of the inhabitants of the southern slopes of the Polish Uplands to move north to the Holy Cross Mts. and the forests of the Mazovian plain or to the Subcarpathian and Carpathian basins where there were thick forests.

During the early Middle Ages, like Wielkopolska, the Małopolska Upland was a centre where Polish statehood was taking shape. In the areas on the upper reaches of the Vistula and in the Nida Valley there was a large tribal centre of the Vislanes, the oldest state organization on Polish territory known from historical sources, with its main centres in Wiślica and Cracow. The Sandomierz Upland came within the territory of another tribe, most probably the Lędzice (Lendizi), and the Lublin Upland was a zone where Polish and Ruthenian tribes struggled for influence.

The seizure of Silesia and the basin of the upper Vistula by the Great Moravian State and, later, by the Czechs made it a foregone conclusion that Wielkopolska was to be the leading force to unite the Polish lands into one state organism. However, already under the rule of Bolesław Chrobry (The Brave) (992–1025), after Małopolska and Silesia had been regained, the southern frontiers of Poland ran along the Sudety and Carpathian Mts. Cracow assumed a more important role, becoming the capital of the state in 1037. In the period when Poland was divided into a number of duchies (1138–1320) it was the capital of the indivisible grand duchy ruled by the senior member of the dynasty as a supreme ruler vested with sovereign authority. After Poland was united, Cracow became the city where the coronation of Polish kings was held and the capital of the kingdom.

The last of the Piast rulers Casimir the Great (1333–1370) completed the task of uniting Poland and extended her frontiers to include Halicz Ruthenia. He also introduced a number of reforms that strengthened the central authorities and military strength of the country and put the state apparatus and economic life of Poland in order. The number of towns and villages grew rapidly and trade and handicrafts developed. The Cracow, Proszowice and Sandomierz were the most densely populated in the country. Cracow had a population of more than 10,000 and became a big centre of economic and cultural life. In 1364, Casimir the Great founded the Cracow Academy, one of the oldest universities in Europe, the second after the Prague University in central Europe. The period of flourishing development which started then was to last till the end of the 16th century.

The economic development of the southern parts of the Polish Uplands was accompanied by expansion to the sparsely settled area of the Holy Cross Mts. and surrounding forests, where hunters and forest bee-keepers had settled long before. The inhabitants of the forests, who were the subjects of princes, retained their personal and economic freedom much longer than the population of the agricultural areas. At the turn of the 14th century the settlements of the knighthood had only just penetrated to the fringes of the Łysogóry Range. In addition to the authority of the princes, the influence of the Church had also penetrated from the parishes founded in fortified settlements and monasteries. The Cistercian monks who had settled there in the 12th century were particularly active. They drained the swampy valley of the River Kamienna and then started wide-scale production of iron, using the local ores and water power gained by building dams on the River Kamienna and its tributaries. The example of the Cistercians was later followed by others, both lay and ecclesiatic authorities, setting up smelting furnaces and forges. The mining of copper and lead ores developed in the vicinity of Kielce, Chęciny and Łagów and also the exploitation of the marble round Chęciny.

The development of mining, industry and trade in the Holy Cross Mts. accelerated agricultural settlement, which progressed towards the mountains from the south along the Vistula, from the east along the Łagów Basin and the Kamienna Valley, and from the north and west along the route leading from Wielkopolska to Ruthenia. All over the area between the Vistula and the Holy Cross Mts. numerous churches, monasteries, castles and palaces were built through the ages. The Reformation Movement developed here very strongly, particularly the radical Arians, whose main centres were Pińczów, Raków and Chmielnik.

The development of mining also contributed to the settlement of the unfertile areas of the Cracow-Częstochowa Upland and the poor, forest-grown lands of the Silesian Upland. There was a rapid development of the old lead and silver mines in the vicinity of Olkusz, Trzebinia and Sławków, and also near Tarnowskie Góry and Bytom. On the upper reaches of the Warta, near Częstochowa and Zawiercie a new iron ore mining region developed. Numerous furnaces and forges were set up along the Biała and Czarna Przemsza rivers and Mała Panew. Urban centres were founded or existing ones expanded.

Nevertheless, until the 19th century, the Silesian Upland remained rather sparsely populated.

After Red Ruthenia was incorporated into Poland by Casimir the Great, there was an increase in settlement on the Lublin Upland. The old towns developed and new ones were built. Even so, the Lublin Upland was still poorly populated in the 16th century and settlement on the Roztocze Ridge had only just started. So whereas there are quite a number of Romanesque buildings in the Małopolska Upland and a great number of Gothic buildings, the Gothic style is rarely seen on the Lublin Upland and the oldest buildings are from the Renaissance period.

The union of Poland with Lithuania under the rule of the Jagiellon dynasty (1385–1572), the regaining of access to the sea (1466) after the victories over the Teutonic Knights, and also the privileges granted to the gentry during the 15th century, had an influence on the rate and direction of economic growth.

Conditions were created for activiting the regions situated to the west of the Vistula, there was an increase in the export of Polish corn, the production of which was gradually being taken over by the landed estates, using serf labour.

The Vistula route was the most convenient for this export, which went through Gdańsk. The corn trade contributed to the development of the Małopolska towns on the banks of the Vistula, particularly Sandomierz and Kazimierz Dolny.

Cracow became a big trading city where handicrafts flourished, as well as a centre of art and learning, concentrated round the university, today called the Jagiellonian University.

Nicolaus Copernicus studied there. The affluence of the city in the 16th century is indicated by the magnificent examples of Renaissance architecture and art to be seen there.

The union of Lublin between Poland and Lithuania (1569) and the transfer of the capital from Cracow to Warsaw brought the previously peripheral Lublin Upland into a central position. Lublin became a junction linking Warsaw with Ruthenia and Cracow with Lithuania. It was the seat of the Crown Tribunal, assemblies of the Diet were held there and economic life flourished. On the other hand, the Małopolska Upland was losing its importance and its economy was being limited more and more to agriculture and the transport of corn down the Vistula to Gdańsk. The Swedish wars in the second half of the 17th century as well as the political and economic crisis of the first half of the 18th century brought a decline of towns and industry all over the Polish state. Attempts to achieve a revival in the second half of the 18th century brought a slight improvement, especially the ore mining and iron production in the Holy Cross Mts. Big furnaces were built, which were fired with wood,

as well as numerous iron processing works and the first manufactures of iron ware and weapons.

Exploitation of copper and lead deposits was started again and there was some fruitless prospecting for salt. This area, later called the Old Polish Industrial Basin, became the main centre of heavy industry during the reign of the last of the Polish kings – Stanisław August Poniatowski (1764–1795).

The next stage in the development of the area came after the partitions of Poland, in the autonomous Polish Kingdom created by the Congress of Vienna (in 1815). A complex plan was drawn up at that time for the development and restructuring of the Old Polish Industrial Basin. Although it was not fully realized, a number of mines, blast furnaces, iron foundries were constructed, as well as several dams. Some of the existing works were expanded or reconstructed, housing estates were built for the workers and hard surfaced roads made. The iron industry also developed in privately owned estates.

The decline of the Old Polish Industrial Basin in the second half of the 19th century was mostly due to technological changes, above all because hard coal was used as fuel instead of wood in iron production. From that time on, the main centre of the iron industry moved to the Upper Silesian Coal Basin.

During the period of the partitions of Poland, the Polish Uplands experienced an economic slump. A long section of the frontier of the Austrian-ruled part of Poland ran along the Vistula, thus cutting off Cracow and Sandomierz from a large part of their hinterland; all the towns along the Vistula went into a state of decline and the area next to the frontier of the Russian-ruled part of Poland, deprived of its communication network, vegetated all through the 19th century.

The situation was better in the area adjoining the quickly developing Prussian part of the Upper Silesian Coal Basin, where from the end of the 18th century there had been a steady growth of coal mining and the production of iron, lead and zinc. The development of industry was given added impetus by the construction of the Kłodnica Canal (1792–1812), linking the Basin with the River Odra and, in the 19th century, the opening of railway lines. In the last thirty years of the 19th century the development of the Upper Silesian Industrial Basin was given a big boost by the dynamic economic growth of united Germany. Upper Silesia became a region of big modern industry comprising foundries, engineering, metal and chemical works. The concentration of population in the Basin increased and this led to the spontaneous development of a great industrial-urban agglomeration in which mines, factories, housing estates and transport facilities were intermingled.

The consequences of this spontaneous development were difficulties in expanding industrial works, transport problems, difficulties in ensuring adequate water supplies, damage caused by mining under buildings, as well as increasingly unhealthy living conditions caused by air pollution with dust and gas from the factories and slag heaps and water pollution.

The production of the Upper Silesian Basin was mostly destined for the Polish Kingdom and Austria. In order to evade customs barriers, industrial works were also set up on the other side of the frontier, in the Austrian and above all, the Russian-ruled part of the Basin, called the Dąbrowa Basin, which became the main heavy industry centre of the Kingdom of Poland, also supplying goods to meet the need of the Russian Empire. The Dąbrowa Basin developed even more chaotically, the towns were badly built and poorly equipped with municipal facilities.

As a result of the First World War and the three Silesian Uprisings, the greater part of the Basin, with Katowice, Królewska Huta (now Chorzów) and the Rybnik Basin in the south was ceded to Poland. Bytom, Zabrze and Gliwice remained within the frontier of the German Reich. The potential of the Basin could not be fully utilized by the economically weak Polish state of the inter-war years. Export possibilities were limited and the home market was underdeveloped.

The market demand was further limited by the policy of big concerns and cartels, often financed by foreign capital, which kept the price level high. So coal extraction did not achieve the pre-war level, and the foundries and zinc factories were just vegetating.

The situation was not very good in the other parts of the Polish Uplands either. Deprived of a communication network, the southern part of the Kielce region became a neglected agricultural area. The obsolete industrial works of the Old Polish Industrial Basin were in a state of stagnation. Only the larger towns developed, namely, Cracow and Lublin, and to a less extent, also Kielce.

During the Second World War, the Nazi authorities applied a plunder policy in exploiting the occupied territories. However the war damage was not very great there, with the exception of the belt along the banks of the Vistula and the bridgehead near Sandomierz, where the frontline fighting went on for some time (1944–45).

After the war, almost the whole of the Upper Silesian Coal Basin was returned within the Polish frontiers. It had favourable conditions for growth in the now quickly developing country. The extraction of hard coal for the home market and for export rose dynamically; in 1978, it exceeded 190 million tons. New mines were built and the old ones modernized. The iron and steel industry, the power, engineering, electrotechnical and chemical industries were also expanded and modernized. In recent years mining has been expanded in the Rybnik Basin to extract the coking coal so badly needed by the iron industry. The engineering industry and the power and heat generating industry are also being developed there. However, further concentration of the growing industry in Upper Silesia is being avoided, particularly in the central part of the big industrial-urban agglomeration. With the aim of improving the natural environment, a number of undertakings have been started, above all efforts are being made to prevent air and water pollution. For some time now, the expansion of industry not directly connected with the exploitation of coal deposite has been limited. Big industrial plants are being set up outside the coal basin. In the years 1950–1954 the biggest Polish steel works, and one of the biggest in Europe, was built at Nowa

Huta, which is now a district of Cracow. The foundries in Częstochowa and Łabędy have been enlarged. In 1971, work was started on the construction of the "Huta Katowice" a huge steel works located between Dąbrowa Górnicza and Ząbkowice. The first blast furnace and steel mill started production in 1976. Very large chemical works have been built in Oświęcim and Kędzierzyn. New towns (Nowe Tychy, Nowe Pyskowice and others) and housing estates for the workers of the Upper Silesian Industrial Region are being built outside the coal basin in healthy climatic conditions amid forests.

The development of the Częstochowa Industrial Region has been to some extent connected with the programme for the deglomeration of the Upper Silesian Industrial Region during the last 20 years. The expanded B. Bierut Foundry in Częstochowa supplies 10% of the national production of pig iron. The Częstochowa Region also accounts for 90% of the national production of iron ore, although this is not a significant figure in the general raw material supplies of the iron and steel industry, based mainly on imported ores. Iron ore mining is concentrated between Częstochowa and Wieluń. There are electrical engineering works in Zawiercie and Myszków. The Częstochowa region is also traditionally a textile industry district; most of the factories are in the town of Częstochowa itself. In addition there is a well developed building materials industry, based on the exploitation of local Jurassic limestone and marls. All over the Cracow–Częstochowa Upland there is an expanding lime and cement industry, mainly concentrated round Częstochowa.

On the western edge of the Upland is Olkusz, an old mining centre, which is again coming to life with the construction of a new zinc and lead mine. Cracow and surroundings has become a large industrial centre. The biggest industrial establishment is the Lenin Steel Works at Nowa Huta, which produces more than 6 million tons of steel annually and also various other metallurgical products. Cracow is also a big centre producing machine tools and various kinds of machines, electrotechnical articles, precision tools, chemicals, and also has light industry and food industry factories and a printing industry.

The Old Polish Industrial Basin has undergone a transformation. Iron ore, ceramic and heat-resistant clays, limestone, marble and sandstone are mined there. The existing engineering and metal works have been expanded and new ones built, the main centres are Kielce, Skarżysko-Kamienna and Starachowice, the latter being known, above all, for the production of delivery lorries and vans. The iron foundry in Ostrowiec Świętokrzyski has been enlarged. An important role is played by the cement and lime industry, the biggest centres of which are in Wierzbica to the north and Sitkówka-Nowiny to the south of Kielce. In the southern part of the Sandomierz Upland, near Staszów, sulphur is mined using the underground washing out method. The food industry is also developing, thus activating local agriculture.

The biggest food industry plants are in Kielce, Ostrowiec Świętokrzyski, Częstocice and Dwikozy.

The Lublin Upland is not nearly so industrialized. The most highly developed branch there is the food-processing industry, mainly concentrated in Lublin. The biggest industrial plants are the sugar factories in Rejowiec and Werbkowice (the biggest in Poland). To meet the needs of the farmers, there are factories producing agricultural machines, implements, etc. in Lublin. Lorries and motorcycles are also produced there, and in nearby Świdnik – helicopters. There are engineering and electrotechnical works in Kraśnik, Poniatowa, Zamość and Chełm. In the vicinity of Rejowiec and Chełm there is a big cement producing centre (20% of the national output). In the future a big industrial region will be created in connection with the recently discovered rich deposits of hard coal, which stretch from the frontier with the USSR on the River Bug (near Hrubieszów and Tomaszów Lubelski) north-west to Radzyń Podlaski. The construction of the first mine was started in 1975.

Agriculture in the Polish Uplands is differentiated according to the soil conditions, the extent of industrialization and urbanization, and is also influenced by the previous development level. The changes that took place in upland agriculture following the agrarian reform of 1944, show two basic tendencies. In the industrialized areas and those where industry is being introduced, a large number of small-holders have started working in industry, becoming peasant-workers commuting to work from their farms. Near the big towns more and more farmers are going in for the suburban type of production groving vegetables and supplying milk, sometimes fruit growing and keeping poultry as well. Some farmers are specializing in hothouse or forced vegetable growing. Intensive suburan farming is highly developed in the Upper Silesian Industrial Region, round Cracow and, on a smaller scale, round other large towns and industrial centres.

In areas where there is not so much industry and the soils are poor, the development of agriculture has gone in the direction of cattle and pig breeding, and where the soil is better – increased areas under wheat and industrial crops, above all, sugar beet, rape-seed, barley, tobacco, hops and even medicinal herbs. This is the development line taken by farmers in the southern part of the Małopolska Upland and in the Lublin Upland. However, the excellent natural conditions of these areas have still not been utilized to the full despite the considerable progress made in this direction.

The social and economic development of the country and the Polish Uplands has had an influence on the urban network.

The development of the Upper Silesian Basin led to the creation there of the biggest industrial-urban agglomeration in Poland. More than 2 million people live in an area of about 2,800 sq.km., from Gliwice to Dąbrowa Górnicza. The biggest town of the agglomeration and the capital of the voivodship is Katowice (350,000 inhabitants); more than twelve other towns go to make up the agglomeration (Bytom, Sosnowiec, Zabrze, Gliwice, Chorzów, Ruda Śląska, Dąbrowa Górnicza, Mysłowice, Siemianowice Śląskie, Będzin, Świętochłowice, Czeladź), four of which have a population of more than 200,000 and two of more than 150,000. This urban complex,

a great centre of the mining and iron and steel industry, linked up by a dense communication network, is now undergoing a planned restructuring. In its vicinity, but outside the coal basin, settlements are being expanded and urbanized.

Katowice is not only a big industrial centre, but also has all-round functions of a non-productive nature with a range going beyond the boundaries of the voivodship. Service facilities are also well developed in the other towns of the Silesian Industrial Region, although they are not of such an all-round character. The region has 15 institutes of the Polish Academy of Sciences, 11 ministerial research institutes and 6 schools of higher learning attended by nearly 47,000 students. The biggest of these are the Silesian Technical University in Gliwice and the new Silesian University. The Silesian Research Institute is a very active centre. Publishing activity is developing dynamically and there are numerous theatres, concert halls, etc.

The expansion of the Rybnik Coal Region will contribute to greater urbanization of the south-western part of the Silesian Upland. In order to guarantee good housing conditions for the workers of the mines in this region, new housing estates are being built, leading to the quick growth of towns like Wodzisław, Jastrzębie-Zdrój and others.

The biggest town of the Małopolska Upland is Cracow (about 700,000 inhabitants). This town, which is also a big industrial centre, is known above all for its cultural significance. Closely linked up with the history of the country, it has a radius of influence embracing the whole of south-western Poland. The Old Town and the Royal Castle on Wawel Hill, which are well preserved, constitute a historical complex of great importance and give a survey of architecture and art beginning from pre-Romanesque times. Cultural life in Cracow is dominated by its schools of higher learning of which there are 11 with 66,000 students. The most important of them is the more than 600-year-old Jagiellonian University. Scientific institutes are numerous and a branch of the Polish Academy of Sciences is very active there. Cracow abounds in museums, archives, theatres, literary clubs, etc. and is a big publishing centre. Owing to its specific cultural role, the town is a big tourist attraction.

The second largest voivodship town of the Małopolska Upland is Częstochowa (about 230,000 inhabitants), an industrial centre, important junction and a centre of culture and learning. Its two schools of higher learning are attended by about 7,000 students – future technical experts and economists. The considerable tourist traffic in Częstochowa is of a special character, associated with pilgrimages to the Monastery on Jasna Góra, where there is a very old picture of the Madonna, which has for centuries been an object of religious cult in Poland.

The chief town in the region of the Holy Cross Mts. (164,000 inhabitants) is Kielce, capital of the voivodship and the Old Polish Industrial Basin. This picturesquely situated town is a big centre of industry, services and cultural life. Nearly 8,000 students attend its two schools of higher learning. The regional movement in Kielce is very active. The Museum of the Holy

Cross Mts. Region is known for its rich ethnographic, archeological and geological collections. Apart from Kielce, there are other, smaller industrial towns in the Holy Cross Mts. region that are developing fast. They are: Ostrowiec Świętokrzyski, Starachowice, and Skarżysko-Kamienna. Along the valley of the River Kamienna, in the Końskie district there are numerous workers settlements. On the same edge of the Sandomierz Upland, dropping towards the Vistula, is the historical town of Sandomierz. It is one of the oldest and most beautiful towns in Poland. In the period between the two world wars its was very popular with tourists.

Today, without losing its tourist attraction, it is also developing in the industrial field. It is the site of the biggest window glass factory in Poland, as well as a river shipyard and food industry factories.

The biggest town of the Lublin Upland, capital of the voivodship, is Lublin (291,000 inhabitants). It has grown into an important industrial and cultural centre with 5 schools of higher learning attended by 33,000 students. The cultural traditions of Lublin date back to the 16th century, when it was the seat of eminent humanists of the Polish Renaissance and Reformation movement. In 1944, Lublin was the seat of the first state authorities on the liberated terriotries. Another town on the Lublin Upland – Chełm – is associated with the beginnings of People's Poland. It was here, on July 22nd, 1944, that the July Manifesto of the Polish Committee for National Liberation was proclaimed, outlining the principles on which the people's state was to be built. At present, apart from its administrative and service functions, Chełm is also an industrial town, above all, it is a centre of the cement industry.

The beautiful historical town of Zamość (44,000 inhabitants), also the seat of a new voivodship, is the most important economic centre of the south-eastern part of the Lublin region. But above all, it is a cultural centre with old traditions. It has numerous secondary schools and also a branch of the Lublin University.

The network of voivodship towns and industrial centres in the Polish Uplands is supplemented by smaller towns and settlements servicing the agricultural areas in their immediate vicinity.

Villages are almost non-existent in the Silesian Upland because, owing to the development of industry, the rural settlements have been urbanized. There are very few agricultural villages and the old traditional Silesian style of building, folk costumes and traditions have disappeared, giving way to settlements inhabited by miners and industrial workers; these settlements, with no pretence to style are comfortable and well equipped. In the Cracow-Częstochowa Upland, the villages are scattered and have a characteristic layout: they are built in long belts along the valleys of rivers and streams. In the Małopolska Upland and the Lublin Plateau, the villages have not undergone many changes. Most of them are long row villages or street villages in some places, particularly along the banks of the Vistula, supplemented by little hamlets. Along the upper reaches of the Vistula there are cluster villages and in the Lublin region – double row chain villages. Rural building is done using local materials (timber, stone, gypsum, loess); although timber buildings still predominate, there are more and more buildings of other materials.

All over the whole area of the Polish Uplands there are many attractive places for holiday-makers and tourists. The Lublin Upland has historical Kazimierz Dolny, the Nałęczów spa with its abundant mineral springs and also Zwierzyniec on the River Wieprz. The Małopolska Upland has such spas as Solec and Busko, well known for their saline-sulphur springs. Chęciny and Sandomierz are tourist centres, and numerous tourist trails run along the rocky ranges of the Cracow–Częstochowa Upland. The inhabitants of the Upper Silesian Basin go to the surrounding forests for weekends. More and more tourists are visiting the region of the Holy Cross Mts. attracted by the beautiful scenery and places of historical interest.

The Polish Uplands, with the exception of Upper Silesia, have not got a well developed railway network and in some places there are not enough hard-surfaced roads. The development of communications is an important problem to be tackled in activating this area, so richly endowed by Nature.

The rich natural resources of the Silesian Upland led to the creation in this area of the biggest mining and heavy industry district in Poland. The first written records of mining in Upper Silesia are from the end of the 12th century; it is known, however, that the mining and smelting of silver, lead and iron ores started much earlier. In the 18th century, exploitation of zinc ores was started too. The main wealth of the Silesian Upland, namely, hard coal, had no particular significance then. It was only when wood was replaced by coke in the foundries that the development of coal mining took place. At the turn of the 18th century, two blast furnaces fired by coke were put into operation in Upper Silesia, as the first on the European continent.

The growing importance of coal came in the 19th century with the concentration of industry in the Coal Basin, the influx of population and the spontaneous development of towns. Former villages grew into workers' settlements and new settlements were built. Then they merged with each other and in turn merged with the old towns, creating industrial towns and settlements. Gradually, the area of the central coal basin became one great industrial-urban complex, chaotically built and badly equipped. At present it is undergoing a planned reconstruction. In the Upper Silesian Industrial District, the main role is still played by coal mining, the output having risen more than threefold in the last thirty years; export of coal has also increased more than threefold. The increased output was achieved thanks to the reconstruction and expansion of old mines, the construction of 18 new ones and to the mechanization and automation of mining work (4). At present, Poland is the world's fourth biggest coal producer and the second biggest coal exporter.

The main centre of the industrial-urban agglomeration in Upper Silesia is Katowice, the voivodship capital, an important junction and economic and cultural centre of Upper Silesia. The development of Katowice was connected, above all, with the growth of coal mining. One of the oldest mines there is "Kleofas", which has been in operation since 1822 (5).

4

5

6

In 1865, Katowice was granted the status of town. It was already a rapidly developing industrial centre then, attracting people from the surrounding villages in search of employment. Poor workers districts grew up round the mines and factories, which are now being replaced by modern, comfortable housing estates with a good network of shops (8) and other service facilities. The reconstruction of the town centre is in progress, where modern architecture is evident in the form of tall buildings standing freely along the wide new thoroughfares. These are both blocks of flats and public buildings and facilities. Worthy of note is the big sports and entertainment hall, which has been given the form of a slightly tilted "flying saucer" (6).

In the very centre of the town a monument has been erected in memory of the Silesian Insurgents (7) in the form of three wings, symbolizing the three uprisings of the Silesian people in the years 1919–1921, who were fighting for the restoration of Upper Silesia to Poland.

7

8

9

The aim of the reconstruction of the Upper Silesian agglomeration is, above all, to give its inhabitants better living conditions. In the reconstruction plan, an important part is played by the increase of green spaces. A protective forest belt is being grown round the agglomeration and gardens, parks and children's playgrounds are being laid out in the towns. Between Katowice and Chorzów, on an area that was once waste land because of the subidence caused by the mine workings underneath, an extensive Culture and Recreation Park has been laid out (600 ha.), with various recreational and entertainment facilities, an exhibition pavilion, a planetarium, a zoo and sports facilities, including Poland's biggest stadium with seating for 100,000 spectators. The "Kościuszko" Iron and Steel Works in Chorzów (9) is one of the oldest works that has continued to operate to this day. Its construction was started by the Prussian government in 1795. They gave it the name of "Królewska Huta" (Royal Foundry). The town of Królewska Huta was named after it and was granted municipal status in 1868. Only in 1934, after the localities of Chorzów and Nowe Hajduki had been incorporated into the town, did it receive its present name.

10

Gliwice, situated in the western part of the Basin, is an old town, which received municipal status as early as the 13th century. The Old Town Quarter still has the old mediaeval layout of streets, a rectangular network leading out of the market place, which is surrounded by old-style houses and has an 18th century Town Hall in the centre (11).

The towns of the eastern part of the Basin, that is, the area known as the Dąbrowa Basin, were not nearly so developed. This situation has now changed thanks to the building of the "Katowice" Iron and Steel Works (12), the biggest in Poland. The new works is to produce pig iron and steel to replace the production of the old foundries of Upper Silesia, which will be converted into works engaged exclusively in processing.

This will bring double advantages: thanks to the concentration of production in one modern works, it will be possible to lower the cost of the production of pig iron and steel; on the other hand, the limitation of the production of the old works in the central part of the industrial district will help to reduce environmental pollution there. In 1978, the "Katowice" works started production. Housing estates for the employees of the new works have been built mainly in Dąbrowa Górnicza (13). In order to avoid the further concentration of industry in the Upper Silesian Coal Basin, particularly its central part, limits have been introduced in the expansion of works that are not connected directly with the exploitation of coal, while new works are being built outside the Coal Basin. These include the power station in Łaziska Górne (14), which is outside the protective forest belt.

11

12

13

The deglomeration of industry in the Upper Silesian Basin is being accompanied by the deglomeration of the densely populated towns. Outside the coal basin, new residential districts and even whole towns, for instance Nowe Tychy (15), are being built in healthy climatic conditions. Nowe Tychy was built round the little town of Tychy, which in1950 had a population of less than 13,000. At present, Nowe Tychy has more than 140,000 inhabitants. It is a large urban centre ensuring good housing and living conditions for the workers of the industrial region, who commute to work by bus and train services. No expanded development of industry is envisaged here. The existing factories and works are small ones to meet the needs of the town and surrounding districts. The only exceptions are the brewery that has existed since 1629, one of the biggest in Poland, and known for the high quality beer produced there, and the recently built assembly branch-factory of the Bielsko-Biała Car Works, working in co-production with the mother factory, turning out the small Fiat 126p cars (16).

14
16
15

17

18 In recent years the coal mining industry has been developed above all in the south-western part of the Coal Basin, in the Rybnik area, this being the result of the growing demand for coke. For the Rybnik Coal Basin has coal resources of which 70% is coking coal, more and more of which is being mined despite the difficult conditions of exploitation (the deposits are at a great depth). Out of the total number of 18 coal mines built since the Second World War in Poland, 7 have been built in the Rybnik area and another 3 are shortly to start operating. Altogether the Rybnik Basin has 16 mines with an output amounting to 22% of the total extraction of hard coal in this country (17).

The development of coal mining in the Rybnik area is being accompanied by a growth of residential building and towns. Today, the biggest housing settlements for the miners working in the nearby mines are in Wodzisław and Jastrzębie-Zdrój. The last mentioned is a spa with saline springs, discovered in 1860. In 1950, the number of permenent residents in Jastrzębie-Zdrój was only 1,800. Since it has been expanded by the housing settlements (18) for the Rybnik miners, the population has increased to the present 100,000. It was granted municipal status in 1963.

19

20

In the northern part of the Silesian Upland is Częstochowa which came
into being by the merging of Stara Częstochowa on the River Warta and
the settlement called Częstochówka.

The first mention of these villages in written sources is from the year
1220. In 1337, Prince Władysław Opolczyk, in granting to two brothers
Jaśko and Niczko the foundry built there to exploit the local iron ore
deposits, called Stara Częstochowa a town. On the other hand,
Częstochówka developed chiefly as a settlement providing services to the
pilgrims that came to the monastery (21) on Jasna Góra, built by the
Pauline Fathers, who had been brought there in 1382. In that same year,
the Byzantine picture of the Madonna, famed for the cult that grew up
around it and which to this very day attracts pilgrims from all parts of
Poland, was hung in the monastery church. The monastery surrounded
by defence walls, several times served as a stronghold. The most famous
defence put up by the monastery was during the Swedish "deluge" in
1655, when a small defense force succeeded in repulsing the attacks of
the greatly superior enemy forces.

21

The Jasna Góra Monastery – a great magnet for tourists and pilgrims is also an important monument of Polish national culture. Originally Gothic, after several additions and conversions, it is now predominantly Baroque in style. The decoration of the richly adorned interiors is also mostly Baroque (22). Among the numerous valuable relics there, special mention is due to the fine examples of goldsmithery in the treasury of the monastery, its collections of books and archives, and the oldest printing house in Poland, which has been in operation since the 18th century. Częstochówka gained municipal rights as Nowa Częstochowa in 1717. In 1826, the government of the Polish Kingdom merged Stara (Old) and Nowa (New) Częstochowa into one town and settled craftsmen there, mainly weavers. However, it was only at the end of the 19th century that the textile and metal industries of Częstochowa began their real development. The development of industry attracted more people and the population grew, attaining 137,000 in 1937. After the Second World War, industry in Częstochowa developed very rapidly. Carrying on the old foundry traditions, a new foundry (19) named after Bolesław Bierut was built in the period of the Six-Year Plan (1949–1955). Numerous modern housing estates have also been built. The cultural functions of the town are developing, expressed by the building of the Częstochowa Technical University (20), theatres, the forming of a symphony orchestra and the opening of a museum, etc. In 1975, Częstochowa became a voivodship town.

23

24

In the past many watch towers and castles were built on the rocky, limestone elevations of the Cracow–Częstochowa Upland to guard the territory of Małopolska from the west. Today an attractive tourist route known as the Trail of Eagles' Nests winds among them for about 160 km. All along this route, there is plenty to see – the fantastic isolated limestone residual rocks (inselbergs), historical monuments and unique natural phenomena. Most of the castles are in ruins, the majority having been destroyed during the Swedish wars. The highest elevation of the Upland (alt. 504 m.) is crowned by the once magnificent castle of Ogrodzieniec (23), built in the years 1530–1545 by Seweryn Boner, who was the treasurer of king Sigismund the Old. This castle, which was still preserved in relatively good condition at the beginning of the 19th century, was finally reduced to ruins during the Second World War.

Ojców and its environs (24), now a National Park, particularly the valley of the River Prądnik, which flows through a deep canyon with steep sides, is considered the most beautiful part of the Cracow–Częstochowa Upland. Here there are many Karst springs, underground streems and caves with the fossilized remains of animals that lived in the glacial period and traces of palaeolithic man. The gentler slopes are covered with characteristic vegetation, among which are some unique specimens of the Ojców birch and associations of plants of steppe and mountain origin.

In the upper part of the canyon stands the Pieskowa Skała (Dog's Rock) castle (25), built by Casimir the Great on the rocky promontory known as Pieskowa Skała. It was reconstructed in the 16th century in Renaissance style (26) by the owners of that time – the Szafraniec family. After the castle was revaged by the Swedes, it was rebuilt by the Zebrzydowski family. At the end of the 19th century the castle, which is said to have been lost in card game, was purchased in answer to an appeal by a Polish novelist A. Dygasiński and converted into a holiday hotel. After the last war the castle was restored and now houses valuable collections of Renaissance art. Before the castle rises the rock known as the Club of Hercules.

25

26

27

In the southern part of the Cracow–Częstochowa Upland, on melaphyre rocks of volcanic origin, rise the picturesque ruins of the 14th century Tenczyn castle that once belonged to the powerful Małopolska family of the Tęczyńskis (27).

28

29 In the narrow gorge between the Cracow–Częstochowa Upland and the Subcarpathians, called the Cracow Gate, the magnificent complex of Tyniec Abbey (28) rises over the Vistula on limestone rocks. There was a stronghold here as early as the 8th or 9th century. According to legends, the first castle belonged to the Toporczyk family, who were ancestors of the Tęczyński family, and was taken away from them by Bolesław the Brave and given to the Benedictine monks. According to the chronicles of Jan Długosz, the Tyniec Abbey was founded by Casimir I the Restorer in 1044. The abbot of Tyniec was the superior of all the Benedictine monasteries in Poland, in Silesia and later in Lithuania. The 11th century Romanesque basilica that was destroyed by the Tatars in 1241, was replaced by a Gothic church built in the 15th century. The walls of the Gothic church have remained and are part of the early Baroque church built in the years 1618–1622 which has survived to this day. The Abbey buildings also have many elements of Romanesque and Gothic architecture, which have been discovered in the course of restoration and archeological work there. After the Benedictine Order was dissolved in 1817, the Abbey went to the Jesuits. However, before the Second World War, the Benedictine monks returned to Tyniec.

To the east of Tyniec is the 17th century, early Baroque church and monastery of the Cameldolites which stand on the Srebrna Skała (Silver Rock) of Bielany, which has recently become a district of Cracow (29).

98

Cracow, the former capital of Poland, is a monument to past splendour and yet today it is a large city throbbing with life. Its origins can be traced back to the prehistoric epoch. It was most probably one of the centres of the tribe of Vislanes. Its name is supposed to be derived from the legendary Prince Krak, who founded the town after killing the dragon living in the Wawel Cave. Another legend tells of Krak's daughter Wanda, who did not want to marry a German and surrender her country to him, and chose death in waters of the Vistula. And indeed, long before the founding of the Polish state, there was a big stronghold on Wawel Hill. In the times of the first of the Piasts it was the seat of princes, and later, in the times of the division into duchies, it was the seat of the Prince-senior.

Casimir the Great built a Gothic castle (30) on the remains of the stronghold that existed in the 10th to 13th centuries. In turn, this castle was enlarged and remodelled into a big Renaissance palace in the years 1507–1536 with an arcaded courtyard and columned galleries (31). This courtyard, one of the most magnificent examples of Renaissance architecture in Poland, was built by Polish craftsmen under the supervision of Francis the Italian, Bartolomeo Berecci and Benedict of Sandomierz. The Italian Renaissance forms were imbued with traditional Polish forms, evident in the frame-work of the doors, the lintels, the tiers of columns on the second floor and the protruding eaves, etc. The interior of the palace is richly decorated (32). The painted friezes (among others by Hans Dürer), the mosaic floor, the coffered ceilings, decorative tiled stoves, beautiful furniture, valuable paintings and portraits have been preserved to our times. The most magnificent adornment of the chambers of the Wawel Castle were the famous Arras tapestries, made specially to the order of king Sigismund Augustus, of which there were 356. Only 136 have survived to our times.

31

32 The cathedral, which was also built on Wawel Hill, was remodelled many times. The oldest part of it is the 10th c. pre-Romanesque rotunda of St. Felix and St. Adauctus and the recently discovered foundations of another building of the same period. Next come the remains of the first Romanesque cathedral built in the 11th century and the crypt of St. Leonard from the second Romanesque cathedral built in the 12th century (34). In the 14th century, Casimir the Great built a third, Gothic cathedral (33) encircled with chapels, in which from then on the Polish kings were crowned and buried. The cathedral is a three-nave basilica with transept and ambulatory apse. The decoration of the cathedral is mostly Baroque, but there are also elements from earlier periods. In the main nave there is the tomb of St. Stanislaus with a silver coffin (35) made by Peter van der Rennen in the 17th century and the Gothic tomb of Władysław Jagiełło (36) made by Giovanni Cini in the 15th century. The Sigismund Chapel, built in the years 1519–1544 is a classic example of Renaissance architecture. The main element of the chapel are the tombs of the kings Sigismund the Old made by Bartolomeo Berecci and of his son Sigismund Augustus made by Giovanni Maria Padovano (37). The tomb of the last of the Jagiellons, Queen Anna (38) is also in Renaissance style. It is the work of Santi Gucci.

As early as the 10th century, Cracow was already a populous trading centre developing at the foot of Wawel Hill. After it was ravaged by the Tatars in 1241, the town was completely rebuilt and organized anew on the basis of the foundation charter of 1257 based on the Magdeburg Law. It is from this period that the regular layout of the Old Town dates. An extensive square Market Place was laid out, covering 4 hectares, with a network of streets running out of it (1). In the centre of the Market Place there were stalls, which were later replaced by Cloth Hall, built in the 14th century.

Burnt down in the middle of the 16th century, it was rebuilt and a fine Renaissance parapet was added (40). Only the tall tower has remained of the 14th century Town Hall. In the corner of the Market Place facing it diagonally, is the Church of St. Mary, called "Mariacki" in Polish. It was built in the years 1355–1365 on the site of the previous 13th century church. The greatest treasure of the church is the late Gothic main triptych altar-piece (39) carved in wood by Wit Stwosz in the years 1477–1489. From the higher of the two church towers, a bugle call is sounded every hour, which breaks off suddenly, to commemorate the bugler whose throat was pierced by a Tatar arrow while he was playing the call. Next to the Church of St. Mary is the small Gothic Church of St. Barbara, built at the turn of the 14th century, and a 16th century Jesuit professors' house. The Market Place is surrounded by old burghers' houses.

Since 1364, Cracow has been known for its Academy (now the Jagiellonian University), founded by Casimir the Great, which is one of the oldest in Europe and the oldest in Poland. At the turn of the 14th century the Academy consisted of the Collegium Maius (41), which is now the seat of the university authorities and also houses the University Museum. Today, Cracow has 11 higher schools of learning attended by 66,000 students.

35

36

37

38

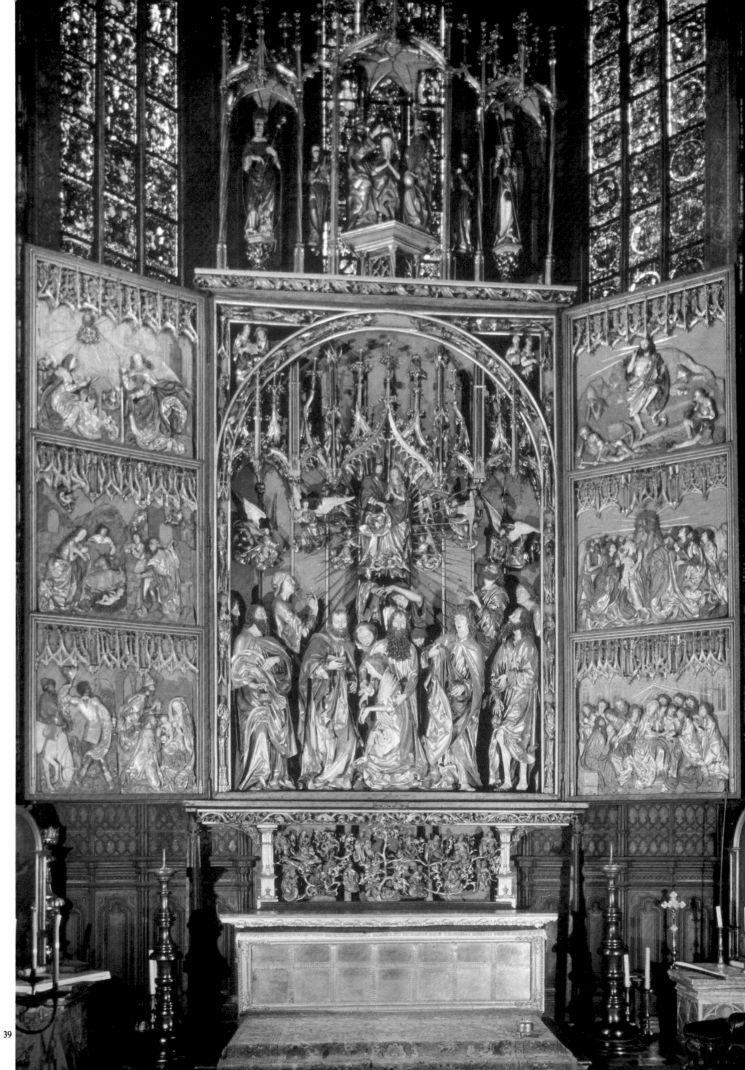

39

40

41 There are so many historical buildings in Cracow that it would be impossible to enumerate all of them, even the most valuable ones. They are sacral and secular buildings. Actually, the whole of the Old Town is one great historical monument on a world scale. It was once surrounded by defence walls more than 4 km. long with numerous towers and gates. The walls were pulled down in the 19th century and a green belt was laid out in their place, known as the Planty Gardens. Small parts of the old fortifications have, however, remained. They are the Barbican built at the end of the 15th century and a section of the defence walls with three towers and the Florian Gate dating back to 1307.
The period of the most flourishing development of Cracow was in the second half of the 15th century and the 16th century, as the capital of the monarchy of the Jagiellons, growing in power and rivilling with the Hapsburgs for the leading place in Eastern Europe. After the capital was moved to Warsaw, and also due to the influence of the political and economic crisis at the end of the 17th century and the beginning of the 18th century, the former splendour of Cracow faded and came to an end. After the third partition of Poland it came under Austrian rule. Following the Vienna Congress it became a Free City for 30 years, but in 1846, it was again incorporated into the state of the Hapsburgs. As a provincial town of the monarchy, its economic development was very slow, but it never ceased to be a centre of Polish national and political life, particularly Polish culture and science. Poles from all three parts of partitioned Poland were educated at the Cracow Academy, and Cracow was the birth-place of new schools of scientific thought, literary trends and new styles in art. At the beginning of the 20th century, the Cracow café "Jama Michalikowa" was the meeting place of artists and writers, not only from Cracow, but from all over Poland, and the excellent Słowacki Theatre (42, 43), which was built in the years 1891–1893 took a leading place in Polish theatrical life.

42

43 44

During the Second World War, Cracow was looted by the occupant and a large number of its treasures of art and culture were taken away. Only a part of them have been regained for Poland since the war. Several monuments were also destroyed, including the monument commemorating the great victory of the united Polish and Lithuanian forces over the Teutonic Knights in the Battle of Grunwald. The monument has been reconstructed and was unveiled in 1976 (44). The town was threatened with terrible destruction, when the Nazis elaborated a plan to blow up the Wawel complex and many other historical buildings. However, thanks to a successful manoeuvre of the Sovie army, the Nazis had to retreat in a hurry and did not have time to carry out these plans. Thus, Cracow is one of the few towns in Poland that managed to preserve its historical building during the war. After the war, Cracow developed quickly. While keeping its position as a scientific and cultural centre, it also became a large industrial centre and also, in view of its valuable historical monuments and geographical position, one of Poland's biggest tourist centres. But the old buildings of Cracow are in need of repairs, so the last few years have seen a big survey and conservation work to save the historical central quarter of Cracow. In 1979, this campaign was made a national issue.

45

46 In the Fifties, a huge Iron and Steel Works, named after Lenin (45), was built just outside Cracow on the site of the village of Mogiła. It was the main investment project of the Six-Year Plan (1950–1955).

The church in Nowa Huta is an example of modern sacral architecture.

The town of Nowa Huta was built for the employees of the Lenin Steel Works between the Works and the town of Cracow. It has since become a district of Cracow and has all the public institutions and facilities to meet the economic, social and cultural needs of the population (49).

To the north-east of Cracow, as far as the Nida Basin, are the fertile and picturesque loess elevations of the Miechów Upland, considered to be one of the earliest settlement areas in Poland (48).

47

48

The Nida Basin, a wide depression dividing the Cracow–Częstochowa and Miechów Uplands from the Holy Cross Mountains, is also an early settlement area. On the gypsum island among the swamps of the valley of the Lower Nida is one of Poland's oldest towns, Wiślica once a tribal stronghold, perhaps even the capital of the Vislanes. In the times of the first Piasts, there was a fortified settlement here that was destroyed by the Tatars in 1241. Casimir the Great built a castle there, surrounded the town with defence walls and founded a Gothic Collegiate Church (49). The Swedish wars of the 17th century led to the town's decline, from which it never recovered.

The castle was pulled down in the 18th century, but the Collegiate Church, which has been rebuilt many times, still stands. During restoration work on the Church, polychrome paintings dating back to the times of Władysław Jagiełło were discovered. During archeological work, many traces of pre-Romanesque, Romanesque buildings and the remnants of the early mediaeval stronghold were discovered.

The Chęciny Chain which constitutes the southern fringe of the Holy Cross Mts., is marked from a distance by the ruins of Chęciny Castle (50), which was probably built in the 13th century. At the beginning of the 14th century this castle was one of the most important strongholds of the country and also the place where nobles held their assemblies. Badly damaged during the Swedish wars, it was still inhabited till the end of the 18th century. The Chęciny Chain built of Devonian limestones, is known for the marble quarried there. A large lime and cement works has been built nearby.

49

50

Not far from Chęciny, a small cave "Raj" (Paradise Cave) has been discovered, which has a wealth of stalactites and stalagmites. It is now visited by many tourists (51).

The people of Kielce are found of making daily excursions into the surrounding hills. A beautiful amphitheatre (52) has been built in an old stone quarry, which until quite recently was still being exploited.

51

52

53

54 The chief town of the region of the Holy Cross Mts. is Kielce, picturesquely situated. The town developed from a trading and market centre, mentioned in chronicles as early as the 11th century. At the tourn of the 11th century it became the property of the Cracow bishops and for a long period was a centre of the large estates owned by the bishops. In 1364, it was granted municipal rights on the basis of the Magdeburg Law. In the 15th to 17th centuries it went through a period of dynamic growth due to the development of the mining and processing of lead, copper and iron ores in the surrounding areas. It was in this period that the beautiful, early Baroque Bishops Palace (53) was built (1637–1641) by Bishop Jakub Zadzik. In the interior of the palace, beamed ceilings with rich polychrome paintings, beautiful plafonds, pictures, portals and fireplaces have all been preserved. At present the palace houses a museum. An older historical building is the cathedral, founded as a collegiate church in the 12th century by Bishop Gedeon. After remodelling, it assumed the character of an early Baroque basilica. In 1789, Kielce became the property of the Respublica. In the period of the Polish Kingdom, Stanisław Staszic did much to promote the development of Kielce. In view of the mining industry developing in the vicinity, he founded the Chief Mining Board in Kielce and Mining Academy. This economic enlivement ended in the middle of the 19th century as a result of the check put on the development of the Old Polish Industrial District and the changes in administrative division that were introduced. The seat of the newly created gouvernement was in Radom. Towards the end of the last century, there was another enlivement of industry in the town and its environs. After the First World War, Kielce became a voivodship town, but even so, until 1945, it remained only a medium sized urban centre which was not very lively in its development. Its real development came in People's Poland, in connection with the dynamic development of industry. The newly built central district of Kielce has given it the features of a big, thriving town (54). The position of the town has made it a tourist centre of growing importance.

56

57

55

The core of the Holy Cross Mts. are two mountain ranges of Łysogóry (55) and Dymińskie, built of hard quartzites of Lower Cambrian origin. Their slopes are overgrown with thick fir forests. On the high ridges there are large boulder fields called gołoborze, the greatest of which is on Mt. Święty Krzyż, which translated into English means Holy Cross Mt. (56). The most beautiful part of the Łysogóry range has been made into the Świętokrzyski National Park, named after Stefan Żeromski, the Polish writer. Also under protection is the larch wood on Mt. Chełmowa, one of the very few woods of Polish larch. The slopes and foot of the Holy Cross Mts. have been cultivated by farmers for a long time, despite the fact that the soil is not very fertile. Narrow fields (61) stretch out from the long villages. In some of them one still sees regional folk costumes being worn (57). The most well known are the red-and-black aprons worn in Bieliny.

The Holy Cross Mts. and the surrounding areas are the cradle of Polish mining and metallurgy the Old Polish Industrial District, with traditions going far back into the past. Copper, iron and lead ores were mined here in ages past. There was a big foundry centre here in the Roman period. Archeologists have discovered remnants of about 2,000 primitive furnaces in the vicinity of Nowa Słupia. In the times of the Great Migration, the foundry centre declined. It was revived again in the early days of the existance of the Polish state, and the development of the "dymarki" furnaces for smelting iron was in the 15th and 16th centuries. Water power from the rivers and streams was used to move wheels of forges and the furnaces were fired with wood. In 1598, the first big smelting furnace using charcoal for firing, and much more productive than the "dymarki" furnaces, was put into operation. It was built by Hieronim Cacci, a foundryman from Bergamo, brought there by Bishop Piotr Tylicki. However, the real development of blast furnaces only came in the 18th century. Blacksmiths forges, tin-smiths workshops, and workshops making axes and pipes grew up round the foundries. The period of the greatest development of the Old Polish Industrial District was in the Twenties and Thirties of the 19th century, that is, the time when Stanisław Staszic and Ksawery Drucki-Lubecki were active there in connection with the planned industrialization undertaken by the autonomous government of the Polish Kingdom and continued after the November Uprising (till 1843) by the Polish Bank. Many specimens of old industrial buildings have survived from those times. In Samsonów on the River Bobrza there are still the ruins of a smelting furnace built in the years 1818–1824 (58). A steam engine was used there to work the bellows and the foundry produced cast iron parts for various machines, boilers and rollers, and – during the Uprisings – also weapons.

In Nietulisko, on the River Świślina, which is a tributary of the River Kamienna, are the ruins of a dam (59) built in 1834. The dammed water, flowing out through canals, was the force used to drive a rolling mill. At Sielpia Wielka, on the River Czarna, the buildings once housing a puddler plant and a rolling mills from the years 1821–1842 have been preserved and also a neo-classic administrative building and a workers settlement. These works were still operating till 1921. In 1934, a Technical Museum of the Foundry Industry was opened there. In the Fifties, there was still a forging hammer worked by water power at Stara Kuźnica.

There are many old industrial buildings of historical interest in the region of the Holy Cross Mts. Most of them stopped operating in the second half of the 19th century, when owing to the introduction of coal for firing foundry furnaces, the foundries using charcoal became obsolete. Only two centres continued production, namely, Ostrowiec and Starachowice, which had railway connections with the Dąbrowa Coal Basin.

Near Samsonów there is the famous old oak Bartek, which is more than 1,000 years old and one of the oldest tress in Poland. The diameter of its trunk is 13.4 m. (60).

61

62

On the borderline between the Holy Cross Mts. and the Sandomierz Upland is the town of Opatów, situated on a hill amid the fertile rolling loess country (61). It was built on the site of the older stronghold of Żmigród, mentioned in chronicles as early as 1189. It is probable that the Romanesque Collegiate Church of St. Martin (62), with additions and gables from the 15th and 16th centuries, was originally built in that early period. In 1237, Opatów and its environs was granted to the Lubusz bishops. In 1282, it was granted municipal status. At the beginning of the 16th century, it was sold to Chancellor Krzysztof Szydłowiecki, who enclosed the town within defence walls and built four fortified gates. The Warsaw Gate with the coat-of-arms of the founder has been preserved.

One of the oldest settlements in the valley of the River Kamienna is Wąchock. The development of the first settlement was due to the activity of the Cistercian monks who were brought there in 1179 by the Bishop of Cracow Gedeon. The Cistercians drained the valley and organized the extraction and processing of iron ore and also the production of mill-stones from the local sands tones. In 1454, Wąchock was granted the status of a town. In the period of the Congress Kingdom, it was an important foundry centre. The factory buildings from that period were destroyed during the last war. But the 12th century monastery and church of the Cistercians has been preserved and is one of the most valuable examples of Romanesque architecture in Poland, with only a few elements of Gothic and Baroque brought in by later additions. The Romanesque chapter-house (63), with its vaulting supported by columns with richly carved capitals, and the early Gothic refectory are particularly beautiful.

At the north-east end of the Holy Cross Mts. there is a town called Szydłowiec, which in the 13th century was the centre of the large properties of the Odrowąż family, who later took from that place the name of Szydłowiecki. Szydłowiec was granted municipal status in 1427. From the Middle Ages, it was a big stone quarrying centre. The sandstone quarried at Szydłowiec, light in colour and fine-grained, was used in building as ornamental facing stone. At the beginning of the 16th century, Mikołaj Szydłowiecki built the impressive late Gothic-Renaissance castle there, which was remodelled in the 17th century by the next owners, the Radziwiłł family. Another beautiful historical building in the town is the late Gothic parish church, built at the end of the 15th century, and the late Renaissance Town Hall, built at the beginning of the 17th century. Another feature of interest in Szydłowiec is the Jewish Cemetery (64) with numerous tombstones from the 18th and 19th century, something rarely met with in Poland now.

63

64

65

On the borderline between the Holy Cross Mts. and the Sandomierz Upland, near the little town of Iwaniska, are the well preserved ruins of one of the biggest magnates residences in Poland, called the Krzyżtopór (Cross and Axe) Castle (65), which was intended to equal the Royal Castle on Wawel Hill with its magnificence. It was built by the Sandomierz Voivode, Krzysztof Ossoliński, to the design of the Swiss architect Lorenzo Senes. It was the owner's wish that the different parts of the castle should symbolize the different parts of the year, so there are four turrets representing the four seasons of the year, twelve large chambers representing the months, 52 rooms representing the weeks, while the number of days in the year is represented by the number of windows. The whole of the Baroque castle was enclosed in a regular pentagonal curtain wall with bastions. Under the castle is a long, two-tiered, vaulted cellar, designed to house the stables. There are well preserved plaques on the wall surrounding the courtyard, which extoll the glory and connections of the family, while family coat-of-arms (the cross and axe from which the castle gets its name) is carved in marble over the gate. Eleven years after it was built, the castle was partly ruined by the Swedes; the remaining part was destroyed by fire in 1770.

To the south of Opatów, on the Sandomierz Upland, is the town of Klimontów. In the 13th century it was a village belonging to the powerful lords of Tenczyn. Klimontów was granted municipal status in 1604, as the property of the Ossoliński family. The Ossolińskis founded the Dominican monastery, that dominates the town in the year 1613, and in the years 1643–1650 – also the impressive Baroque Collegiate Church (66), which still stands today. It was designed by Lorenzo Senes, after St. Peter's in Rome.

On the high verge of the Sandomierz Upland with its deep loess ravines (68), is Sandomierz, picturesquely situated on the Vistula, one of the most beautiful and, at one time, one of the biggest towns in Poland. Its origins as a settlement are very early, traces of Neolithic man having been found there. In the times of Bolesław the Brave, a large important stronghold existed here, which after the feudal division of the country was a ducal capital and then, when the country was united – the capital of the large Sandomierz voivodship. Situated on the crossing point of routes from Ruthenia and Hungary, Sandomierz was many times invaded and ravaged by the Ruthenians, Lithuanians and Tatars. In the years 1200–1207, Prince Leszek the White built a castle, and in 1286, Prince Leszek the Black granted the town municipal status on the basis of the Magdeburg Law, as well as trading privileges, which were later added to by successive monarchs. Casimir the Great enclosed the town with defence walls and reconstructed the castle and the Town Hall. Both sacral and secular building developed there. The flourishing development of Sandomierz came in the 15th centuries, when access to the sea was opened. The town became wealthy from trading in corn and numerous granaries were built along the Vistula. Handicrafts also flourished at this time. After the wars of the 17th and 18th centuries, Sandomierz went into decline, and after the partitions of Poland it became a border town deprived of communications. Its economic situation did not undergo any particular changes in the inter-war period. Fortunately spared from destruction during the last war, with many historical buildings, Sandomierz has become an important tourist centre. The town is developing, new residential districts are springing up both on the high, left bank and the low right bank of the Vistula.

The Oldest part of the town is on two hills divided by the Piszczele Ravine. On the western side is the oldest building in Sandomierz – the Church of St. James, founded by Adelaide, the sister of Prince Leszek the White, and built of bricks, partly glazed, with a magnificent Romanesque portal. The first cathedral in Sandomierz was built in 1120 and was burnt down by the Tatars. The present cathedral was founded as a collegiate church in 1360. Its Baroque pediment dates back to the second half of the 17th century. It has well preserved frescoes in Ruthenian-Byzantine style from the 15th century. Near the cathedral is the 15th century house of Jan Długosz, the well known Polish chronicler. Only the west wing with two Gothic towers has remained of the old castle, which was reconstructed and enlarged several times in the past. In the large Market Place, surrounded by old burghers houses (67) is the beautiful Town Hall, built at the turn of the 13th century and later remodelled in Renaissance style in the 16th century. On the verge of the high bank of the Vistula is the only surviving wing of the Renaissance Jesuit College, founded in 1604 by the voivode Hieronim Gostomski, hence its name Gostomianum. There are many more buildings of historical interest, in fact the whole of the Old Town Quarter, surrounded by the extant parts of the old 14th century defence walls with the Opatów Gate, constitutes a beautiful and valuable complex of Romanesque, Gothic and Renaissance architecture. In recent years, the historical central district of Sandomierz has undergone a general survey, as a result of which many buildings of historical interest have been exposed and renovated and now fulfil new, more suitable functions.

67

68

On the western border of the Lublin Upland, in the Vistula Valley is the historical town of Kazimierz Dolny, beautifully situated amid loess ravines (69). It is one of the most charming spots in Poland, quite unique as regards it architecture and landscape. The white buildings round the Market Place are concentrated in the place where the high right bank of the Vistula forms a steeply sloping, green escarpment. From the Market Place the street run up and down hill, lined with houses surrounded with orchards, branching out in various directions all over the whole width of the valley right down to the water's edge. Above the houses nestling in the valley, rise the rowers of old churches, and above them all stand the white ruins of the castle and watch-tower perched on a hills. Thus it is not surprising that artists busy with paint and brush are a constant element of the Kazimierz landscape, and that Kazimierz is a favourite haunt of writers and artists. The name of the town is generally associated with Casimir the Great although its history goes back to earlier times. It is, however, a fact that Casimir the Great granted the town municipal status and built a fortified castle there. The position of the town favoured its development. There was a crossing point here across the Vistula on the trade route from Lwow to Silesia and Wielkopolska. Corn was carried by raft down the Vistula to Gdańsk. So in the 16th century, Kazimierz was an important river port where corn from Lublin Upland was loaded onto rafts. It was then that its well known granaries were built (71) and the corn trade brought fortunes to the merchants, whose richly ornamented houses, such as the one belonging to the Przybyła family (70) or the one known as Celejowska still stand today as evidence of the prosperous past. The times of flourishing development ended in the second half of the 17th century, when the situation of the country was getting worse. In the inter-war period, the beautiful scenery and architecture of Kazimierz, the beautiful sandy beach by the Vistula and the surrounding orchards, made the town a favourite summer holiday place. Kazimierz suffered considerable damage during the Second World War, but work was soon started after the war to restore it. The buildings of historical interest were carefully repaired and in some cases restored. The new buildings were designed to fit in with the architectural style of the town, and holiday homes, pensions and hostels were built to accomodate the large number of tourists who thronged to the town.

72

73

The Lublin Upland is gently rolling country with
a network of river valleys, the hills intersprersed with
shallow ravines (72). To the north, its verge drops 20–30 m.
The fertile soils, rendzinas, chernozems based on loesses,
and brown soils, have been partly responsible for the early
felling of the forests. The villages are usually large, of the
double-row chain type.
Agriculture dominates here, the main crops being wheat,
suggar beet, tobacco, hops (73) and oleaginous plants.
Industry is mainly connected with the processing of
agricultural produce, and has only developed here in
recent decades.

74

75 76

Since the 12th century, the main centre of the Lublin Upland has been Lublin, situated on the River Bystrzyca, a tributary of the River Wieprz, amid the gently rolling loess hills. The town grew up from a stronghold on the Polish-Ruthenian border. Destroyed many times by invasions of Ruthenians and Lithuanians, it was granted municipal status in 1317. Casimir the Great built a castle there, surrounded the town with defence walls and granted it privileges. The significance of Lublin increased greatly after union of Poland with Lithuania. It then became an important economic, political and cultural centre. Trade with Lithuania and Ruthenia thrived and the Lublin fairs drew merchants from various countries. It was in Lublin that the Polish-Lithuanian councils, meetings and Diet assemblies were held, and it was in this town that the Lublin Union, uniting Poland and Lithuania, was concluded in 1569. The Crown Tribunal was located there in 1578. The Cossack and Swedish wars, plagues and fires, brought the decline of the town. In the 19th century, Lublin was a gouvernement seat, which brought another period of development. In 1877, after the building of a line linking it with the railway network, industry began to develop there. The first Polish government after the period of partitions was formed in Lublin on November 7th, 1918. In the inter-war period, new factories and cultural institutions appeared in the town. The Second World War brought considerable material damage and human losses to Lublin. After the liberation in 1944, until Warsaw was freed in January 1945, Lublin acted as the capital of Poland. The first higher school to be opened in liberated Poland was the Maria Curie-Skłodowska University in Lublin. The town developed very quickly after the war, first and foremost due to its growing industrialization. In 1951, a lorry factory was opened there. The town developed in other respects too, becoming the main economic, university and cultural centre of south-eastern Poland. The town has grown, enlarged by new residential (75) and industrial districts. On the tenth anniversary of liberation, Lublin completed the reconstruction of the Old Town Quarter, where there are numerous buildings of historical interest (2, 74). The most valuable of these include: the Town Hall, built in the 13th century, many times remodelled and enlarged, the last time in 1781 by Domenico Merlini in Classicist style, the Renaissance and Baroque burghers houses, parts of the old defence walls with the 14th century Grodzka and Cracow Gates and the 16th century Trynitarska Gate, and the Dominican church dating back to 1342, which after many alterations now has a Renaissance character, with Baroque towers and a few elements of the older, Gothic building. The cathedral, which was once a Jesuit church built in the years 1586–1603, is a beautiful example of Renaissance architecture, with a Classicist portico by Antonio Corazzi, dating back to 1819. There are several monastery complexes built between the 15th and 17th centuries outside the Old Town Quarter. On a hill near the Old Town is the castle (75). All that has remained of the original castle built by Casimir the Great is the tower and the Gothic Holy Trinity Chapel, founded by Władysław Jagiełło about 1385, with its vaulting supported by one pillar and beautiful Ruthenian-Byzantine style polychrome paintings (77). Since its reconstruction in the 19th century, the castle has assumed a Neo-Gothic style. During the Nazi occupation, the castle was turned into a terrible prison, through which about 400,000 people passed. At Majdanek, a suburb of Lublin, the Nazis set up an extermination camp in 1940. The first transports of Soviet prisoners were brought there in 1941. Later, transports arrived there from all over Poland and other occupied countries of Europe. In the winter of 1941, the first gas chambers and the crematorium started "work". While it existed, the camp exterminated at least 360,000 persons of more than 20 nationalities. After the war, the site of the camp was made into a Museum of Martyrology, and an impressive monument was raised to the memory of its victims (78).

77

78

79

80

Chełm, a former Ruthenian stronghold built on a chalk hill, was incorporated into Poland by Casimir the Great. But it was only in the 16th century that it began to develop as an important trade centre. The wars in the 17th century badly damaged the town. In the 19th century, industry began to develop there, mainly processing of agricultural produce. After the liberation in 1944, it was the first seat of the Polish Committee of National Liberation and it was here that the Manifesto of the Committee was published, laying the foundations for the new system. The cretaceous limestone deposits here became the basis for the developing cement industry in Chełm and nearby Rejowiec (80). The agricultural area to the south of Chełm has the most fertile loess chernozem soils in Poland, with numerous privately owned (79) and state farms.

In this region is the former town of Uchanie, today a small market centre, where there is a late Renaissance church with two chapels and beautiful stucco decoration, built about 1625 on the site of an earlier Gothic church (81).

Zamość is the main urban centre of the southern part of the Lublin region. It was founded in 1580 by Jan Zamoyski, Chancellor and Hetman. The town was designed as a stronghold magnate's residence and a centre of the vast estates of the Zamoyskis; it was built to the design of Bernardo Morando of Padua and strongly fortified with bastioned defence walls of the old-and-new-Italian systems by Andrea del Aqua. Thus, the most impressive building of the town of Zamość was the magnificent magnate's palace. The town developed rapidly due to trade. It also became an important centre of intellectual life. In 1593, Jan Zamoyski founded an Academy, which was a branch of the Cracow Academy. During the wars of the 17th century, the stronghold effectively resisted the attacks of the Cossacks and Swedes. In 1810, the town and its stronghold was taken over by the government of the Congress Kingdom, and later by the Tsarist authorities. In 1866, the stronghold was pulled down. The town and its population suffered greatly during the Second World War. During the occupation, Zamość was the centre of the area that the Nazis took for German colonization, so the extermination policy towards the Polish population here was particularly cruel. There were 3 extermination camps in Zamość and its vicinity. Many thousands of people were executed in the Zamość Rotunda.

The carefully preserved large Market Place with the Town Hall built in the years 1639–1651 (83), surrounded by burghers houses with arcades, is a pearl of Renaissance architecture. The Renaissance-Baroque Collegiate Church of St. Thomas, designed by Morando, has also been preserved, as have the arsenal building, a Greek-Catholic church and a synagogue dating back to the 17th century, and the castle, which was enlarged and remodelled in the 18th century. Some parts of the powerful defence walls and bastions still stand today.

The Roztocze Ridge (83) is a long upland about 15 km. wide, linking the Lublin Upland with the Podole Upland. The northern part of the Roztocze Ridge, with loess soils, is practically devoid of forests, but the higher, southern part, with no loess cover, is thickly grown with fir and beech forests. The waters of the streams flowing down from the Roztocze Ridge have carved out numerous valleys and ravines. In the north there are associations of xerophilous steppe vegetation. Part of the Roztocze Ridge is a National Park.

82

83

The Sudety Mts. and the Silesian Lowland

1

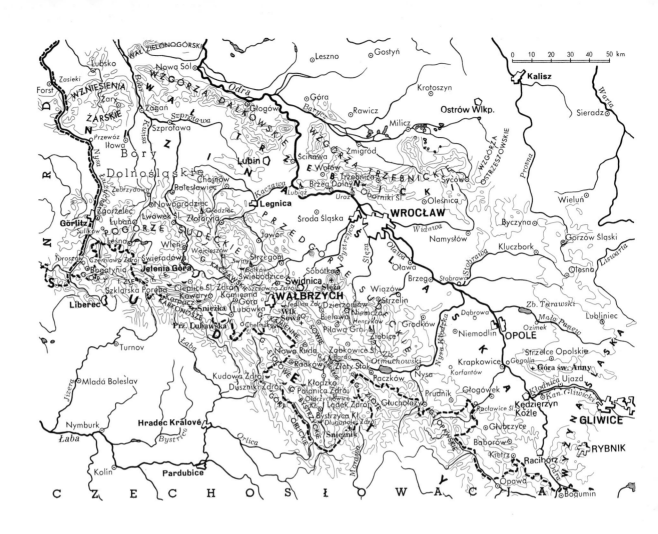

This is an area comprising two parts with quite different natural features, namely, the Sudety Mts., which are part of the Bohemian·Massif, and the Silesian Lowland, which is usually included in the Central European Plain. Despite these differences there are natural links between the two parts, and above all, historical and cultural ties,which make it an inseparable whole – historical Silesia. In the Middle Ages, apart from Wielkopolska and Małopolska, it was one of the three mother provinces of Poland. From the 14th century, when separated from the rest of Poland, it was subjected to intensive germanization. It was returned to the Motherland after the Second World War and today plays an important part in the economic and cultural life of the country.

Several times in their geological history the Sudety Mts. underwent uplifting, levelling and folding processes, so they are not high mountains, but greatly varied. The mountain chains are divided by wide intermontane basins or deep valleys. Almost every ridge or massif is a separate unit, differing from the others in structure and relief. They form a range about 300 km. long and 50 km. wide, stretching in a south-easterly direction from the upper Elbe to the Moravian Gate, composed of three basic parts, the western, middle and eastern Sudety Mts., and also the Sudety Foreland and Foothills.

The Western Sudety are mainly built from old crystalline rocks and extend from the Lusatian Gate to the Lubawka Gate. They form four chains grouped round the large Jelenia Góra Basin, namely, the Kaczawskie Mts., the Izerskie Mts., the Rudawy Janowickie Mts. and the Karkonosze Mts., the latter being the highest of the Sudety (Śnieżka, alt. 1601 m.). The peaks of the Karkonosze are covered with Goulder fields and their relief is varied by glacial forms such as hollows, hanging valleys and lakes, and the characteristic mushroom and club-like forms, towers and pinnacles created by weathering.

The Middle Sudety, situated between the Lubawka Gate and the Kłodzko Basin, comprise the central subsidence basins of the Sudety Mts. and the surrounding mountain massifs. In the north are the old Sowie Mts. (Great Sowie alt. 1014 m.) and their extension – the Bardzkie Mts. In the south there are two parallel chains – the Bystrzyckie and Orlickie Mts. (alt. up to 1115 m.), partly built of crystalline rocks and partly from cretaceous sandstone. The inside of the central basin of the Sudety Mts. is filled with a variety of sedimentary and extrusive rocks, creating a number of uplifts like the Wałbrzyskie Mts., the Kamienne Mts. and the very picturesque, rocky Stołowe (Table) Mts. The large Kłodzko Basin (alt. 350–450 m.), dividing the Middle Sudety from the Eastern Sudety, is filled with the youngest Pleistocene and Holocene formations.

The larger part of the Eastern Sudety, extending to the Moravian Gate, are within the boundaries of Czechoslovakia. Only parts of the Śnieżnik Group (alt. 1425 m.), the Złote Mts. (990 m.), the Bialskie Mts. (1125 m.) and Opawskie Mts. (890 m.) come within Poland's frontiers.

A very marked faulted verge divides the Sudety Mts. from the Sudety Foreland. It is highest in the Middle Sudety, where the Sowie and Bardzkie Mts. border directly with the Foreland.

The Western and Eastern Sudety are separated from this verge by an intermediary zone called the Sudety Foothills, the western part of which is an extensive undulating plateau (alt. 300–400 m.) with slender basalt cones protruding from it here and there.

The Sudety Foreland does not differ much from the Sudety Mts. as regards geological structure, but there are differences in height and landforms. The Foreland was not uplifted in the Tertiary epoch like the Sudety Mts. and has preserved its archaean relief characterized by the protrusion of isolated abrupt residual hills build up with hard rocks above the old surface, which was levelled to an altitude of 200–300 m. and later covered with layers of Tertiary and Quaternary deposits. The highest of these hills is Mt. Ślęża (alt. 719 m.).

The foundation of the Sudety Mts. is an archaean pre-Cambrian rock core, which was later covered with layers of sedimentary and igneous rocks formed from various lavas from the Paleozoic to the Quaternary epochs. This archaean core only appears on the surface in the Sowie Mts. in the form of gneiss and crystalline schists. The crystallized limestones formed in the same epochs in the region of Sławniowice to the south of the River Nysa, in the vicinity of Lądek-Zdrój and in the Kaczawskie Mts. near Wojcieszów are quarried as marble or raw material for the lime industry. The small deposits of rich iron ore (magnetites and hematites), most of which have already been exploited and exhausted around the Karkonosze Mts. and in the Kaczawskie Mts. are most probably of Cambrian origin. In successive later epochs various kinds of sediments were deposited in the Sudety and were afterwards transformed into the sandstone, quartzites, shale, greywacke and conglomerate found in the Kaczawskie Mts. and in the vicinity of Kłodzko. At the close of the Silurian epoch, the Sudety were folded by powerful earth movements, which brought outflows of acid magma (granites) and alkaline magma (gabbro, dunite and peridotite). The granite intrusions, later transformed into gneiss or granite-gneiss, occurred above all in the northern and eastern fringes of the Karkonosze and Izerskie Mts., and also in the Śnieżnik massif. The outflows of alkaline magma mainly occurred in the Sowie Mts. and the Sudety Foreland. Among the alkaline magma transformed into igneous rocks (in the vicinity of Sobótka and Ząbkowice) there are beautiful serpentine rocks and numerous chalcedony, opals, hyalites, nephrites, exploited as semi-precious stones. Magnesites occur here too, and also iron, nickel and chrome ores.

In the Carboniferous epoch, the deepening sea covered wide areas of Opole Silesia and later various parts of the Sudety Mts., depositing thick layers of shales, conglomerate and sandstone. During the next successive uplift of the Sudety (Hercynian Orogeny), thick layers of rock material washed down from the mountains covered the surrounding basins overgrown with tropical flora. This led to the creation of the Wałbrzych (Lower Silesian) Coal Basin, one tenth the size of the Upper Silesian Basin and with coal deposits 50 times smaller. The coal deposits there are estimated at 1,200 million tons, going down to a depth of 1,000 m. The importance of the Wałbrzych Coal Basin is due mainly to the fact that about 40 per cent of its resources consist of coking coal.

Huge magma outflows accompanied the earth movements in the Hercynian epoch, traces of which are the granites of the Karkonosze Mts., the Strzegom and Strzelin massifs and the environs of Kudowa and Kłodzko, the syenites of the Niemcza and Złoty Stok massifs and the later veins and outflows of porphyre and melaphyre, which formed the Kamienne Mts. and are frequently found in the Wałbrzyskie Mts. too. The granite rocks are of the greatest economic importance, which are used for road construction and building. The magma intrusion caused mineralization processes of the surrounding rocks, which led to the formation of small veins of ores, mostly polymetallic. These deposits, which have been exploited through the centuries, are not of economic importance today, only supplying small amounts of baryte. More important are the Upper Permian (Zechstein) sedimentary ores created by the weathering and washing down of mineral ores, which were deposited in shallow piedmont lakes or at the bottom of the nearby sea. The ore-bearing marls and shales formed in this way, mostly containing copper, occur in the central basin of the Sudety Mts., near Nowa Ruda and Silesian Chełmsko and in the Sudety Foothills between Bolesławiec, Złotoryja and Jawor. The rich copper ore deposits discovered after the Second World War between Głogów and Lubin in the Silesian Lowland are of similar origin. Other deposits of the Zechstein Sea are marls and limestone and also the gypsum and anhydrite deposits exploited in the Bolesławiec and Złotoryja area.

The limited range of Triassic and Jurassic formations in the Sudety Mts. and over a large area of the Silesian Lowland indicate that this area was then land. In the Opole area, the Triassic layers are covered with cretaceous formations, mainly marls, exploited by the cement industry. The cretaceous sandstone forming the Stołowe Mts. and occuring around Bolesławiec, Lwówek and Złotoryja is excellent building material.

In the Tertiary epoch the Sudety were upelifted again. This caused considerable dislocations along the whole length and breadth of the mountain massif. One of them separated the Foreland of today from the Sudety Mts. The Foreland was later covered by swamps and shallow lakes, where sand and silt deposits washed down from the mountains accumulated, and this in turn led to the formation of deposits of brown coal in many places. The biggest deposits (40 to 80 m. thick) were found in the Turoszów Basin. During the Tertiary epoch the Sudety Mts. underwent intensive weathering processes, which resulted in the formation of white kaolin clays in the hollows of the granite massifs of Strzegom, Ślęża and Strzelin and in the gneisses of the Sowie and Izerskie Mts. The purest quality clay is used for the production of porcelain and the inferior clays for technical ceramics. The Lower Silesian ceramic industry also makes use of the Tertiary clays of the Sudety Foreland.

The Alpine mountain building processes were accompanied by volcanic activity, traces of which can be seen in the numerous basalt cones, layers and veins found everywhere and particular-ly in the Sudety Foothills, between Zgorzelec and Lubań, near Złotoryja and Jawor.

Between the Sudety Foreland in the south, the Trzebnica Ridge in the north and the Silesian Upland in the east stretches the wide, rather flat area known as the Silesian Lowland. Its deep substratum, of Paleozoic and older formations, is partially covered by Triassic sediments which are overlaid by thick Tertiary deposits and these are covered by layers of clay and silt brought there by glaciers. In the west, a large area of the Lowland is occupied by alluvial cones formed by the outwash of the rivers of the Sudety Mts. The Silesian Lowland is separated from the Wielkopolska Lowland by the Trzebnica Ridge, a moraine elevation rising about 100 metres above the surrounding country.

With the exception of a small part of the Orlickie and Karkonosze Mts., the whole of the Sudety Mts. and the Silesian Lowland lies in the Odra Basin into which the Sudeten rivers flow from the south, namely, the Osobłoga, Nysa Kłodzka, Oława, Ślęża, Bystrzyca, Kaczawa, the Bóbr with Kwisa and the Lusatian Nysa, and from the north – the Kłodnica, Mała Panew, and Stobrawa (from the Silesian Upland) and the Widawa (from the Trzebnica Ridge).

The Sudety have a mountain climate, the differences depending on the altitude, the exposure of the mountain slopes and the prevailing winds. Low atmospheric pressures often bring masses of Polar-maritime air from the west and north west, due to which the climate of the Sudety is cooler and more humid than that of the Carpathians. Cloudy weather is frequent here, as are mists and strong winds. The rainfalls, exceeding 650 mm. in the foothills, increase with altitude, reaching 1,000 mm. and more in the mountains. Snow lies a long time there, and Mt. Śnieżka is snow-capped for 200 days of the year. The intermontane basins and the Sudety Foreland are warmer and have more sun. Storms and torrential rains are frequent in the Sudety Foreland. The Silesian Lowland is one of the warmest areas of Poland. The average temperature for the whole year is above 8.5 °C and the winters are short and mild, almost without snow. Spring is moist and the summers are long and warm. The growing season lasts for 220 days or more. The rainfalls vary between about 550 mm. to over 600 mm.

The varied geological conditions, relief and climate, and various plant associations that once covered the Sudety Mts. and Silesian Lowland, have led to the creation of greatly differentiated soil conditions. In the Sudety Mts., the shallow skeletal soils characteristic of mountainous areas predominate. These are not cultivated very often by farmers due to the steepness of the mountain slopes. The soils in the Sudety basins, created on the basis of alluvial and post-glacial gravel and sands, are not very fertile. Only the centre of the Kłodzko Basin has better, podsolic soils. The Sudety Foreland has more differentiated soils, and so has the Silesian Lowland. On the left bank of the Odra, large areas are covered with fertile brown or podsolic soils, created on loess or loess-like substrata or fine silt deposits brought there by water. In some places there are patches of heavier podsolic soils on a clayey substratum. To the south of

Wrocław there is a large area of black earths. To the north, west and east, light podsolic soils become more frequent and areas of loose sands, light clayey sands and bog soils make their appearance. Only in some places are there patches of tighter silty loamy and clayey soils, and even brown soils of loess origin. Tighter podsolic soils are also found on the Trzebnica Ridge. The Odra and Nysa valleys are covered by alluvial soils.

The plant life of the Sudety Mts. and the Silesian Lowland has undergone great transformations. Only the highest parts of mountains have retained a more natural character. In the Sudety upper regel forests occur at an altitude of 900–1,250 m. Mountain slopes at an altitude of 450 to 1,000 were formerly overgrown with luxuriant lower regel forests, to the west – with mixed beech-fir-spruce forests, in the Kłodzko Basin with mixed deciduous forests with a predominance of beech trees. Over large areas these forests have been replaced by uniform spruce forests. There are raised peat bogs overgrown with dwarf spruce or dwarf mountain pine on the gently undulated Sudety mountain tops and some of the levelled slopes. Many relics of tundra flora are found there, such as the cloudberry, Laponic willow, dwarf birch, crowberry, etc. The Sudety have their own specific mountain fauna, among which is the Mornel peewit, and many of the same species that are found in the Carpathians. The area at the foot of the Sudety Mts., up to an altitude of 450 m., was formerly overgrown with beech forests with quite a large percentage of fir, oak, maple, mountain elm and linden trees and on the poorer soils – mixed forests with a predominance of pine and a large percentage of deciduous forests. These forests have also, to a large extent, been turned into uniform spruce or pine forests.

On the fertile soils of the southern part of the Silesian Lowland there were once gronds (mixed hornbeam and oak forests) and oak forests, of which very little has remained. In the northern part there were dry, fresh and bog–pine forests. A large area of dry pine forests (Lower Silesian Forest) has remained to this day. Bog pine forests also occur quite frequently there. The Odra Valley and the lower reaches of its tributaries were once grown with mixed marsh woods, the remains of which can be seen near Racibórz, between the Oława and Wrocław, and also in the vicinity of Wołów and Środa Śląska.

The fauna of the area has also changed greatly. The local larger fauna have practically disappeared, the only ones to survive being the hare, fox, polecat and weasel. Stags and roe-deer have survived under protection. Fallow deer, mouflon, rabbits and pheasants have been brought there from abroad.

Due to favourable natural conditions, the Sudety Foreland and the Silesian Lowland were an area where people settled as early as the Palaeolithic Age. In the Neolithic Age agriculture made its appearance on the fertile soils of the Lowland. It attained a high level in the period of the Lusatian culture. In the year 500 B.C., Silesia was invaded by the Scythians, and about 400 B.C. by Celtic tribes, who left traces of the first iron smelting furnaces. In the Roman epoch, agriculture and iron smelting developed quickly. At that time the Amber Route leading from the Mediterranean to the Baltic ran through Silesia.

In the early Middle Ages, numerous Slav tribes lived in Silesia. The largest tribe, the Ślężans, set up a political organization round Wrocław, which later embraced the whole of Silesia. For many centuries, the Bohemians and Polanes rivalled with each other for Silesia. Incorporated into the Polish state at the end of the 10th century, it became the scene of Polish-German battles at the beginning of the 11th century. It was then that fortified castles were built along the frontiers with Germany and Bohemia. The threat to Silesia increased during the time of the feudal fragmentation of Poland. Left to fend for themselves, the Silesian princes became vassals of the Luxemburg Dynasty reigning in Bohemia.

The position of Silesia near the western frontiers of Poland meant that progressive methods of husbandry came to Silesia earlier than to other parts of Poland. In the 13th century the process of organizing existing towns and setting up new ones according to "German Law". In these well built towns protected by defence walls, handicrafts and trade flourished. This period saw the building of churches, monasteries and castles, among which the castles of the Silesian princes are worthy of note. The biggest role was played by Wrocław, situated at the crossing of the trade routes from west to east and south to north, which from the year 1000 was a bishopric capital.

For a long time settlement developed along the Odra and on its left bank within the boundaries of the Silesian Lowland and part of the Sudety Foreland around Śleża and the Strzelin Hills. Slowly settlers penetrated into the Kłodzko Basin and moved along the River Bóbr towards the Sudety Mts. The forest grown regions bordering on this area to the south and north were not settled on a large scale until the 13th and 14th centuries. The settlement of the border forests of the Sudety and the Lower Silesian Forests was even slower, for they were deliberately kept inaccessible.

Meanwhile the settlement of the Sudety Foreland and Foothills progressed well. A colourful description of agriculture in these parts has been preserved in a 13th century book, known as the Henryków Book. In addition to the growing of crops, including flax, sheep rearing was common, and this led to the development of numerous centres making woollen cloth. Very often colonization was connected with the exploitation of mineral deposits. There was an increase in the extraction of iron, copper and zinc ores, and even gold (Złoty Stok).

When Silesia came under Bohemian rule, a fact Casimir the Great was forced to recognize in 1348, this did not have any great influence of the national character of Silesia for some time. The situation changed after the Hapsburgs began to reign in Bohemia. Gradual germanization of the Silesian towns and gentry, and also the Silesian princes was started. In any case, during 150 years the Silesian rulers of the Piast dynasty gradually died out (the last of the dynasty died in 1675). Silesia continued its economic development, although from the turn of the 15th century the growth rate was slower. Trade was not so lively and the landed estate economy that replaced the manorial system became more widespread. The Thirty Years War (1618–1648) caused great damage. The population of Silesia diminished by more than 30%, a lot of land lay fallow and the towns went into decline.

As Silesia became more and more germanized, its contacts with Poland got weaker or ceased to exist. The cultural ties with Cracow, where numerous young men from Silesia were still being educated in the 16th century, were broken. The Polish character of the population was most affected in Lower Silesia, but in the countryside there were still numerous concentrations of Polish population still standing firm there, for the rural population withstood the germanization process the longest. The germanization campaign was intensified after Silesia was incorporated into Prussia in 1742. From that time on feelings of Polish nationality were suppressed severely by the Prussian administration, the clergy and the schools. In spite of this strong germanization pressure, the majority of the inhabitants of Upper Silesia and the Opole region resisted all efforts to denationalize them. As late as the 19th century, Polish literary and scientific works were still being published in Wrocław, and also school textbooks of the Polish language, because the German merchants needed to know the language for their trade contacts with the Polish villages.

The growth rate of industry in Lower Silesia and the Opole region was slower in the 19th century than in Upper Silesia. Coal mining developed in the Wałbrzych Basin, 'Wrocław became a big industrial centre, but the technically obsolete textile industry in the Sudety Mts. area declined. A centre of the cement industry grew up in the Opole region. There was a development of the building materials industry, the ceramic, glass and printing industries, and above all the food processing industry, connected with the speedily growing agricultural production. But the majority were small and medium size enterprises, mainly light industry factories, concentrated in Wrocław, Opole and the Sudety districts. The northern areas bordering on Wielkopolska were neglected. This relatively slow growth rate of industry in Lower Silesia situated on the peripheries of the German state, caused an outflow of population to the west. Most of those who left were of German nationality. Wrocław, Legnica and Jelenia Góra were among the very few immigration centres.

The 19th century brought a revival of Polish national consciousness among the people of Silesia, and in its wake came an even better organized resistance to germanization. An expression of the people's feelings of belonging to Poland were the three uprisings of the Silesian population and the results of the plebiscite in 1921. Despite the heroic struggles of the people of Opole, Opole Silesia and part of Upper Silesia remained within the Reich.

In the interwar period, the part of Silesia under German rule did not have favourable conditions for development due to its peripheral position and the fact that it was cut off from Polish markets. The germanization pressures, steadily growing in the Twenties, became a ruthless battle against the Polish element under Hitler's rule. Despite this, about 860,000 persons declared themselves of Polish nationality when Silesia was returned to Poland in 1945.

The last phase of the Second World War caused great destruction in Lower Silesia and the Opole region. The towns suffered considerably, particularly Wrocław, industry and the communication network. Farms were abandoned and the fields lay fallow. The least damage was done to the Sudety region, liberated after the capitulation of the Reich. At the beginning of 1946, about 1,400,000 of the German population were repatriated to Germany. Silesia was settled by Polish population.

In 1950, out of the total of about 2,500,000 inhabitants of Lower Silesia and the Opole region, 20% were Polish autochthons, 31% repatriates from the USSR, 4% repatriates from other countries and 45% were people resettled from other parts of Poland. The majority of people settling in the Western Territories were young, so the natural population increase remained at a very high level here for a long time.

In subsequent decades Silesian towns have been reconstructed from war ruins, the rural areas have been populated and developed. Industry has been rebuilt and expanded and so has the system of communications. Lower Silesia and the Opole region have become important in the economic and cultural life of the whole country.

In the Sudety Mts. and Silesian Lowland, the following industrial districts are developing: the Sudety, Wrocław, Opole and Legnica-Głogów districts.

The biggest and most extensive is the Sudety Industrial District, embracing the Wałbrzych and Jelenia Góra Voivodships and a small part of Legnica Voivodship, and producing 6% of the national industrial output, which places it fourth after the Upper Silesian, Łódź and Warsaw industrial districts. Industry in the Sudety District is differentiated, the biggest role being played by industries utilizing local raw materials and traditional branches of industry that existed in that area before.

The Wałbrzych Industrial District, based on the coal deposits situated between Wałbrzych and Nowa Ruda, was already developed a long time ago. At the beginning of the 19th century coal extraction there was twice as much as in Upper Silesia. At present the Wałbrzych Coal Basin only supplies 2% of the national output of hard coal, but the importance of this coal is its high caloric value and above all, the large percentage of coking coal produced there. Brown coal is mined mainly near Turoszów in the extreme south-west of the district and of Poland. The two open-cast mines supply 60% of the national output of this raw material, which is mainly used for power generating.

The mining and processing of metals, developed in the Middle Ages, has almost ceased to exist as the deposits of ore have been practically exhausted. Small quantities of nickel ore are still extracted near Ząbkowice and of barite ore at Boguszów.

The mineral industry is also closely connected with local raw materials. There has been a particularly intensive development of industry producing building and road construction materials. The main centres of this industry are in the belt stretching from Bystrzyca Kłodzka, through Kłodzko, Wałbrzych, Strzegom, Strzelin, Jawor, Złotoryja and Lwówek to Lubań. The largest granite quarries are in Strzegom and Strzelin. In the Kaczawskie Mts., near Wojcieszów, there are numerous limestone quarries, and also marble quarries and masons workshops.

Another well developed sector of the mineral industry are glass and ceramic works. Of the more than 60 glass works in Poland, the majority are in the southern and western parts of Lower Silesia. Particularly worthy of mention are the crystal glass works at Stronie Śląskie (the biggest producer of crystal glass in the world), Szklarska Poręba and Szczytna. Technical and optical glass is produced in Jelenia Góra. The glass works in Wałbrzych is a big producer of blown glass products, reinforced glass and mirror glass. Table porcelain is produced in Wałbrzych and Jaworzyna Śląska and in the vicinity of Wałbrzych and Jelenia Góra – technical porcelain.

The textile industry, a characteristic branch in Lower Silesia for centuries, is very well developed in the Sudety Industrial District. In the past woollen cloth and linen was produced. At present cotton fabrics predominate. The biggest textile centres are at the foot of the Sowie Mts., in Dzierżoniów, Bielawa and Pieszyce. There are also important textile mills in Wałbrzych, Lubań and Kamienna Góra. In Dzierżoniów, the clothing industry is also well developed. Carpets are made in Kowary. In the Sudety Industrial District a less important role is played by the engineering industry, but its share in the production of the district is growing. The biggest centre of this branch of industry is in Świdnica, where machines and installations for the chemical and food industry are produced (including complete sugar refining plants), goods wagons, electrical measurement apparatus, etc. Mining machines are made in Wałbrzych and textile industry machines – in Kamienna Góra and Dzierżoniów. Dzierżoniów is also a producer of radio sets. Ząbkowice Śląskie is a centre of the electrotechnic industry and precision instruments are made in Jelenia Góra and Świebodzice.

The chemical industry is not very well represented in the Sudety Industrial District. The only big chemical plants is in Jelenia Góra. It is an important producer of cellulose and viscose fibres and of pharmaceutical preparations. The timber industry is well developed, with numerous works in the Kłodzko, Kamienna Góra and Jelenia Góra Basins and near Lubań. There are furniture factories in Świdnica and Olszyna Lubańska and a match factory in Bystrzyca Kłodzka.

The biggest centre of the food industry is Kłodzko, but there are food processing factories in many other places too. There are numerous sugar factories all over the area where sugar beet is grown (from Racibórz to Legnica).

The Opole Industrial District has many different branches of industry, the engineering and electrical engineering industries predominating. Industrial machines and installations are produced in Opole, Nysa, Strzelce Opolskie and Brzeg. Nysa is also a producer of mini-buses and delivery vans. Jelcz produces buses and Brzeg – electric motors. High pressure boilers are produced in Racibórz and machine tools in Kuźnia Raciborska. In the old iron smelting centre of Ozimek on the Mała Panew there are now modern steel works and iron foundries. Kędzie-

rzyn is an important centre of the chemical industry and Zdzieszowice has a coking plant.

There has been a strong development of the mineral industry, represented by several big cement works in Opole and its surroundings and numerous lime quarries near the border with the Silesian Upland. Krapkowice on the Odra is known for its production of cellulose and paper. In the southern part of the Opole Industrial District there are textile mills, the main centre being in Prudnik. Otmęt has one of the biggest footwear factories in Poland and Brzeg is another big centre of the leather industry. The biggest food processing factories are in Opole and Racibórz.

The big industrial centre of Wrocław, together with the nearby towns of Oława, Jelcz, Oleśnica, Brzeg Dolny and Siechnice, form the Wrocław Industrial District. The electro-power industry is developing there, but the most important branch is the engineering industry, with Poland's only electric railway rolling stock works ("Pafawag") and a computer factory ("Elwro"), also the Wrocław works produce building machines, generators, electric motors, and the "Hutmet" works produce non-ferrous metals from scrap metal. In Oleśnica there is a railway rolling stock repair works, and Siechnice has a foundry producing ferrochromium.

The chemical industry is concentrated in Wrocław, Brzeg and Oława. Wrocław is also a centre of the clothing, leather, paper and food industries. It also has a river shipyard. The leather industry is also developing in Oleśnica.

The new Legnica-Głogów Industrial District is a very specialized one, based on the mining and processing of copper. There are three copper mines between Złotoryja and Bolesławiec (exploiting rather poor deposits), which were reconstructed after the last war, and the new Lubin-Głogów Basin, where the recently discovered rich copper ore deposits are being exploited. Three mines have been constructed here during the last twenty years: in Lubin, Polkowice and Rudna, and the construction of a fourth is being completed at Sieroszowice. The ore is processed in the works at Legnica, opened in 1954, and at Żukowice, near Głogów, opened in 1971. Poland is now one of the biggest copper ore producers in the world and has first place in this respect in Europe.

As regards other branches, this district has engineering works, light industry and food factories and enterprises of the mineral industry. In the western part of the District, there is a large centre of the glass and ceramics industry in Bolesławiec. The textile industry in the vicinity of Żary and Żagań has fine old traditions.

The Silesian Lowland and the Sudety Foreland are one of the areas with the most productive agriculture in Poland, supplying large quantities of produce to the market. The share of large state farms is considerable (30–40% of arable land) and the individual farms are larger than in the Subcarpathians and the Silesian Upland. It is also the only area of such a size in Poland where there is a marked predominance of the cultivation of wheat and sugar beet over the rye-potato pattern. The farmers attain high yields of wheat, sugar beet and rape-seed. Maize is also widely cultivated here. There is also a large cattle population, bred mainly for meat.

Agriculture in Opole Silesia has a particularly high level of productivity. In the southern and western parts of this area there is intensive output of wheat, sugar beet and milk. In the north, the share of potato crops and pig and cattle breeding increases. The productivity of the land is among the highest in the country and the incomes of the farmers are also among the highest in Poland. Good results are attained by the farmers in the area between the River Odra and the Sudety, in the central belt stretching from Racibórz to Legnica where wheat and sugar beet are grown. In the Sudety Mts. the share of wheat and sugar beet decreases in favour of the cultivation of rye, oats, potatoes and flax, but cattle breeding, particularly sheep, is more highly developed. In the northern part of the Silesian Lowland, where the soil is not so good, the farmers grow rye and potatoes instead of wheat and sugar beet. The yields are lower, as are other indices of agricultural production. On the other hand, the forest economy plays a more important part.

The Sudety Mts. and the Sudety Foreland constitute an important recreational and curative area with many spas. They have excellent conditions for this, namely, beautiful scenery and valuable mineral springs, which have been exploited for a long time at well organized spas. Szczawno, Kudowa, Duszniki, Polanica, Długopole, Czerniawa and other spas are famed for their acidulous waters. In Lądek and Świeradów, the ferrous-acidulous waters are radio-active. Some of the mineral springs in Duszniki, Kudowa and Lądek have traces of arsenic acid, valuable in some cures. Cieplice and Lądek are known for their warm springs. Many places have a good curative climate (Szklarska Poręba, Karpacz, Bierutowice, Polanica). After the Tatra Mts., the Karkonosze Mts. are the second most important winter sports area in Poland. There are large numbers of recreational and tourist centres all along the Sudety range and on the Sudety Foreland, which are very popular holiday resorts.

The main centre of the economic and cultural life of Lower Silesia is Wrocław (pop. about 600,000), one of the three big provincial capitals (with Cracow and Poznań) of Poland. The town of Wrocław developed on the site of a very old settlement, dating back at least to the Neolithic Age. It was already a big centre of trade and handicrafts in the 13th century. For centuries it was an important link in trade between Poland, Bohemia and Germany. Incorporated into Bohemia in 1335, and later into Prussia in 1741, Wrocław maintained strong cultural and scientific ties with Poland, particularly with Cracow. The 19th and 20th centuries brought increasing germanization pressures. Despite this, Wrocław remained an important centre of Polish culture, the seat of many Polish associations and organizations. In the last phase of the war, in 1945, Wrocław was very badly damaged (70% of the buildings and 80% of its industry lay in ruins). The scars of war have now healed, industry has been built up again and expanded and the most valuable historical buildings have been carefully reconstructed. Wrocław, which is a voivodship town and a big industrial centre, also plays the role of the scientific and cultural capital of the south western part of Poland. It has eight higher schools of learning attended by nearly 46,000 students, numerous scientific centres of the Polish Academy of Sciences and ministerial research institutes. Wrocław also has valuable library collections, archives, museums, an opera house, operetta and theatres. The Wrocław Laboratory Theatre of J. Grotowski is an experimental group well known in the world, with many followers. H. Tomaszewski's mime theatre has won world fame, too.

Opole is an important regional centre (pop. over 110,000). It was the centre of a densely populated area as early as the 10th century and for several centuries it was the capital of an independent duchy. The accelerated development of the town in the 19th century was connected with the growing industrialization of Upper Silesia, when the Opole cement industry met the need for supplies of cement to that industrial district. Opole was also an important centre of Polish life, effectively resisting germanization pressures. Opole was badly damaged in the last war (60% of its buildings lay in ruins), but was reconstructed in the post-war years and is now a thriving industrial town, an important junction and a lively cultural centre. It has two higher schools of learning (attended by more than 7,000 students) and numerous cultural institutions. Opole is the seat of the well known Silesian Institute and the active Opole Scientific Society.

The second biggest voivodship town in Lower Silesia after Wrocław is Wałbrzych (pop. 132,000), a big mining and industrial town. Silver and lead ores were mined there as early as the 14th century. In the 15th and 16th centuries Wałbrzych was a well known centre of the textile industry. At the end of the 18th century it gained importance in connection with the coal mined there. Glass and porcelain were also produced there. Apart from its administrative and industrial significance, it is now a centre providing services, some of which cater for the needs of tourists.

Legnica (pop. 87,000) became a voivodship town only a few years ago (1975). It was once a trading settlement, the seat of castellans and later the capital of a duchy ruled by the Silesian Piasts till 1675, when it passed into the hands of the Hapsburgs, who ruled there till Silesia was incorporated into Prussia. In the 15th and 16th centuries it was an important linen producing centre. Later till the 18th century it was known as a centre producing Arras tapestries. Apart from its administrative functions, Legnica today is an industrial town, a junction, cultural centre, and provides services to the surrounding areas.

Another young voivodship town is Jelenia Góra (pop. 85,000). In the Middle Ages it was known for the production of woollen cloth, then, in the 15th century it began to produce fine fabrics exported to many world markets and the glass industry began to develop there. In the 19th century, Jelenia Góra became a tourist centre. It is still an industrial town and tourist centre, and its significance is growing as a cultural centre. There is a branch of the Wrocław Higher School of Economics in Jelenia Góra.

Apart from the voivodship towns, there are other towns of

various sizes that are developing fast in Lower Silesia. Some of them are already thriving industrial towns, and others are developing in the same direction. They also provide services, including tourist facilities, and some of them are nodes of communication. However, the leading towns are those whose development is based on industry. The largest of these include: Świdnica (pop. 55,000) and Nysa (pop. 40,000), and the quickly growing towns of the copper basin: Lubin (pop. 58,000) and Głogów (pop. 45,000). Bolesławiec, Dzierżoniów, Bielawa, Brzeg and Oleśnica are large industrial centres. A fast developing border town is Zgorzelec, which is divided in two by the Polish-German state frontier. Nine other towns with a population between 20 and 30 thousand are gaining significance, generally in connection with the development of industry; the growth of 18 more (pop. 10–20,000) is connected with industry or their service function for surrounding areas. The network of towns in the Sudety Mts. and the Silesian Lowland is well developed and varied. The network is denser in the Sudety (in the intermontane basins), the Sudety Foreland and in the southern part of the Silesian Lowland, getting sparser towards the north-west.

Most of the Silesian towns have buildings of historical interest, the remains of defence walls and fortifications, burghers' houses, churches, castles and palaces. Many of them testify to the Polish character of the area and old Polish traditions.

The Silesian villages have in general preserved the old spatial layout. The most frequently met with are green villages, street villages and chain linear villages. The green type villages, usually 1–2 km. long, are built along roads, widening in the centre where there is an oblong market place. This old layout is also seen in many towns that have developed from villages. Green villages are generally found in the flat country along the left bank of the Odra. A rather smaller number of street villages (similar in layout but without the market place and forked roads) are mostly found in the northern part of the Silesian Lowland. Both layouts are characteristic of the oldest Slav settlements in the period preceding the colonization according to German Law. The chain villages were built at the time of this colonization. They extend for 3 to 4 kilometres in long double rows along the valleys of rivers and streams. These villages link up in an almost uninterrupted chain, sometimes as much as 20 km. long. The chain type villages predominate in the Sudety Mts. and the western part of the Sudety Foreland. They were mostly built in the 13th and 14th centuries as a result of the colonization of forest areas. On the right bank of the Odra, particularly to the north of Opole, one quite frequently meets scattered villages and small hamlets. The rural buildings are mainly of brick, sometimes of stone or half timbered with plaster or clay, but these are not so frequent. In the mountains, to the south of the Kłodzko Basin and in the Kamienna Góra Basin, a small number of old wooden buildings have been preserved. Another separate type of rural settlement are those which have grown up in the place of old landed estates. They consist of farm labourers' cottages and farm buildings grouped round the old manor house of the former land-owner. Today, these are mostly state farm centres, found all over the Silesian Lowland, the largest number being in the flat country round Wrocław and in the vicinity of Oleśnica.

5

6

The main river of the Silesian Lowland is the Odra. Its source is in the Sudety Mts. on the Czechoslovak side, at an altitude of 624 m. It flows down to half that altitude very quickly, for 54 km. and below Racibórz becomes a lowland river. All the Silesian rivers flow into the Odra. The left bank tributaries, namely the Opawa, Osobłoga, Nysa Kłodzka, Oława, Ślęza, Bystrzyca, Kaczawa, Bóbr, Kwisa and the border River Lusatian Nysa all have their sources in the Sudety Mts. The right bank tributaries have their sources in the Carpathians (Olza), the Silesian-Małopolska Upland (Mała Panew, Stobrawa) or in the Kocie (Cat) Hills (Trzebnica Hills), like the rivers Widawa and Barycz. The Odra (5), regulated along its entire length, canalized in parts, is the best waterway in Poland. The Gliwice Canal, built in the years 1933–1939, which replaced the 19th century Kłodnica Canal, is of great economic importance. It links the Upper Silesian Coal Basin with the Odra, and through the Odra, with the Baltic Sea. The Odra also serves as a waterway from Czechoslovakia to the Baltic, and the port at Koźle at the end of the Gliwice Canal is a loading point. The goods transported along the Odra are mainly coal, aggregate, iron ore and pyrites, and also apatites and phosphorites.

A characteristic feature of the past in Silesia was its considerable feudal devision, which went much further here than in other historical regions of Poland. The number of duchies ruled by the prolific Silesian branch of the Piast Dynasty was well over a dozen, not counting the duchies belonging to the Church. At the time of the greatest feudal division, the number of duchies in the Opole Land alone was seven. The capital of one of them was Racibórz, an old settlement once belonging to the tribe of Gołęszyce. In the times of the first Piasts, it was a stronghold guarding the crossing of the Odra on the trade route from Bohemia to Poland, and a trading settlement grew up there. It was the capital of a Piast duchy in the years 1172–1336. In the years 1337–1521, the Przemyslids of Bohemia ruled the duchy and in the years 1521–1532 – the last of the Opole Piasts, Jan. In 1552, the Duchy of Racibórz was incorporated directly into the Bohemian Crown lands. Racibórz was granted urban status before 1235. The town became wealthy from trade, had large stores of salt and was known for its corn exchanges. Handicrafts flourished there. During the Thirty Years' War, the town was badly damaged. In 1742, together with the whole of Silesia, it came under the rule of the Prussians. The next period of development of the town came in the middle of the 19th century, when Racibórz became a railway junction and industrial centre. The people of Racibórz always maintained lively cultural contacts with Poland. In the years 1919–1921, they participated in the Silesian uprisings, but did not succeed in their efforts for unification with the Motherland. In the inter-war years, Racibórz was a lively centre of Polish life. During the Second World War, the town suffered great destruction (80% of its buildings). After the war it was quickly rebuilt. Industry also made a quick recovery. The reconstruction work also included the most valuable historical buildings, among others, the Renaissance burghers houses in the Market Place (6). A reminder of the old Piast rulers is the partly ruined 15th century ducal castle, built on the site of the original stronghold, later enlarged, and in the years 1603–1635, remodelled in Renaissance style, as well as the remains of the old

defence walls, several churches originally Gothic, and reconstructed several times.

On the borderline between the Lowland and the Silesian Upland rises the Chełm Ridge, built of shelly limestone, the highest point of which is the basalt cone called St.Anne's Mount (alt. 404 m.). At its foot, amid the old Basalt quarries, a huge amphitheatre was built. On top of St. Anne's Mount is a Monument to the Silesian Insurgents (4), the work of the well known Polish sculptor Xawery Dunikowski, to commemorate the struggle of the Silesian insurgents for unification with Poland in 1921.

7

8

Opole voivodship is one of the best developed agricultural regions of Poland. The very productive individual farms of the region provide food to the industrial-urban agglomeration of Upper Silesia. On the fertile soils of the Silesian Lowland and Sudety Foreland stretching along the left bank of the Odra, individual and state farms grow large quantities of wheat and sugar beet. This is the only region in Poland where wheat predominates over rye. One of the best state farms in the area is Kietrz (7).

A very interesting and original example of wooden sacral building in the Opole region is the pilgrimage church of St. Anne in Oleśno (8). It grew out of the original small church built in 1528, which was enlarged by the addition of several Baroque chapels onto it according to a star groundplan in 1670. The walls and roof are shingle-covered. Inside there is a historical late Gothic triptych altarpiece from the beginning of the 16th century.

9

10

11

Opole is in the eastern part of the Silesian Lowland, on the River Odra. It was the old centre of the Opolan tribe. Archeological research has revealed traces of very early settlement here. In the 10th century it was a stronghold. From the times of Bolesław the Brave, Opole was the seat of castellans. In 1202, it became the capital of a separate duchy, and in 1217 it was granted urban status. It developed mainly from trade with Ruthenia and Bohemia. In 1327, the Opolan prince Bolko II, like most of the Silesian princes, became a vassal of the Bohemian Crown. Pledged as a security to the Polish king Władysław IV, Opole served as a refuge for his successor Jan Casimir during the Polish-Swedish war ten years later. In 1740, the town was taken by Prussia, which in 1816 made it an administrative seat (Regierungsbezirk). A big break-through in the economic life of Opole came with the opening of a cement there in 1857, one of the first in Europe, which utilized the local deposits of cretaceous marls.

Despite the big influx of Germans and the germanization policy of the Prussian government, most of the inhabitants of Opole retained their Polish character. In the inter-war years, Opole was a strong centre of Polish life. It was badly damaged during the Second World War, particularly the historical central district, which was painstakingly reconstructed after the war (2).

Several Gothic-Renaissance houses with Baroque facades still stand in the Market Place (9). Among the valuable buildings of historical interest are the Franciscan monastery, in which there are tombstones of the Opolan princes, and the Dominican monastery, as well as the 15th century Gothic collegiate church (now a cathedral), which was built on the site of a small wooden church founded by Bolesław the Brave in 1024. All that remains of the castle of the Opolan princes, built in the years 1228–1231 is the 14th century Gothic tower. Opole is today a fest developing voivodship town and also a strong industrial and cultural centre. The town is growing and there are new buildings with interesting modern architecture, to mention the theatre (10) and the amphitheatre (3).

The cement industry is being developed, the most recent addition being the new Górażdże Cement Works (11).

The ancient Slav settlement of Nysa grew up at the crossing of important trade routes from Poland to Bohemia. Tradition has it that before 1015, in the time of Bolesław the Brave, there was a chapel of St. James there, one of the earliest Christian places of worship in Silesia. From 1201, Nysa became the capital of the Duchy of Nysa, which belonged to the bishops of Wrocław. At the beginning of the 12th century, next to the old settlement, a new one was built on the other bank of the Nysa Kłodzka, which in 1308 was granted urban rights under Flemish Law. In the middle of the 14th century, the Duchy of Nysa became a vassal state of the Bohemian Crown. And at this time the town was surrounded by defence walls with towers and turrets. In the 17th century, the famous Jesuit college was opened here, which was attended by the Polish kings Michał Korybut Wiśniowiecki and Jan Sobieski. At the end of the 15th century, Polish was still being generally spoken there. The growing prosperity of the town was conductive to the development of cultural life. Nysa was ravaged during the Thirty Years' Was and the Austrian-Prussian wars and in the 18th century came under the rule of the Prussians, who enlarged its stronghold. In 1810, the properties of the bishops were secularized. Up till the end of the 19th century, the spatial expansion of Nysa was checked by the fortifications. After the construction of a railway line in the 19th century, the metal industry developed here and to this day plays an important role in the town. During the Second World War, the town was badly damaged. Many of the valuable historical buildings have been reconstructed (12): the church of St. James from the 13th–14th centuries (13), the Jesuit church and college, the monastery of the Holy Sepulchre, the Municipal Weighing House from the beginning of the 17th century, parts of the 14th century defence walls and the later 17th century fortifications with bastions, and also Renaissance and Baroque houses.

14

Paczków, on the River Nysa Kłodzka, is one of the most beautiful historical
towns of Silesia. Founded in 1254 by Thomas, Bishop of Wrocław, of Polish
origin, according to Flemish law (like Nysa), it was part of the "state" of the
bishops. In the middle of the 14th century the town was surrounded by
double defence walls. In 1428, Paczków was taken by Hussite troops and used
for a time as a point of resistance. The town lived through a period of
flourishing development in the 16th century as a centre producing cloth,
which was exported to Bohemia, Moravia and Austria. The Thirty Years' War
and the Prussian-Austrian wars of the 18th century brought destruction to the
town. The loss of its markets after Paczków was incorporated into Prussia
caused the decline of the cloth industry. Paczków escaped destruction in the
Second World War and has retained its characteristic appearance of
a mediaeval town (14) surrounded by walls with three gates and 19 turrets. It
is dominated by the Gothic defence church with its massive tower. In the
Market Place, amid Renaissance and Baroque burghers houses, stands the
impressive Town Hall in Classicist style with the Renaissance tower that was
preserved.

The Kłodzko Basin (15), the largest inter-montane basin in the Sudety Mts.
divides the Eastern Sudety from the Middle Sudety Mts. It is elongated and
irregular in shape running from north to south. The River Nysa Kłodzka flows
through the centre of the basin. The floor of the basin is undulating and
covered with fertile soils. The climate is mild, so there was an early
development of agriculture in the basin. Some of the settlements are
industrialized, there are valuable mineral spings in many of them, but all of
them are known for their beautiful scenery, and consequently the Basin is one
of the most frequently visited recreational areas of Poland.

15

The main centre of the Basin is Kłodzko (16), one of the oldest Silesian settlements, mentioned in chronicles from the year 981 as a stronghold on the Polish-Bohemian border. In the year 1114, it was already referred to as a town. It was granted urban status in the second half of the 13th century. Together with the whole of the Kłodzko Land, it changed hands between the Bohemians and the Poles a number of times, finally to become a fief of the Bohemian kings as a separate unit, often ruled by the Silesian Piasts. In 1458, the Bohemian king George of Podiebrad granted the Kłodzko Land the status of an independent county. For a long time the contacts of Kłodzko with Poland were lively, particularly with Cracow. In the 14th century, the famous Florian Psalter, which is one of the oldest surviving works written in the Polish language, came into being at the monastery of the Augustinian Fathers. Thanks to its position on the route leading from Cracow to Bohemia, trade and handicrafts developed in Kłodzko. For a certain time also it had the right to strike coins. The development of the town was checked by Thirty Years' War. After the war, the Austrians built a powerful fortress in Kłodzko. After Silesia was occupied by Prussia, the Kłodzko fortress was enlarged and strengthened by Frederick II. In 1807, it successfully resisted the attacks of Napoleon's forces. Today, rebuilt from war destruction, Kłodzko is a lively economic and cultural centre. The old quarter of the town is built on the slopes of the Nysa Kłodzka valley, the narrow streets running down towards the river. The oldest relic of the past in Kłodzko is the Gothic bridge built in the years 1281–1390, later ornamented with Baroque statues of saints. Also worthy of attention is the 15th century Gothic church of the Knights of St. Jonh of Jarusalem and the 17th century Franciscan church and monastery. In the centre of the sloping Market Place, amid Renaissance and Baroque burghers' houses, stands the Town Hall, which was completely reconstructed in the 19th century, leaving only the preserved late Renaissance tower dating back to 1654. Over the town rise the ruins of the 18th century fortress that was built on the site of the former settlement and castle.

16

17

The spas of the Kłodzko Basin are very popular. In the eastern part of the Basin, in the valley dividing the Góry Złote (Gold Mountains) from the Śnieżnik massif, lies Lądek-Zdrój. It is a historical town, founded most probably in the second half of the 13th century. There are some beautiful Baroque burghers' houses with arcades (17) surrounding the Market Place and an old stone bridge over the River Biała.

Tradition has it that the spa in Lądek-Zdrój is just as old as the town, but it was only in the 19th century that it developed on a large scale. It is situated one kilometre to the east of the town on sunny mountain slopes. It has warm sulphate springs with the highest radio-active content in Poland and valuable therapeutic muds. The picturesque surroundings (19) and mild mountain climate add to the attractions of the spa, regarded as one of the most beautifully situated in the Kłodzko region. So it is not surprising that more and more sanatoria and holiday homes are being built there (18).

18

19

Międzygórze, situated near the frontier with Czechoslovakia, at the foot of the Śnieżnik massif at an altitude of 570–670 m., in the sheltered, deep valley of the River Wilczka, is an attractive climatic and holiday resort. The first settlement was founded in the 15th century by wood-cutters and charcoal burners. In the 19th century it developed as a climatic resort. The excellent, health-giving climate and attractive position amid forests (20) are invaubale in treating chest troubles and provide good conditions for rest and recreation. In the winter the good skiing conditions attract winter sports enthusiasts. The biggest attraction in the vicinity of Międzygórze is the biggest waterfall (28 m.) in the Sudety Mts. (21).

22

23 In the part of the Kłodzko Basin to the west of the Nysa Kłodzka river, there are more spas than in the eastern part. The most well known of these include: Polanica-Zdrój, Duszniki-Zdrój and Kudowa-Zdrój. Duszniki, on the River Bystrzyca, between the Bystrzyckie Mts. and Stołowe Mts. was granted municipal status in 1324 and was at first a small centre of handicrafts and trade. In the 15th century, the mining and smelting of iron ore developed here and lasted until 1879. In the 16th century, the production of cloth was developed and also of paper, the latter being of particularly fine quality. The wooden building of the paper mill built in 1605 (22) still stands today. Although the mineral springs here were already known in 1408, the spa was only developed there at the turn of the 18th century. It has warm acidulous springs and an acidulous earthy-iron spring, now called Chopin's Spring, in connection with the fact that the young Chopin went there for a cure in 1826. While there, he gave two concerts and his stay there is commemorated by the Chopin Festival held in Duszniki every year in August. The spa also has therapeutic muds.

Duszniki can also boast of some historical buildings. In the Market Place and neighbouring streets there are a number of Baroque houses dating back to the 17th and 18th centuries. Nearby is the parish church built in 1708, with a pulpit of original design in the shape of a large fish.

Kudowa-Zdrój is in a wide basin sheltered from the north and east by the Stołowe Mts. As a town, it is very young, having only achieved this status in 1945. On the other hand, as a spa, it is one of the oldest in Europe. Its earthy acidulous-alkaline and ferrous-arsenic springs were probably known as far back as 1581. The first written records of the spa are dated 1622, and the first baths were built there in 1636. The spa also has a carbonic anhydride spring and deposits of therapeutic mud. Kudowa-Zdrój has a large, modern physiotherapy centre, many sanatoria and health-cure-holiday homes as well as the biggest and most attractive pump-room in Lower Silesia. The treatment facilities are concentrated in a beautiful park (23). It is also a good base for making excursions into the nearby hills and Stołowe Mts. The most interesting relic of the past in the vicinity is a chapel dating back to 1776 in the village of Czermno, which is covered with thousands of human sculls and crossbones from the times of the Thirty Years' War.

The Stołowe (Table) Mts. (24) are a characteristic group of mountains of the Middle Sudety, built of Tertiary sandstones forming two layers, one on top of the other, divided from each other and the surroundings by perpendicular rocks. The top layer consists of several isolated, cracked blocks that have undergone weathering and formed labyrinths and interesting rock forms (25). The highest of these mountains is Mt. Szczeliniec, from which there is a wonderful view of the Kłodzko Basin. On the southern slopes of the Stołowe Mts. there are luxuriant mixed forests with a large part of beech trees. At the foot of the Stołowe Mts. on the north side is the big village of Wambierzyce, which is remarkable for its impressive basilica in late Italian Renaissance style (26). The basilica was built in the years 1724–1730 and has an eliptic dome and a richly decorated late Baroque interior. It was built as a place for holding indulgence feast days. Apart from the church, on the mountain sides, there are chapels of various epochs, which form the Way of the Cross.

The most westerly part of the Middle Sudety Mts. are the Wałbrzyskie Mts. (27) formed by a number of porphyre domes dividing old sedimentary rocks, among which there are deposits of hard coal. Coal mining was started here earlier than in Upper Silesia. As early as 1366, Bolko I, prince of Świdnica, granted several of his courtiers the privilege of mining coal. Documents have survived in which there is mention of mines operating in the 16th century. The greatest development of coal mining in the Wałbrzych Basin was in the 18th century and the first half of the 19th century. At the beginning of the 19th century this basin was still supplying more coal that the Upper Silesian Basin. After 1873, its role was greatly diminished. Today, the value of the Wałbrzych Basin consist in the fact that a large part of its resources is coking coal.

26

27

28

29 The capital of the Wałbrzych Basin is Wałbrzych (28), a big mining and industrial town. Already in the 12th century a forest settlement existed here, inhabited by hunters and forest bee-keepers. Later a small stronghold was built there. It was enlarged by Prince Bolko I of Świdnica at the end of the 13th century. A mining and trading settlement developed at the foot of the stronghold. The founding of the town on the basis of the Magdeburg Law took place about 1400. In the course of the next few centuries, cloth making and linen weaving developed in Wałbrzych. The growth of the town was quicker in the 19th century in connection with the expansion of industry there. Before the First World War, it was already a big urban centre built up in the chaotic, unplanned way, typical of spontaneously developing industrial towns. The Second World War spared the town, so the Wałbrzych mines and factories were able to start production immediately. Today, Wałbrzych is the biggest town of Lower Silesia after Wrocław. New, modern residential districts have grown up round the Old Town. The cultural and educational functions of the town have also grown. As from 1975, Wałbrzych has been a voivodship town.

Not far from Wałbrzych, above the deep valley of the stream Pełcznica on the verge of the Wałbrzych Mts., is the settlement of Książ, with a monumental castle (29) towering over it, surrounded by magnificent beech woods with clumps of rhododendrons. From the architectural point of view, the castle is a mixture of various styles. The oldest part are the remains of the former Romanesque frontier stronghold built at the end of the 13th century by Bolko I, prince of Świdnica. In the 14th century, the castle was the property of Bolko II, and next of the Bohemian kings. At the beginning of the 16th century the castle passed into the hands of the Hochberg princes of Pszczyna, related to the Piasts, and remained with them till 1939. In the years 1548–1555 the Hochbergs remodelled the castle in late-Gothic-Renaissance style, and in the 18th century enlarged it in Baroque style. Another remodelling at the beginning of the 20th century added fin de siècle elements to it. During the years of the Second World War, another remodelling of the castle was started so that it could be used by Hitler as one of his seats. The interior of the castle was greatly damaged then, when gigantic dungeons were drilled under the castle. Now, the systematic rebuilding, reconstruction and conservation of the interiors that have survived is restoring the castle to its former splendour (30).

31

In the Lubawa Gate, dividing the Middle Sudety, from the Western Sudety Mts. is the village of Krzeszów, where in 1242, Princess Anna, widow of Henry the Pious, founded a Benedictine Abbey with the aim of colonizing the Sudety Mts. The Abbey was transferred to the Cistercians in 1292 by Prince Bolko I. In the 17th and 18th centuries the church and abbey were considerably enlarged. The church, which is now a parish durch, is one of the most beautiful Baroque buildings in Silesia. It has a magnificent facade (31), two towers with heavy cupolas and an interior with rich Baroque-Rococo style decoration. Behind the presbytery is a two-domed late Baroque burial chapel of the Świdnica princes, and in it the 14th century Gothic tombs of Prince Bolko I and Prince Bolko II and their wives. The princes are shown holding shields with the Silesian Piast eagle (32).

The main urban centre of the vast Jelenia Góra Basin is Jelenia Góra (34), which was originally a settlement round a fortified castle built in the years 1108–1111 by king Bolesław the Wrymouth. It was granted municipal status most probably in the middle of the 13th century. In the 14th and 15th centuries, apart from trade there was a development of mining and iron smelting the production of glass and also weaving, which later (16th to 18th centuries) took first place in the economic life of the town. The finest materials (batiste, voile), not produced anywhere else in Silesia, were made here. From the end of the 16th century, the biggest cotton fabric markets were held in Jelenia Góra and the materials produced there were sent to the most important European markets. The glass production of the Middle Ages developed into the production of polished crystal glassware. After the town was incorporated into Prussia, its economic development was checked and the beginning of the 19th century saw the decline of the weaving trade there. The next period of development came in the second half of the last century and was connected with the development of industrial textile mills, the ceramics and paper industries. During the Second World War the town did not suffer greatly. In the course of the last thirty years it has become a large industrial town with various industries and an important administrative, cultural and educational centre. It is also a base for tourists visiting the Western Sudety Mts. Its historical buildings, particularly the Market Place with its Town Hall built in 1747, surrounded by Baroque houses with arcades, add to the attractions of this beautifully situated town.

32

Another town in the Lubawa Gate, at the foot of the
Kamienne Mts. near the frontier with Czechoslovakia, is
Chełmsko Śląskie. It grew up from a customs post on the
Silesian-Bohemian border. Till 1289, it belonged to Bohemia,
after that it became part of the Piast duchy of Świdnica and
shed its fate together with the whole of Silesia. Its greatest
period of development came in the 17th and 18th centuries as
a large weaving centre. It was in those times that the old
burghers houses in the Market Place were built, and also the
Baroque parish church and the wooden, arcaded houses of the
weavers, concentrated in two groups, known as "The Twelve
Apostles" (33) and "The Seven Brothers".

33

34

To the south of Jelenia Góra, at the foot of the Karkonosze Mts., is the Chojnik Castle (35) built on a steep hill. A small wooden hunting castle existed here as early as the 13th century. In the years 1353–1364, Prince Bolko II built a brick castle here, which was later turned into a strong fortress. After the death of Prince Bolko, the castle was bestowed on the powerful Schaffgotsch family. After a fire in 1675, it never regained its former splendour. In the west reconstructed part of the castle there is now a tourist hostel. There is a marvellous view of the Jelenia Góra Basin and the Karkonosze Mts. from the castle.

The highest massif of the Sudety Mts. are the Karkonosze (36), the main range of which is built mostly of granite. The Karkonosze Mts. have an altitude of 1350–1450 m. Only a few high peaks rise above the tops of the ridges. They are built of very resistant crystalline schists. The highest peak (1605 m.) is Śnieżka (37), on which there is a tourist shelter and a meteorological observatory (38). From the summit of Śnieżka there is an extensive view of the Jelenia Góra Basin. A specific feature of the Karkonosze Mts. are the numerous scattered groups of rocks, some of them taking fantastic shapes. They include the group called Pielgrzymy (The Pilgrims), otherwise known as The Three Crags (39). There are traces of the Glaciation period in the form of rocky hollows (cirques) with steep jagged sides and the beautiful montain lakes in them. Mały Staw (Little Lake) below the peak of Śnieżka is in one of these hollows with steep slopes rising up to 200 m. (40). The Karkonosze ridges are covered with mountain meadows and numerous clumps of dwarf mountain pines. The highest parts of the Karkonosze Mts. on the Polish side have been made into a National Park.

37

38

39

In the extreme south-east of Poland and Lower Silesia, by the frontier with the German Democratic Republic, is the Turoszów Basin, which is the southern part of the depression known as the Lusatian Gate. The Basin is filled with Miocene deposits with rich deposits of brown coal. The deposits of brown coal within Poland's frontiers are estimated at 900 million tons. This coal is exploited on a wide scale in two open cast mines – Turów I and Turów II, the first of which was built before the war and the second in 1963. The annual output of these mines is more than 23 milion tons of brown coal, of which about 4 million tons are exported to the German power station at Hirschfelde, situated on the other side of the frontier River Lusation Nysa. The rest of the coal is used as fuel for the local power and heat generating plant in Turoszów (41).

The Sudety Foothills, to the north of the Western Sudety Mts. are of upland character, rising to an altitude of 200 to over 500 m. and are built of various rock formations. The Foothills comprise several parts differing as to their geological structure. One part are the Izerskie Foothills between the Lusatian Nysa and the Bóbr rivers, another the Kaczawskie Foothills situated between the Bóbr and Nysa Szalona rivers. The Kaczawskie Foothills are mostly built of sedimentary rocks, over which protrude cones of volcanic origin. The highest of these is Ostrzyca (alt. 501 m.) a basalt mountain in the vicinity of Złotoryja of beautiful regular shape, the remains of volcano from the Tertiary period (42). Parts of the mountain slopes are covered with luxuriant deciduous forests and other parts with rocky debris. Owing to its characteristic vegetation and rock forms, Ostrzyca is a nature reserve.

41

42

On the borderline between the Kaczawskie and Izerskie Foothills, on the River Bóbr, is Lwówek Śląski, one of the oldest towns of Silesia. It was granted municipal status in 1209 by Henry the Bearded, the prince, who for a certain time ruled over most of the Polish lands. Later Lwówek belonged to the princes of Świdnica and Jawor. Situated on a trade route leading from Germany through Wrocław and Cracow to Ruthenia, it became a thriving centre of trade and handicrafts. The most flourishing development of the town was in the 16th century and the beginning of the 17th century, in connection with its growing significance as a centre of crafts, particularly linen and woollen cloth making. At that time, Lwówek was one of the most populous towns of Silesia. During the Thirty Years' War, the town was almost completely destroyed. Later in the 18th century, Lwówek again became quite an important centre making yarn, but its population was less than half of that in 1618. The Second World War brought a lot of destruction to the town and many historical buildings were lost. Of those that have remained, mention is due to the Gothic church with its beautiful portal, the Gothic-Renaissance Town Hall with a vaulted entrance hall (43), and also parts of the former defence walls with turrets.

To the east of the Kaczawskie and Bolków–Wałbrzych Foothills, on the River Nysa Szalona, is Bolków, a former trading settlement, today an industrial town and a summer holiday and tourist centre. The town nestles at the foot of a hill of green schists, on the top of which stands one of the most strongly fortified castles in Silesia (44), built at the end of the 13th century by Prince Bolko I of Świdnica. Today it is partly ruined. The town takes its name from that of the prince, who took a special interest in its welfare. Despite numerous fires and the destruction caused by the Hussite wars and the Thirty Years' War, Bolków has preserved its mediaeval layout and historical character. On the northern side of the Market Place there are 16th and 17th century burghers houses with arcades. The remains of the 14th century defence walls give an idea of the system of fortifications linking the town with the castle.

43

44

To the north-east of Bolków, among the Strzegom Hills, which are part of the Sudety Foreland, the concentration camp of Gross Rosen was set up near the village of Rogoźnica. In the Thirties, German opponents of fascism were sent there, but by the end of the Second World War prisoners of various nationalities were kept there, who had to work in inhuman conditions in the nearby granite quarries. The number of Gross Rosen victims is estimated at about 200,000. A monument was erected on the site of the camp after the war to commemorate those who were murdered there (45).

Świdnica, on the River Bystrzyca, amid the fertile country of the Sudety Foreland, is one of the most important towns of Lower Silesia. It was already the seat of castellans in the 12th century. It was granted municipal status in the 13th century. In 1291, it became the capital of the independent Duchy of Świdnica. The town developed under the care of the Silesian Piasts, particularly during the rule of Prince Bolko II. In the 14th to 16th centuries, it was a significant centre of handicrafts and trade, having close contacts with Poland. The decline of the town started with the Thirty Years' War. Frederick II, the Prussian king, turned it into a fortress town. After the destruction of the fortifications in 1867, Świdnica again began to develop. One of the most valuable historical buildings in Świdnica is the Baroque Protestant half-timbered church construction, built in the years 1656–1658, on a cross fround-plan with a wreath of chapels (46).

45

46

On the Sudety Foreland, in the wide depression between the Sowie Mts. and the Ślęża massif, an urban-industrial agglomeration has grown up, the largest textile industry centre of Lower Silesia. The agglomeration comprises the towns of Dzierżoniów and Bielawa and the settlements of Pilawa Górna, Pieszyce and Ostroszowice. The main centre is Dzierżoniów (47). Founded in the 13th century, this town was already famed for the linen made there in the 16th century, and later also for its woollen cloth. The persecution of Protestants during the Thirty Years' War caused many of the weavers to emigrate. In the second half of the 19th century, the weaving craft gave way to textile mills. Today, apart from the textile industry, Dzierżoniów also has its electrical engineerings works. The well known Diora radio factory is in Dzierżoniów. The central district of the town has a chess-board layout, with old houses, and the remains of its former defence walls (13th c.), partly replaced by gardens. The beautiful Gothic parish church has also been preserved with remnants of its 13th century façade. Other buildings of interest are the Classicist Protestant church built at the end of the 18th century, the old burghers' houses built in the 16th to 18th centuries and a large part of the town walls.

The Sudety Foreland is a gently rolling plain covered with loess-like sediments, over which rise several isolated massifs having the character of residual hills built of hard crystalline rock. They are the massifs of Ślęża, Strzegom and Strzelin, which supply valuable stone for building and road construction. The granite quarry in Strzelin is one of the biggest (48).

47

48

At the foot of the western side of the Strzelin massif, on the River Oława, is Henryków, a settlement founded by Prince Henry the Bearded near the Cistercian Abbey also founded by him in 1225. At the end of the 13th century, the Abbey chronicler wrote the first known sentences in the Polish language in the book known as "Księga Henrykowska" (The Book of Henryków), which has survived to this day in Wrocław. The Book of Henryków is a valuable source of historical knowledge about the social and settlement relations in 13th century Poland. The Cistercian Abbey was remodelled in Baroque style in the 17th century and at this time the early Gothic abbey church (13th c.) was also given Baroque additions (49).

49

50

51

The Ślęża massif, built of gabbro and granitic rocks, is the highest elevation of the Sudety Foreland, rising as an isolated cone to an altitude of 500 m. Its culmination is the peak Mt. Ślęża (51) also called Sobótka (alt. 718 m.), on which there was an ancient settlement which originated from the times of the Lusatian culture. In the 8th to the 11th centuries it was the main place of the pagan cult of the Ślężane tribe, from which the name of Śląsk (Silesia) is derived.
The mountain top was surrounded by stone ramparts, the remains of which can still be seen today, as well as the stone sculptures of tribal cult (50) that have also survived. There is a beautiful view over the Wrocław Plain from the top of Mt. Ślęża.

On the high bank of the River Odra on the eastern fringe of the Wrocław Plain is the town of Brzeg. There was already a stronghold here in the 11th century, around which a settlement and fishing village grew up. Brzeg was granted municipal rights in 1248 from Prince Henry III of Wrocław, and in 1311 became the capital of the separate Duchy of Brzeg. The duchy remained separate until the death of George William, the last of the Silesian Piasts in 1675. Brzeg's most prosperous period was in the 16th and 17th centuries. It was then a big centre known for the production of woollen cloth and Gobelin tapestries. It was in this period that many beautiful Renaissance buildings were erected, such as the Town Hall dating back to 1570, the Odra Gate from the years 1595–1596, the fortifications with bastions, built in the 17th century and the burghers' houses. In the middle of the 16th century, the castle of the Brzeg princes (13th–14th c.) was reconstructed leaving very little of the original castle. Damaged badly by the Prussian troops in 1741 and partly pulled down, the castle was later used as a warehouse. During the fighting in 1945, Brzeg suffered great losses. Part of the castle was burnt down then. The two-storey façade of the castle gatehouse (52), which survived is adorned with figures of Silesian princes and also coats-of-arms and plaques.

Situated right in the centre of the Silesian Lowland, Wrocław is one of the oldest Polish towns and, for ten centuries, it has been the main historical centre of Silesia. It grew up on the site of a very old settlement, dating back to Neolithic times. At the beginning of its history, Wrocław was one of the centres of the Ślężane tribe, at the end of the 9th century, it probably belonged to the great Moravian state, and in the 10th century it was under the rule of Bohemian princes for a time. About 990, at the latest, it was already part of the Polish state. It must have played an important role then, judging by the fact that in 1000, Bolesław the Brave founded there one of the three episcopates subject to the Gniezno Church Metropolis. The oldest settlement developed on the islets between the overflow arms of the River Odra. In the 11th century the seat of the princes and of the bishopric was on Tum Islet. In the middle of the 12th century, under the rule of Bolesław the Wrymouth and his descendents – the first Silesian princes – Wrocław lived through a period of prosperity as their capital. Tum Islet and the neighbouring Piasek Islet became too small for the developing town. So at the turn of the 12th century, the town moved over to the left bank of the Odra. Rebuilt from the revages of the Tatar invasion in 1241, the town was then granted municipal status on the basis of the Magdeburg Law. The town was enclosed in defence walls in the 13th and 14th centuries, and the new town centre was the Market Place which still exists today. Owing to its position at the crossing of important trade routes from Ruthenia to the West and from southern Europe to the Baltic, it continued to develop. Despite the feudal division into duchies, it was still an important centre of Polish political life. In the 13th century, the princes of the prosperous Duchy of Wrocław aimed at uniting the Polish lands under their rule. In 1327, the last of the Piast princes of Wrocław Henry VI, together with several other Silesian princes, became vassals of the king of Bohemia.

After Henry's death in 1335, the Duchy of Wrocław was incorporated directly into the Bohemian Crown lands. At that time, Wrocław was one of the biggest towns in Europe. From the middle of the 14th century it belonged to the Hanseatic League. The town became very wealthy from trade with Poland, Bohemia and Germany.

The town continued to develop and many Gothic buildings, both sacral and secular were erected. Among them, special mention is due to: the magnificent Gothic cathedral (54) on Tum Islet, the construction of which was started in 1244, on the site of the former Romanesque cathedral from the 12th century; the Holy Cross church (1288–1350), one of the most valuable Gothic buildings in Poland (53), which once contained the tomb of its founder Prince Henry IV Probus (55), which is now kept in the Wrocław National Museum; the monasteries and durches of the Augustinian Fathers and Nuns on the Piasek Islet, and in the main part of the town – the churches of St. Mary Magdalene, St. Elizabeth and others, and also the magnificent Town Hall (56), first built in the middle of the 13th century and enlarged and remodelled in the 19th and 20th centuries. Today it is one of the most beautiful secular Gothic buildings in Wrocław. In 1526, Wrocław came under the rule of the Hapsburgs. In the 16th to 18th centuries, Wrocław went through a period of flourishing economic growth, which was temporarily slowed down during the Thirty Years' War. The town still continued to develop. Many Renaissance and Baroque buildings were erected at this time. The partly preserved and partly reconstructed burghers houses in the Market Place date back to this period, as do a number of churches and monasteries, among them the Baroque monastery (1675–1715), now used as the Library of the Ossolińskis National Institute, where valuable collections of manuscripts and old prints are kept, and the building of the Jesuit College from the early 18th century, which is now the seat of the Wrocław University (57), founded in 1702. It is one of the most beautiful Baroque buildings in Central Europe. Among the University halls, the Leopoldina Aula is remarkable for its beautiful frescoes (58). In 1741, Wrocław came under Prussian rule and germanization pressures were intensified, but in spite of this it remained a centre of Polish culture for a long time and the Polish language was still in everyday use till the middle of the 19th century. In the inter-war period, the Poles of Wrocław were still carrying on lively social and cultural activity, which even continued in Hitler's time, despite the heavy repressive measures appied by the authorities. The 19th century brought the quick economic growth of the town. Numerous factories and works were built, as well as new districts densely built up with apartment houses. The southern districts, which were better built, are from the early 20th century. The final battles of the Second World War brought terrible destruction to the town. The Nazi troops, surrounded by the Soviet Army, put up a stubborn defence, burning one district after another as they withdrew from their positions. With the coming of People's Poland, the town was quickly rebuilt from ruins and is now developing very rapidly.

56

57

58

One of the first industrial works to be rebuilt and enlarged was the "Pafawag" Railway Car Factory (59). Many other factories and works were built anew and Wrocław now has new higher schools, educational, scientific and cultural institutions and new residential districts (60). The town is one of the three provincial capitals of Poland (the other two being Cracow and Poznań). The historical layout of the Old Town quarter, which has been painstakingly reconstructed (1) with many valuable specimens of architecture and relics of culture, the beautiful green parks and the situation of the town have also made Wrocław a tourist attraction.

59

60

The wide valley of the River Odra was once grown with luxuriant marsh forests. The varieties typical of these forests are alders, poplars, willows, elms and ash trees, and they have a luxuriant undergrowth. Today they are something rare. The few remaining woods of this kind have survived in the vicinity of Racibórz, Koźle, between Oława and Wrocław (61) and near Środa Śląska and Wołów.

To the north-east of Wrocław is the town of Oleśnica. In the 11th century, on the site of today's town, there was a prince's stronghold with a trading settlement round it, through which a trade route from Wrocław to Wielkopolska ran. The oldest mention of Oleśnica in chronicles is from the year 1189, and the first source material concerning the markets held there is dated 1214. Written records from 1248 refer to it as a castellan's seat. During the period of feudal division into duchies, Oleśnica first belonged to the Duchy of Wrocław, then to the Duchy of Głogów. In 1240, Prince Henry II of Wrocław built a castle on the site of the old stronghold. In 1255, his successor Prince Henry III, granted Oleśnica urban rights according to the Środa Law. In 1312, as a result of more feudal divisions, a separate Duchy of Oleśnica was created. After the death of the last of the Piast princes, in 1492 Oleśnica passed into the hands of Bohemian Podiebrads. In 1649, it was inherited by the princes of Würtemberg, and in 1802, became the property of the Hohenzollerns. In the 16th century, Oleśnica was a vital centre of the Polish Reformation Movement. There were still many Polish Protestants living in the surrounding area up to the middle of the 19th century. In addition to Wrocław and Brzeg, Oleśnica was also a centre publishing Protestant printed matter in Polish. The town suffered serious damage during the Thirty Years' War and lost its previous importance. A symbol of the former splendour of Oleśnica is the large ducal castle (62), enlarged and remodelled into a Renaissance residence by Jan of Podiebrad, the grandson of George, king of Bohemia.

A circular tower is all that remains of the original 13th century Piast castle. There is an arcaded courtyard inside the castle and a covered walk leading from the residence to the Gothic church.

61

62

Trzebnica, situated among hills, was once the tribal centre of the Trzebowians, who inhabited the northern part of Silesia. At the beginning of the 12th century, it belonged to the Silesian potentate Piotr Włostowic. In 1207, Henry the Bearded and his wife Hedvig (canonized as a saint) founded and richly equipped the first Silesian convent of Cistercian nuns, the abbesses of which were members of the Piast line up till the 16th century. The town was ravaged several times by wars and fires. In the 18th century the spinning of linen yarn developed there. Trzebnica was a town with a large concentration of Polish population. It was badly damaged in the Second World War, but a large Gothic church that once belonged to the Cistercians survived. It has beautiful Romanesque portals (63), and in the chapel are the tombs of the founders of the convent and a number of other members of the Piast family.

West of Wrocław, in the Silesian Lowland, is the historical town of Legnica. The stronghold of Legnica, mentioned in chronicles of the year 1149, guarded the crossing of the River Kaczawa and its tributary Czarna Woda. At the turn of the 12th century, a fortified castle was built on the site of the old stronghold, which successfully resisted the Tatars in 1241. In the years 1242–1675, Legnica was the seat of the Legnica princes. It was granted municipal status in 1252. In the years 1281–1321 defence walls were built round the town. After the Thirty Years' War, the town declined. In 1675, after the death of the last Silesian Piast, George William, prince of Legnica and Brzeg, it passed into the hands of the Hapsburgs. In 1741, it was incorporated into Prussia. After 1870 it grew considerably as an administrative seat and a centre of trade, handicrafts and small-scale industry. It was badly damaged during the Second World War; among others, the Piast castle was burned down and all that remains of it today are two towers and the richly carved Renaissance East Gate dating back to 1532 (64). Near the castle is the 15th century Głogów Gate, with a sundial, the remains of the former fortifications. There are also several historical sacral buildings in Legnica, the most interesting being the Mausoleum of the Piasts in St. John's church, which once belonged to the Franciscans and later to the Jesuits. There are some beautiful frescoes in the cupola of the Mausoleum, depicting scenes from the history of the Poland of the Piasts. Today, Legnica is a voivodship capital and centre of the economic and cultural life of the western part of the Silesian Lowland. The town is developing and new residential districts are growing up around it.

63
64

Due to the active geological past of the Sudety Mts. various kinds of ore deposits were formed there, such as copper, and also zinc, lead, silver and even gold. However these deposits were either too small to have has any economic significance, or have been exhaused as a result of long exploitations, at least from the early Middle Ages. In the period of the Zechstein Sea, when the recently uplifted Sudety Mts. bordered on the sea, the vein ores in the mountains, washed out by water, were deposited in the sea or in shallow piedmont lakes, forming large deposits of marls or schists with a greater or lesser content of these ores. The sedimentary deposits of ore-bearing shales were known in the Sudety Foothills between Bolesławiec, Złotoryja and Jawor as early as the 16th century, but their exploitation was only started in the years 1863–1883. Due to the small copper content and the drop in copper prises on the world markets, the mining of these ores was stopped. It was only in 1935, in connection with the arming of Nazi Germany, that interest was again shown in them. During the Second World War, several mines were built there and also ore-washing plants. In 1943, the output from these mines was 400,000 tons. During the hostilities, these mines were flooded.

66 After Silesia was restored to Poland, work was immediately started to resume the mining of these ores. In 1951, production started again. In 1954 a copper works was opened in Legnica. In 1965, the output of ore reached 2.4 million tons and the production of copper was 37,000 tons. This met about 20% of Poland's demand for copper. The discovery of new, abundant deposits of ore-bearing marls and shales of the same origin, more to the north between Lubin and Głogów, brought a momentous turn in the copper mining industry. These deposits, with a higher copper content that those of the old basin, occur over an area of about 200 sq.km., but they are deeper down (600–1000 m.) and the water and geological conditions are difficult. In spite of this, work was started on building mines in 1960. By 1968, two mines has been set in motion, in Lubin (66) and Polkowice, and 1974 a third in Rudna. The fourth mine is under construction. Ore extraction in 1975 was about 17 million tons, of which 90% came from the new mines. Two thirds of the ore is processed in the much bigger copper works near Głogów (65), which was opened in 1971. In 1975, both copper works produced a total of about 250,000 tons of pure copper. This sufficed to meet not only the increased home demand, but also to export more than one third of this output. As regards copper resources and output of the mines, Poland is today first in Europe. Apart from copper, the ore-bearing deposits also contain small amounts of other valuable metals, such as silver, nickel, cobalt, vanadium and molybdenum, which makes them additionally valuable.

The discovery of these deposits, along with the other big discovery – sulphur – is the greatest success of Polish geologists in the last thirty years.

67

On the high bank of the Odra, not far from the place where the river changes its course and flows north towards the Wielkopolska Lowland, is the former Cistercian Abbey at Lubiąż (67). The Abbey was built in 1163. The Cistercian monks were brought there by Prince Bolesław the Tall. The Abbey was given its present Baroque form in the years 1690–1720, when it was reconstructed and enlarged after the devastation caused by the Thirty Years' War. It is one of the largest monastic buildings in Poland, with an elevation 223 m. long and about a thousand cells. Among the Abbey buildings is a Gothic church dating back to the first half of the 14th century, which was also remodelled in Baroque style. In the Gothic ducal chapel in 1312 there are tombstones of Piast princes. During the Second World War, the Abbey was partly destroyed, but the polychrome paintings and Baroque sculptures survived.

The Wielkopolska Lowland

1

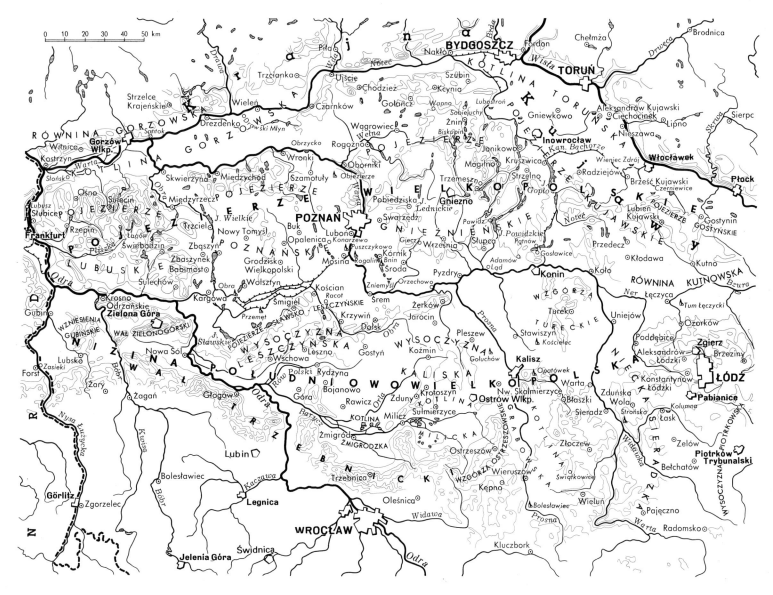

2

3

The Wielkopolska Lowland is part of the Central European Plain, which extends from the North Sea, through the Netherlands, North Germany and Poland and then joins the East Baltic Lowland which constitutes the western part of the Great Plain of Eastern Europe. Historically, this area embraces Wielkopolska (Polonia Maior), the cradle of the Polish state, the lands along the middle reaches of the Odra, including part of the Lubusz land, the northern part of Silesia and the eastern fringes of Lusatia. Today, Wielkopolska is one of the most evenly and best developed areas of Poland.

The Central European Plain owes its present relief, substratum and character mainly to the action of the Scandinavian Glacier. The change to a colder climate and increased precipitation caused great masses of snow to accumulate in the Scandinavian mountains, which under pressure turned into ice at the close of the Tertiary Epoch (about 600,000 years ago). A glacier, created in this way at the beginning of the Quaternary Epoch, started moving westwards, southwards and eastwards, reaching as far as England, the mountains of Central Germany, the Sudety Mts., the Carpathians and parts of central Russia, its tongues moving even further south along river valleys. In the Alps, Pyrenees and Carpathians, mountain glaciers formed simultaneously and moved down towards the plains. Successive fluctuations in temperature caused the glacier to retreat or advance again southwards. These recurrent advances, called glaciations, are known to have occurred four times. There were intervals between them known as interglacials.

As it moved the ice-sheet destroyed and levelled out the pre-Quaternary land forms, burying them under the masses of rock debris carried from Scandinavia or collected on the way. This mixture of clay, sand, gravel and stones, known as boulder clay, is the material which went to build the flat ground moraines and the ridges of end moraine, which mark the extent of glacial penetration each time. The water flowing under the ice-sheet destroyed, carried and deposited the rock material, creating various kinds of fluvial-glacial deposits. The most common of these are the outwash plains (sandr) forming extensive plains of sand and fine-grained gravel at the head of the glacier. Eskers – long, high, narrow ridges are built of coarse-grained gravel and sand. The fine silt deposited in the ice-dammed lakes formed at the head of the glacier later turned into layers of varve clays. In the periglacial climate the deposited material underwent weathering processes which wore away the original glacial forms. In addition these formations were denuded in the interglacial periods by water, carrying this material much further afield. In this way the Lowland was covered with glacial deposits of varying thickness, in some places more than 200 m. deep.

On Polish territory the glacial deposits extended as far as the Sudety Mts. and the Carpathian Foothills, marking the extent of the glaciation, known as the Cracow Glaciation (Mindel), which covered earlier formations with its deposits. However, most of the deposits left by the Cracow Glaciation were covered with younger deposits or washed away, revealing in some places in the south of Poland older geological formations. The next glaciation, known as the Middle Polish Glaciation (Riss) extended to the Sudety Mts. However, in the east it dit not extend further than the edge of the Polish Uplands. The deposits left by this glaciation are not thick. They were to a large extent destroyed or transformed, producing gentler, rounded forms. The last glaciation, known as the Baltic Glaciation (Würm) covered the northern part of Poland up to the line of: Zielona Góra––Leszno–Konin–Płock–Nidzica–Grajewo. The glacier did not retreat continuously, but with several recurrent advances (stadials). During the period of the Middle Polish Glaciation, the Warta Stage was an evident recurrent advance which reached a line running along the Trzebnica Ridge – Wieluń – the latitudinal section of the Upper Warta – Łódź and the Lower Pilica–Siedlce–Bielsk Podlaski. Particularly evident is the last recurrence of the ice-sheet within the Baltic Glaciation, which is known as the Pomeranian Stage. Its range is marked by the well preserved end moraines of the Lakeland and the extensive outwash plains stretching south. The Wielkopolska Lowland lies between the end moraine belt of the Warta Stage and the southernmost point of the Pomeranian Stage of the last glaciation.

Retreating northwards, the glaciers blocked the natural flow of rivers from the south to the sea for a long time, directing them westwards, where they found an outlet in the vicinity of today's Bremen or Hamburg. The melting glaciers, supplied abundant waters to the rivers which carved out the wide pradolines, that became broader in some places to form the great ice-dammed lakes. The remains of these lakes today are the basins found in some of the pradolines. The Wielkopolska Lowland is cut through by three of these pradolines: the Barycz-Głogów Pradoline in the south, the Warsaw-Berlin Pradoline in the centre and the Toruń-Eberswalde Pradoline (which is the largest and widest) in the north. The system of pradolines has an influence on the course of the rivers flowing through the Wielkopolska Lowland. Some sections of the main river of the area, the Warta, flow through the Warsaw-Berlin and Toruń-Eberswalde pradolines. A river of specific interest in the Wielkopolska Lowland is the Obra, which initially flows through many river beds to the west through the wide marshy Warsaw-Berlin Pradoline, then divides into two arms, of which one (the Gniła Obra) continues on its westerly course and flows into the Odra, and the other (North Obra), turns north and flows into the Warta.

The bottoms of the pradolines are flat, often marshy or with peatbogs, sometimes sandy, with dunes. As in the course of time the water in the rivers diminished and the river beds became deeper, river terraces were formed along the banks. The lowest of them (flood plain terrace) is today the bottom of the pradoline, covered with alluvial silt or sand carried there when the river waters are higher. The older terraces higher up, also formed from alluvial deposits, mark the old level sand course of the former valley bottoms. These erraces are now dry, and if they are sandy, dunes are commonly found.

In the depressions created by the action of glaciers or the melting blocks of dead-ice left behind, lakes were formed, which are gradually disappearing as more and more alluvial deposits fill them up or they became overgrown with vegetation, turning into marshland or peatbogs. These in turn are either slowly drying up or have been drained by man. Today, the area of the Wielkopolska Lakes does not exceed 30% of the original area. They are grouped in the northern part of the Lowland. Many of them, in the deep troughs created by the flow of glacial waters, form long chains of so-called finger lakes. The biggest of these is the Gopło Chain, which is about 70 km. long. Lake Gopło, the biggest in Wielkopolska (23.4 sq.km.) and tenth as regards size in Poland, is long (26 km.) and narrow (0.25–2 km.) and not very deep (15.7 m.). Further chains of finger lakes are found more to the west. A long chain is formed by the Zbąszyń Lakes, through which the North Obra flows.

The relief of the Wielkopolska Lowland is the result of all these processes. The landscape of this area today is made up of flat or slightly undulating plains of ground moraines with here and there chains of end-moraines and outwash plains, low weathered eskers, numerous depressions filled with lakes or peatbogs in the north, wide pradolines, often with sand dunes or peatbogs and the narrow transverse valleys formed by the rivers of today. In this rather monotonous lowland landscape one can distinguish three latitudinal units, namely: in the south, the lakeless Wielkopolska Lowland, in the middle – the Wielkopolska Lakes, and in the north – the Warta-Noteć Pradoline. Although the glacial deposits of the Wielkopolska Lowland are not thick, the surface formations and the courses of the rivers do not have much in common with the deeper geological substratum. In the south this substratum is uplifted as the pre-Sudety ridge of Triassic and Jurassic rocks. In the centre, the older formations are buried deep beneath the Cretaceous and Tertiary deposits which reappear near the surface in the form of the big Kujawy-Pomerania anticlinorium built of Jurassic and Cretaceous formations, which is an extension of the Holy Cross Mts. As a result of several uplifts, faults and fissures appeared in the Jurassic rocks, through which salt from deep strata of salt deposits worked its way up forming salt domes or plugs. Over a dozen salt domes have been discovered in the Wielkopolska Lowland in the vicinity of Kcynia, Wapno, Inowrocław and other places, and judging by the occurrance of saline waters (Ciechocinek, Aleksandrów Kujawski, Pyzdry, the vicinity of Łęczyca, Ozorków and elsewhere) there must be more of them.

Apart from deposits of table and potassium salts and of gypsum, the Zechstein Sea deposits often contain crude oil and natural gas, traces of which have been known for a long time in the area of the Kujawy salt domes. Over ten years ago, the first deposits of Zechstein oil in sufficient quantities for exploitation were discovered near Krosno on the Odra, and natural gas was found near Nowa Sól and Ostrzeszów. The Jurassic limestones, which are near the surface in the Kujawy region, have been utilized for some time by the lime, sugar and chemical industries. In 1954 deposits of Lower Jurassic iron ore were discovered near Łęczyca.

Deposits of Miocene brown coal of varying thickness are of Tertiary origin. Exploitation of these deposits was first started in the Lubusz land and neighbouring parts of Silesia. After the Second World War, rich deposits of this raw material were discovered in the vicinity of Konin, Turek, Łęczyca, Łódź and Bełchatów. The deposits of brown coal are often separated by layers of pure quartz sands – an important raw material for the glass industry. In some cases these sands turned into deposits of compact quartz sandstone, which is quarried near Ostrzeszów for use in the iron and steel industry. The rich, plastic, limeless clay of Tertiary origin, which occurs in many places just under younger deposits is an excellent raw material for ceramics. As regards Quaternary raw materials, the bog iron ores found in some places in the river valleys have long been exploited, and also boulder stones, gravel, sand, clay and peat.

The fact that the surface formations are almost entirely of glacial and post-glacial origin, the lack of variety of these formations and the generally dry, warm climate have resulted in a fairly uniform type of soils in the Wielkopolska Lowland. Podsolized soils predominate, mainly light and medium podsolic soils originating from boulder clays or clayey and loamy sands under a pine forest cover. In the west and south-east light and sandy podsolized soils predominate. Large areas of these soils are forest covered, today mainly pine forests, which have been planted by man. Here and there the remains of the natural fresh or mixed pine forests have survived. The heavy loam and silt soils are found above all on the higher ground around Kalisz, Leszno and Poznań. These soils were once covered with oak-hornbeam forests called gronds, and even oak forests, but very little of them remains today. Not much has remained either of the once luxuriant mixed forests that grew on the fertile black earths of the Kujawy region and on the alluvial soils of the Warta, Prosna, Barycz river valleys and the middle reaches of the Odra. The alder forests once growing in the more peaty parts of the Odra and Noteć valleys have also disappeared. Their place has been taken by meadows and pastureland. In some places due to bad melioration, these areas have been drained too dry and have turned into idle land overgrown with weeds.

Drainage and felling of forests led to a decrease in rainfall. At present it is not more than 500 mm. annually in the eastern part of Wielkopolska. An indication of the dry climate is the appearance in many places, particularly in the Kujawy region, of xerophytic plants (the dwarf steppe cherry, feather grass and spring adonis) and the appropriate small fauna, insects and snails.

The Wielkopolska Lowland is an area of early settlement. Man came to this area in the Old Stone Age (Palaeolithic). In the early Neolithic the western and central parts of the Lowland in particular were densely settled and primitive agriculture and animal breeding began to penetrate from the south. Traces of numerous settlements have remained from those times, often situated on islands in lakes or amid bogs, or on river promontories. Tombs have been discovered containing the remains of pottery, woven materials and tools. In the late Neolithic tilling the land was already common.

In the Bronze and Iron Ages, Wielkopolska was one of the main centres of Lusatian culture. A famous example of that culture is the fortified settlement of Biskupin dating back to 600–500 B.C. and comprising more than 100 dwellings inhabited by 1,000 to 1,200 persons. At this time iron tools were already known in Wielkopolska. At first they were brought there from other places, but later in the la Tène (150 – 0 B.C.) and Roman (90–400 A.D.) periods they were made from local bog-ore. Coulters with iron fittings were already being used in agriculture. In the Roman period, the great amber route passed through this area, running along the River Prosna and Gopło Lakes towards the mouth of the Vistula. The ancient town of Calisia (Kalisz today) mentioned by Ptolomaeus (2nd cent. A.D.) was most probably on this route and perhaps Słupca and Kruszwica too.

The invasions of Germanic tribes and next the Great Migration towards the close of ancient times caused an economic regress in Wielkopolska, which lasted till the early Middle Ages. In the following period agriculture developed, going from the slash and burn system to the current fallow system. Animal breeding and handicrafts developed. The smelting of iron and other metals became a common practice. An ever denser network of settlements sprang up on the fertile land, particularly in the Kujawy region. From the areas surrounding Lake Gopło legends originated telling of the beginnings of Polish statehood. As early as the 9th century round Gniezno, Poznań and Kalisz, there was a tribal centre of the Polanes, separated by forests and swamps from Małopolska, Silesia and Pomerania. Led by the Piast Dynasty, the Polanes, undertook to unite the lands of the western Slavs, on whom they imposed their name of Poland (Polska). The three generations that came between the legendary founder of the Piast Dynasty – Ziemowit – and the first Christian ruler – Mieszko I, succeeded in extending their rule over the Kujawy (Cuyavia), Sieradz, Łęczyca and Mazowsze lands. The next stage was the inclusion of Pomerania and then Silesia and the old land of the Vislanes – Małopolska. Bolesław the Brave, son of Mieszko I, the first Polish king, established the western frontier of Poland along the Odra and then started expansion into neighbouring Bohemia, Moravia and Ruthenia. These political conquests were followed by colonization. Already in the Early Middle Ages, the Polanes had control of the water nodes of the Vistula, Brda and Noteć and had settled in the Krajna and Chełmno lands. Moving northwards along the Vistula, they were confronted by the Pomeranian expansion coming from the west. In the south, the Polanes settlement moved along the Prosna and Upper Warta, towards Silesia. After their conversion to Christianity, the monasteries started to play an important role in colonization, systematically cultivating land wrested from the forests, growing crops, breeding cattle and developing fishing. The progress of settlement was marked by fortified places. The threat from Germany led to the construction of a whole system of strongholds and defence walls along the western frontier. For several centuries an important role was played by the big fortified settlement of Lubusz, defending the state from invaders crossing the Odra. The Piast princes also fortified their southern frontier (along the Obra and Barycz), separating Wielkopolska from Silesia, which was more easily accessible to the Germans, and the northern frontier along the Warta and Noteć rivers, separating Wielkopolska from Pomerania.

By the 9th century, all the larger strongholds were surrounded by settlements of craftsmen and traders. The development of handicrafts and trade sometimes exceeded the needs of the stronghold, thus justifying the creation of the first towns. In the 10th century, Gniezno and Poznań already had about 4,000 inhabitants each. Traces of pre-Romanesque buildings have survived in these towns. From the 11th century, one-nave churches without aisles or in the form of a cross appeared in Wielkopolska, using stone blocks, modelling them on West European buildings. In the first half of the 13th century, bricks began to be used for building. They were later commonly used in numerous Gothic buildings.

Taking advantage of the relaxation of vigilance after the death of Bolesław the Brave, the Bohemian ruler Břetislav invaded Wielkopolska in 1039, pillaging Gniezno, Poznań and Giecz. The devastated Gniezno land lost its political primacy. Although the capital of the state was then transferred to Cracow and Poland was divided up into feudal duchies, Wielkopolska, undisturbed by her neighbours for two centuries developed well. Settlements were established on the basis of the new law, which strictly defined rent in kind or money. This led to the introduction of the three-field system, water mills and windmills were widespread and gardens, vineyards and hop-fields made their appearance. Existing towns expanded and new ones were built.

The unification of the Polish state with Cracow as its capital, but excluding Silesia, Pomerania and the Lubusz land, caused the centre of political and economic life to move eastward and in connection with this the eastern areas of Wielkopolska assumed more importance. However, these areas were soon after to be invaded by the Teutonic Knights from the nearby Chełmno land. In Kujawy, Polish knights defeated the Teutonic Knights at Płowce in 1331, but this did not prevent the Teutonic Order from occupying Kujawy in 1332. It was regained for Poland 13 years later by Casimir the Great. Then followed a period of relative peace. Casimir the Great took a particular interest in the development of towns. Traces of development in that period are seen in numerous Gothic churches and secular buildings in Wielkopolska. The Toruń Peace Treaty of 1466 resulted in the return to Poland of Gdańsk Pomerania and the Chełmno land. From then on, Polish products – corn, salt, timber, potash and pitch – could be transported without any obstacles along the Vistula to the Baltic ports. This trading brought wealth to the towns along the banks of the Vistula. The advantages brought by exports to western Europe encouraged the land-owning gentry to take up farming, which led to a departure from the old manorial rent system of free copyholders in favour of the estate system based on corvée. However, in Wielkopolska, the estates of the nobles never grew to such a size as those in other parts of Poland, so the contrast between the rich magnates and the poor peasantry was not so sharp here. The towns went on developing too. In the 16th century, projects for the "Improvement of the Respublica" came from Wielkopolska. Education and culture went through a period of flourishing development. Apart from Poznań, an important role was played by Leszno – the centre of the Wielkopolska Reformation Movement. Handicrafts developed in the towns, particularly wool weaving. This period is marked for numerous Renaissance buildings, and later, Baroque buildings in the towns, as well as the castles and palatial residences of the rich Wielkopolska noble families.

The Swedish invasions, civil wars and natural disasters of the second half of the 17th century and the beginning of the 18th century brought a lot of destruction, but in the Enlightenment Period, Wielkopolska developed favourably again; being much more prosperous than other parts of Poland, with the resulting higher standard of living and better quality building in towns and villages alike. The burghers set up manufactures, mostly producing woollen materials. Textiles were exported to Silesia, Bohemia, Prussia and even to Russia and China.

The fortunes of the Lubusz land were different. It had been wrested away from the motherland five centuries earlier. Occupied by the Germans, it became a springboard for German expansion to the east, intended to cut Poland off from her access to the sea, while in the south the aim was Silesia. The German occupation of this region was also an obstacle to the development of trade contacts between the eastern provinces of Poland and Silesia with Pomerania and western Europe. This was the basis of the development of Gorzów Wielkopolski and Frankfurt-on-Odra, which blocked the transport of Polish goods along the Odra and Warta rivers to Szczecin. The process of germanization in the Lubusz land was more rapid than in other parts of Poland.

The first partition of Poland in 1772 cut off Wielkopolska's access to the sea and the part of Kujawy on the River Noteć came under Prussian rule. After the second partition in 1793, Prussia seized the whole of Wielkopolska. In the Napoleonic period it did for a short time come within the boundaries of the Duchy of Warsaw (1806–1815), after which, by virtue of the decisions of the Congress of Vienna, most of Wielkopolska again came under Prussian rule as the Grand Duchy of Poznań, while the eastern part of Wielkopolska went to Russia as part of the autonomous Polish Kingdom.

In the occupied territories the new authorities, issuing successive "regulation" edicts, made social relations in the rural areas uniform with those prevailing in Prussia. The process of enfranchisement of the peasants was completed by the edict of 1850. The Wielkopolska textile industry and also the paper and brewery industries and others, could not stand up to the competition of Prussian industries. The original autonomy of the first years of the Duchy of Poznań, was limited after 1830 and withdrawn altogether after the Wielkopolska Uprising, in the time of the Springtide of Nations (1848). The loss of autonomy was accompanied by persecution of Polish patriots, germanization of the administration, courts of justice and

schools and an intensification of German colonization. The Polish population, not having access to employment in state administration offices, turned their energies to economic activity. They set up trading firms, industrial enterprises and credit banks, sometimes based on the cooperation of the big land-owners and burghers. Polish scientific and cultural institutions were developed.

The speedy economic development of Germany after 1871 had an influence on the economy of Wielkopolska. The demand for labour and agricultural produce on the part of western and central Germany, which was undergoing the process of industrialization and urbanization, brought in its wake the emigration of population from the eastern provices of Prussia, which had been assigned the role of a food producing region for the empire. This was further promoted by the intensification of agriculture in Wielkopolska, the development of the food processing industry and other branches of industry serving agriculture. The network of railways and roads was developed. The timber industry, the main centre of which was Bydgoszcz, situated on an important river route for floating timber from the lands under Russian and Austrian occupation, also developed well. The increased productivity of Wielkopolska agriculture brought wealth to the big land-owners and larger peasant farms. The landless peasants and small holders from these areas emigrated to the western and central provinces of the Reich. The growing shortage of manpower was made good by employing seasonal farm hands from the Polish Kingdom and Galicia. Among those emigrating to the west were a large part of the German settlers and this weakened the German element in Wielkopolska. Wishing to counteract this, Bismarck set up a Colonization Commission in 1886, which was to buy up land and transfer it to German settlers on very favourable terms. The activity of the Commission was, however, energetically opposed by the Polish community. Despite national oppression and thanks to the cooperation of the land-owning gentry, rich peasant farmers and burghers, the amount of land in Polish hands did not decrease but even increased.

The economic development of the eastern part of Wielkopolska that came within the boundaries of the Polish Kingdom was quite different. Before the November Uprising (1830–1831), the policy of planned industrialization introduced by the autonomous authorities gave birth to the nucleus of the Textile Industry District in Łódź and its vicinity. Craftsmen from the western part of Wielkopolska, Silesia and Saxony were encouraged to settle and work there. A particularly flourishing development of this industrial district took place after the abolition of the customs barrier between the Polish Kingdom and the Russian Empire in 1850 and the construction of railway lines making Polish goods accessible to the absorbant Russian market. The main centre of the industrial district – Łódź – became a typical early capitalist industrial town, chaotically and badly built with insufficient public facilities and without cultural institutions. There were striking contrasts between the palatial residences of the factory owners and bankers and the miserable hovels of the factory workers. This town, which in

1910 had a population of 400,000, did not – apart from using manpower – have any strong ties with the surrounding areas. Łódź only became a voivodship town after Poland regained independence in 1918. In 1939, the town had a population of 650,000.

The rebirth of the Polish state brought the unification of the Wielkopolska region into one political and economic organism. However, up to the outbreak of the Second World War, the disproportions between the more economically developed Poznań region and the areas coming within the Polish Kingdom in the period of the partitions continued to exist. Industrial Łódź, which was deliberately ravaged during the First World War by the Germans, was very slow in building up its industry again, experiencing difficulties because of the loss of the Russian market. On the other hand, the loss of German markets had a bad effect on agriculture in the Poznań region, despite the fact that farming there was still on a higher level than in other parts of Poland.

After the September defeat in 1939, Wielkopolska together with part of Mazovia and Małopolska, was incorporated into the Reich. These areas were not subjected to such a severe policy of plunder economy as the other parts of Poland, but very severe repressions were imposed on the inhabitants. Soon after they marched in and took possession, the Nazis murdered the most active representatives of the Polish population. Intellectuals, land-owners and some of the peasant farmers were deported to the General Gouvernement and their place was taken by German repatriates from the East. After the liberation of Poland in 1945, the population of Wielkopolska went to work very quickly to rebuild their region from the ravages of war. Poznań suffered the greatest war damage.

The establishment of the western frontier of Poland on the Odra and Nysa rivers, brought back to Poland the areas on the middle reaches of the Odra – a part of the former Lubusz land. These areas were settled with Wielkopolska population and then by Polish repatriates from the USSR. The new arrivals started work to remove the ravages of war and build up the economy again. The damaged towns were brought back to life and are now developing favourably as centres of economic and social life. Most of the land is now in the hands of individual Polish farmers and a large part of it (more than 40%) is now cultivated by state farms. In comparison with the other parts of Wielkopolska, agriculture here occupies a smaller percentage of the land, for it is one of the most forested areas of Poland. Forests cover more than 45% of its area.

In Wielkopolska proper, the dominant type of farming is peasant farms of 7 to 15 hectares. There are quite a large number of bigger farms and also state farms, which supply the peasant farmers with seeds, breeding stock and also market a large amount of their surplus production to meet the needs of towns. The cooperative farm movement is developing well there, too. Agriculture in Wielkopolska is very productive and the methods of farming are up-to-date and efficient. Rational rotation of crops and abundant fertilizing is wide-spread in the region. Agricultural work is largely mechanized there.

Most of the farms specialize in growing rye and potatoes and also keeping dairy cattle and pigs, the latter being mainly orientated towards export production of bacon. On the more fertile soils of the Kujawy region and further south in the Leszno voivodship, the rye-potato orientation is replaced by rye and sugar beet and even wheat and sugar beet cultivation, the sugar beet plantations being connected with the highly developed sugar industry there. An important crop, particularly in the Kujawy region, is malting barley. Also a lot of rapeseed and fodder crops are grown there. The highest yields are obtained in Kujawy and part of southern Wielkopolska. The yields are lower in the eastern area of the Lowland. A slower rate of development has been noted in the Lubusz land where the people started farming on poor sandy soils in an area badly damaged during the war.

Industry is concentrated mainly in the eastern part of Wielkopolska. Apart from the formerly existing branches of industry and industrial centres, new ones are quickly developing. The biggest is the Łódź Industrial District, comprising Łódź, Pabianice, Zgierz, Aleksandrów, Konstantynów and Ozorków. The textile industry founded and developed in the 19th century is predominant in this district, employing about 60% of all those working in industry. It is one of the biggest centres of this industry on a world scale and Poland's biggest textile centre, producing nearly 60% of the home output of cotton fabrics and nearly as much woollen fabric. The rayon industry is also developing and production of synthetic fibres is significant. Altogether, this industrial district produces 40% of the total output of textiles in Poland, and three quarters of it is made in the town of Łódź. The fabrics produced in the district are exported to several dozen countries of Europe, Asia, Africa and America. The clothing industry uses the materials produced there. Among the new branches of industry, the most important is the engineering industry, producing textile and mining machines, as well as boilers, machine tools, electrotechnical, telecommunication and film projecting equipment. The chemical industry is growing in importance, represented by the dyestuffs factory at Zgierz, the pharmaceutical works at Pabianice and the rubber factory in Łódź.

The Konin Industrial District is much more recent, based on the open cast mining of brown coal, started in 1958. For the utilization of this raw material a complex of three power and heat generating plants have been built in the coal basin, their combined output exceeding 2,800 MW, and this in turn made possible the starting up in 1966 of the aluminium works at Maliniec. There is also an electrical engineering works in Konin and a clothing factory in Turek. Not far away, to the east of Konin, there is a new salt mine at Kłodawa.

The nucleus of a new industrial district has just come into being in the Bełchatów region, where a large open-cast brown coal mine is under construction. Piotrków Trybunalski is an important centre of the textile, glass and engineering industries.

The main raw material of the Kujawy Industrial District are its deposits of salt. The main centre of the district is Inowrocław. It has a well developed soda industry based on salt processing, and also engineering works, mineral works and food industry factories. Janikowo is another salt processing centre. Other towns in Kujawy, even small ones, are developing industries, above all food processing and production of building materials. Bydgoszcz, in the north west of the Kujawy region is known for its well developed engineering, chemical, leather, clothing, food and timber industries.

Poznań is a big, fast developing industrial centre of Wielkopolska. The dominating position, is held there by its engineering works, among which is the "H. Cegielski" Metal Works, which grew from a small agricultural machine factory founded in 1846 into today's important works producing railway rolling stock, ships engines and Diesel railway engines, machine tools, etc. The chemical industry, clothing, leather and food processing factories in Poznań are also developing fast. Numerous timber and food processing factories and mechanical works have been built in the vicinity of the town. At Luboń, near Poznań, there is one of Poland's biggest artificial fertilizer plants.

Other centres of industry of Wielkopolska are Kalisz (textile, food and engineering works), Ostrów Wielkopolski (engineering works), Włocławek (cellulose and paper industry, nitrogen fertilizers), Gniezno (leather and footwear industries), Piła (metal and timber industries). Almost all the smaller towns of Wielkopolska are centres of the agricultural and food industries, leather, clothing, building materials and engineering industries, producing to meet the needs of the rural areas.

The degree of industrialization of Wielkopolska gets smaller towards the west. In the areas on the middle reaches of the Odra an important centre of the chemical industry (synthetic fibre) is Gorzów Wielkopolski, which also has light industry and engineering plants. Kostrzyn on the Odra has a big cellulose and paper factory. Zielona Góra and Nowa Sól are centres of the engineering and textile industries, with fine old traditions.

There are more textile factories in other places in the southern part of Zielona Góra voivodship, which come within the bounds of the Lower Silesian Textile Industry District.

The towns of Wielkopolska are mostly well built and equipped with public facilities, and also well serviced in the field of handicrafts and trade network.

The main centre of the whole Lowland is Poznań (pop. about 540,000), one of the biggest and oldest towns of Poland, a big industrial, trade and cultural centre. Its eight higher schools of learning, headed by the university, are attended by 44,000 students. There are numerous research institutes there. The Poznań Friends of Science Society has been operating for more than a hundred years now. Poznań's rich museum collections, its Opera House, Philharmonia and theatres, known for their high artistic level, testify to the lively cultural life of the town. With its thousand years' traditions, Poznań has many historical buildings and works of art, despite the devastation brought by the last war. The central district was almost 75% destroyed. The economic and cultural influence of Poznań extends far beyond the boundaries of the voivodship. It is one of Poland's three provincial capitals. Abroad, Poznań is known as the place where the International Poznań Fairs are held every year, attended by many firms from all over the world.

Łódź, the second largest town (pop. 825,000) has a smaller range of influence than Poznań. Although the beginnings of Łódź can be traced back to the Middle Ages, it is a young town, not very much more than 150 years old. It owes its position to its industry. Despite the damage of both world wars to its industry, it is still one of the biggest textile industry centres in the world. Since the last war, Łódź has assumed new expanded administrative functions and is the seat of a number of scientific and cultural institutions. It has a large university, the only State Higher Film, Television and Theatre School in Poland and four other higher schools of learning. There are 33,000 students attending these schools. Scientific centres are developing there, among them, 10 industrial research institutes. The cultural life of the town is flourishing with its several theatres, Opera House, Operetta, and Philharmonia. Łódź also has museums known for their fine collections of modern art.

The third biggest town of the Wielkopolska Lowland is Bydgoszcz (pop. 340,000). In the 16th century, the town was a large corn and salt trading centre. In the 19th century it grew into a big industrial and trading centre and has remained so to this day. With the biggest river port in Poland, it is an important communication centre. In addition to its economic functions, Bydgoszcz is also a growing cultural centre. The Festivals of Old Music held in the Philharmonic Hall known for its excellent accoustics, have made a name for themselves in the world. Bydgoszcz figures in the history of the last war as the place where the Nazis carried out the first mass execution of civilians.

Apart from the above mentioned towns, there are nine more voivodship towns in the Wielkopolska Lowland of varying size. Mention is due to ancient Kalisz (pop. 96,000), a lively industrial and cultural centre with many historical buildings, both of the Middle Ages and later times. There are also many buildings of historical interest in Włocławek (pop. 97,000), which in the 11th century was one of the most powerful fortified settlements in Poland and was for a time the capital of the Kujawy bishops. It developed due to trade on the Vistula and, like many other towns, declined during the wars against the Swedes. Today it is an important industrial town. The voivodship towns of Gorzów Wielkopolski (pop. 99,000) and Zielona Góra (pop. 95,000) are about the same size. They are the main urban centres of the area on the middle reaches of the Odra and their population has greatly exceeded that of the pre-war years. The medium sized voivodship towns include Piotrków Trybunalski (pop. 70,000), with fine old traditions, and many buildings of historical interest. Its present development is due to industry. Konin (pop. 62,000) is another town which owes its present development and importance to industry, becoming the capital of a new industrial district. Piła (pop. 54,000), badly damaged during the war, is not only an industrial centre, but above all an important junction. The two smallest voivodship towns of the Wielkopolska Lowland are Leszno (pop. 46,000) and Sieradz (pop. 24,000). They are both industrial towns and both have an interesting history. Leszno is famed for its role as a centre of Protestant culture. Sieradz was once the seat of an independent duchy, and later up to the partitions of Poland a voivodship town.

There are some larger towns which do not have the function of voivodship seats. They are: Inowrocław (pop. 64,000), Gniezno (pop. 59,000), and Ostrów Wielkopolski (pop. 56,000). They are old service centres, well industrialized, which are also centres of trade and culture, etc. Together with other smaller towns, which till 1975 were district towns, they supplement the urban network of the Wielkopolska Lowland. All over the area there are many small urban centres servicing a small area. The network of towns in the area along the Odra river is more sparse than in the other parts of the Lowland. The frontier on the Odra and Nysa runs through several towns (Słubice, Gubin, Zasieki), leaving a smaller or larger part on the Polish side.

Apart from the Łódź Industrial District, which is surrounded by a circle of industrial satellite centres, Wielkopolska does not have many specialized towns. Most of them are small settlements linked either with industry, or serving as junctions, recreational and health resorts. The most well known of these resorts are Inowrocław, Ciechocinek and Łagów Lubuski.

Rural settlement in Wielkopolska is characterized by nucleated villages. There are many row villages and street villages. Green villages are not met with so often, most of them being in the west. Only in the pradolines and in the southern parts of Kujawy rural settlement is generally more scattered. Everywhere one sees settlements that have grown up on the old landed estates, most of which have been turned into state farms. Some of these settlements, which are of historical interest, having a castle or palace, have been recognised as monuments of our national culture and have been made into the seats of cultural institutions.

The Wielkopolska Lowland is the cradle of the Polish state. It was here, between the Warta and Vistula rivers, that the oldest fortified settlements of the Polanes developed in the 8th and 9th centuries. This was the nucleus of the Polish state, the historical area mentioned in the first chronicles as "Polonia" and, from the second half of the 13th century, as "Polonia Maior". The Polish name for this area was Wielka Polska (literally translated, Great Poland, understood as Old), and later, as from the middle of the 15th century Wielkopolska.

It is an area of very old settlement, dating back to the Neolithic Age. Among the numerous traces of the old settlers one of the most valuable relics – of international importance – is the fortified settlement from the times of the Lusatian culture, originating in the early Iron Age (about 550 B.C.), discovered in 1933 on a former island, today the peninsula of Lake Biskupin, near Żnin (4). Excavation work revealed the ground-plan of the settlement and the tools, ceiling ornamentation and other objects found there enabled scholars to reconstruct the life of its inhabitants. This large oval settlement, surrounded with an earth and timber rampart with a breakwater, was crossed by 12 streets that were linked up by a circular one on the outskirts. Along the timber paved streets there were 105 wooden houses (8×9 m.) with fireplaces in the centre and common gable walls (5). The settlement had a population of about 1,000, whose occupation was agriculture and animal breeding. The remains of craftsmen's workshops have also been found. On the basis of these archeological finds, several houses (4) and part of the defence rampart and breakwater have been reconstructed.

One of the places associated with the period when the Polish state was taking shape is Ostrów Lednicki, the biggest island in Lake Lednickie, to the east of Gniezno. On the island are the remains of a fortified settlement (6) with the ruins of a church and a ducal seat. Archeological excavations on the island have revealed traces of human settlement dating back to the 7th century. In the 9th and 10th centuries, there was a small stronghold with an earth and timber rampart there. It was surrounded by a settlement inhabited by craftsmen. At the turn of the 10th century, on the site of the former stronghold, a church was built there of boulder stone on a ground-plan in the form of a Greek cross, the roof being supported on four pillars, as well as a rectangular storeyed palace with a hall measuring 14×14 m. and a chapel. Tradition has it that Bolesław the Brave was born at Ostrów Lednicki, and it is said that he received the emperor Otto III there. The palace was destroyed in 1039, during the invasion of Prince Břetislav of Bohemia; the chapel survived till the 15th century and the trading settlement till the end of the 12th century. On another smaller island, called Ledniczka, there are traces of a fortified settlement. There was a castellan's stronghold there, which was destroyed in the 15th century.

Giecz was also one of the most important tribal centres of the Polanes. In the times of Mieszko I, there was a powerful stronghold there, which was destroyed when Břetislav of Bohemia invaded the Polish lands in 1039. Archeological excavations in the remains of the fortified settlement have revealed the foundations of a palace and chapel resembling the one on Ostrów Lednicki (2).

6

7 The main centre of the Polanes and the first capital of the Polish state united by Mieszko I was Gniezno (8). Its name is derived from the Polish word gniazdo (nest) and is associated with the legend about the eagle's nest found by Lech, the common ancestor of the Poles. In 1000, the emperor Otto III was sumptuously received by Bolesław the Brave when he came to Gniezno as a pilgrim to visit the tomb of the bishop Wojciech (Adalbert), who lost his life during a mission in Prussia and was soon after canonized as a saint. The emperor recognized the independence of the Polish ruler and as a symbol of this presented him with a crown. Also at that time the Gniezno Archiepiscopal Metropolis was founded, independent of the German hierarchy, to which the newly created Bishoprics in Cracow, Wrocław and Kołobrzeg were to be subordinated. The political role of Gniezno diminished shortly afterwards when, after the devastation of the town during the invasion of Břetislav of Bohemia in 1039, King Casimir the Restorer transferred the capital of the state to Cracow. But it still remained – and has done to this day – the seat of the Church authorities in Poland. In 1243, Gniezno was granted municipal status. Its economic development, despite devastation by the Teutonic Knights in 1331, lasted until the Swedish wars in the 17th century, which brought the decline of the town. There was another period of economic enlivenment in the 19th century. The oldest parts of the town are Lech's Hill – the place where the former stronghold stood – and the area of today's Market Place, where there was already a market before the town received municipal status. The Old Town quarter has retained its old urban layout and many historical buildings. The oldest of them, the pre-Romanesque church where, in 973, Dubravka, the wife of Mieszko I was buried, was burnt down in 1018. The second, Romanesque cathedral was built by Bolesław the Brave. A Gothic cathedral (7, 8) was erected on its foundations in the years 1342–1372, and in the 17th and 18th centuries it was remodelled and surrounded by a wreath of Renaissance and Baroque chapels. This cathedral was burnt down in 1945. It has been rebuilt in its old form. The most valuable of the numerous relics in the cathedral are the bronze doors (about 1170–1180) covered with reliefs showing scenes from the life and death of St. Adalbert (3).

The chief town of the Wielkopolska Lowland is Poznań. It is situated in the valley of the River Warta at a place where there was a convenient river crossing. As early as the 9th century, between the River Warta and its tributary Cybina, in the place today known as Ostrów Tumski (Tum Islet) there was a stronghold, under whose protection a settlement grew up. In the middle of the 10th century, the Poznań stronghold was enlarged and made into a powerful fortress, also fulfilling, apart from Gniezno, the functions of a capital. After Poland was Christianized in 966, it became the seat of the first Polish bishopric. After 968, a pre-Romanesque cathedral was built on Ostrów Tumski, and later a Romanesque cathedral was erected on its site (1058–1079). This was followed by a Gothic cathedral (1346–1357), which was later enlarged and altered. After it was burnt down in 1945, the Gothic style was re-introduced during the reconstruction (9). The Poznań stronghold, devasted by Prince Břetislav of Bohemia (1039), became one of the capitals of the Wielkopolska line of the Piast Dynasty in the period of feudal divisions. The town began to grow. On the right bank of the River Cybina, a settlement grew up called Śródka, which in 1230 was given municipal status. However, neither Ostrów Tumski nor Śródka had enough room for any great development, and the Wielkopolska prince Przemysław I transfered the economic centre of the town to the left bank of the Warta. In 1253, left-bank Poznań received its foundation charter on the basis of the Magdeburg Law. Defence walls were built round the town and at the turn of the 13th century the Gothic Town Hall was erected. Poznań, which was granted many privileges, developed rapidly, outdistancing Gniezno, and became the chief town of Wielkopolska.

In the 16th and 17th centuries, it was one of the biggest trading towns in Europe. It also had a well developed network of handicraft workshops.

The town was expanded and many alterations and additions were made. In the years 1550–1560, the Town Hall was remodelled in Renaissance style, with beautiful interior decoration (11). At the end of the 16th century, the population of Poznań was 20,000. The trade contacts of the Poznań merchants extended from Western Europe to the Middle East, and even China. Poznań was also an important centre of education and culture. In 1518, the bishop J. Lubrański founded an Academy here – a branch of the Cracow Academy. In the 16th century, the influence of the Reformation Movement was strong, but already in the first half of the 17th century, it became a centre of the Counter-Reformation. The Swedish wars and plagues brought a decline of the town. It began to develop again in the Enlightenment Period, when trade began to boom and numerous manufactures were started, mostly textile mills. After the second partition of Poland (1793), Poznań came under Prussian rule. In the Duchy of Warsaw it was the capital of a department, and after the Vienna Congress (1815), having been incorporated into Prussia again, it became the capital of the Grand Duchy of Poznań.

In the second quarter of the 19th century, Poznań grew into an important centre of science and culture. In 1829, E. Raczyński founded a library (12) in the years that followed, several printing houses were opened, as well as publishing houses, book shops and lending libraries. In 1857, the Poznań Friends of Science Society was formed. After 1831, the autonomy of the Duchy was restricted and, following the Wielkopolska Uprising of 1848, it was completely withdrawn. Despite germanization pressure, Poznań remained Polish. The organic system of work prevailed in Poznań, giving priority to the economic and cultural development of the community. And it was in this spirit that the numerous Polish organizations developed their activity in the second half of the 19th century. This was a period of economic growth for the town. Its main function was trade and also services to the agricultural population of Wielkopolska. Also, Poznań's contacts with other towns developed, particularly with Berlin, Wrocław and Szczecin, facilitated by the development of a network of hard-surfaced roads and the railway. Handicrafts flourished and so did industry, above all the processing of agricultural produce and services to the agricultural population. The small workshop founded in 1846 by H. Cegielski grew into a factory making agricultural implements.

The 20th century saw the considerable territorial expansion of the town. After the secularization of Church property in 1797, the nearby land which had once been under the jurisdiction of the Church and the monasteries was incorporated into the town. Further possibilities of development were created by the pulling down of the mediaeval fortifications, but these possibilities were shortly to be limited by the building of a fortress with a citadel, forts and ramparts. The Poznań fortress was one of the strongest within the frontiers of the Prussia of that time. The defence walls were only pulled down in the beginning of the 20th century, and then there came a successive expansion of the area of the town. Its development continued. Above all, privately owned tenement houses were built there. After 1892, on the initiative of the municipal authorities, who were under the thumb of the Germans, the construction was started of a number of impressive buildings modelled on similar buildings in Berlin.

12

13

14

15

The First World War raised hopes of regaining independence. On December 27th, 1918, the Wielkopolska Uprising broke out and a few days later came the liberation of Poznań. The town was not damaged, had a population of 187,000 and had medium and small-scale industry, a large network of handicraft workshops and was also a lively centre of trade and services. Despite the development of industry, the trade functions of the town continued to predominate all through the inter-war period. In 1921, the Poznań Fair was organized there for the first time, and then took place annually. As from 1925, the Poznań Fair assumed an international character.

In the field of culture, a momentous turn came with the founding in 1919 of the Poznań University. The following years brought the opening of more higher schools, namely the Higher School of Engineering, the Higher School of Commerce, the Poznań Conservatoire and the School of Decorative Art. Poznań grew into one of the leading centres of Polish scientific and cultural life. Its territory expanded and the population in 1939 was 275,000.

The Second World War brought the difficult period of German occupation to the town, with arrests, deportation and the destruction of national monuments of culture. The fighting in the last stage of the war caused considerable damage. The historical central district of the town was 80% destroyed. With the organizational talent and industriousness typical of the people of Poznań, they speedily rebuilt their town (by 1950) and started its development. New higher schools of learning were opened and cultural life blossomed again. The International Poznań Fair (14) became an event of world significance. There was a strong development of industry, with the H. Cegielski Works (15) still in the lead. It now produces modern ships engines, Diesel locomotives, machine tools, implements, etc. The town has grown and the population is now over half a million. A new central district has been built (3) and new residential districts have sprung up. The important trading functions of the town mean that there is a large inflow of visitors, including foreign guests, which has made it necessary to develop the hotel network. Among the new hotels are "Merkury" and "Polonez" (16) and also the "Novotel" (17), of interesting architectural and functional design. The destroyed historical buildings have been reconstructed and in many cases restored to their former appearance. They are mainly in the Old Town quarter and on Ostrów Tumski. The Old Town has retained its mediaeval urban layout. In the historical Town Hall, there is now the Museum of the History of Poznań. Next to the Town Hall are the former houses of the stallkeepers, dating back to the 16th century. The burghers' houses from the 16th to 18th centuries round the Market Place have also been rebuilt and carefully restored to their former appearance. Among the valuable buildings of historical interest in the Old Town are the churches: the 13th century former Dominican church of St. Adalbert, the Gothic church of Corpus Christi (founded by Władysław Jagiełło) and the Baroque churches of the Carmelites and Franciscans, as well as the parish church. Ostrów Tumski, the second historical complex of Poznań, where the dominating feature is the cathedral, also suffered badly during the Second World War. It has been carefully rebuilt and today is an attraction drawing many tourists. Next to the cathedral is the Collegiate Church of St. Mary dating back to the 15th century, the Psalter House (1512), the building of the former Academy from 1519 (9) and canons' houses.

16

17

The old town of Kórnik, situated to the south-east of Poznań, was successively owned by many Wielkopolska families. In the years 1426–1450 it was granted municipal status, but the town did not develop. It owes its fame to the museum and library founded by Tytus Działyński. The museum contains rich and valuable collections of sacral and secular art from the 15th century, archeological and ethnographic collections, as well as natural science exhibits from Poland and other countries. The library, with more than 100,000 books and a collection of Polish prints from the 16th to 18th centuries, is at the same time a scientific and publishing institute. The museum and library are in the 16th century castle, which was remodelled in the 19th century in the style of English Neo-Gothic (18). In 1924, the last owner, W. Zamoyski, presented the castle together with its art collections and estate to the Polish nation. The castle is surrounded by a park, first laid out in the 16th century in the Italian style, later changed to French style, and in the 19th century to English style. Today it is the largest dendrological park in Poland (about 10,000 trees and shrubs, both Polish and exotic), constituting a basis for the work of a scientific centre – The Institute of Dendrology and Pomology of the Polish Academy of Sciences.

The chief river of the Wielkopolska Lowland is the Warta, the biggest right-bank tributary of the Odra. Along a large part of its course, flowing west, it follows the Warsaw-Berlin Pradoline. The river meanders there with many bends. In some parts, the valley is boggy and full of old river beds (19). In the vicinity of Śrem, the Warta changes its course and flows north, cutting through the upland belt towards the Toruń-Eberswalde Pradoline and forming a narrow gap valley.

20

21

To the south of Poznań, in the former Raczyńskis palace at Rogalin, there is another museum with collections of furniture, sculptures, paintings and elegant porcelain from the 16th to 19th century, as well as historical relics, both Polish and foreign. The 18th century Baroque palace, with Rococo and Classicist elements added in the 18th and 19th century (21), now belongs to the National Museum in Poznań. It stands in a beautiful park, laid out in the 18th century, partly in French style and partly English. There is a mausoleum-chapel of the Raczyński family in the park, dating back to 1820, a copy of the Roman temple in Nimes. The park ends with the largest complex (about 900) of huge old oaks (up to 9 m. in diameter) in Poland (20), the remains of a former marsh forest. The most magnificent oaks have been given the names: "Lech", "Czech", and "Rus", after the three legendary brothers who were the ancestors of three Slav nations.

Also to the south of Poznań is the Wielkopolska National Park (22), which embraces an area of beautiful forest-grown moraine hills, amid which there are more than a dozen lakes. Predominant here are fresh pine or mixed forests, dry pine forests being rare in this area. The Park covers an area of about 100 sq. km. Inside it, there are several protected nature reserves of flora and fauna and several places of a recreational-holiday character.

The Town Hall in Jarocin was built at the end of the 18th century, after a great fire that destroyed the town. In the middle of the 19th century it was enlarged and has remained in this form till today (23). It is one of the very few historical buildings of this pretty town that has survived. Jarocin is mentioned in chronicles as a town as early as 1257, when it was given to Castellan Jan of the Zaremba family by Bolesław the Pious, prince of Wielkopolska. The town changed hands a number of times, remaining a privately owned one till the end of the 18th century. Frequent fires and plagues and, in the 17th and 18th centuries, the looting by armies passing through it, ruined the town and its inhabitants. The most recent devastation was caused by the Germans in 1945. The steady development of the town has only taken place during the last thirty years.

Between Jarocin and Kalisz, there is another former magnate's residence which is now a branch of the National Museum in Poznań. It is the old castle of the Leszczyński family at Gołuchów on the River Ciemna, a tributary of the River Prosna (24). This late Renaissance, three-wing castle with an arcaded courtyard was created at the beginning of the 17th century as a result of the enlargment of a Renaissance residence built half a century earlier, of which the corner turrets have remained. In the years 1872–1885, the castle was completely remodelled by Izabella Działyńska, née Czartoryska, in the French Renaissance style with the addition of original architectural and sculptured elements from the 15th to 17th century, brought from France and Italy. The interior decoration and furnishings (25) were modelled on the interiors of French palaces. The Czartoryski family accumulated valuable collections of European and Middle East art in the castle. The park surrounding the castle, with its numerous Polish and exotic trees, is today a nature reserve.

22

23

Rydzyna – once a privately owned town belonging to the Wierzbno-Rydzyńskis, then to the Leszczyńskis and Sułkowskis – was granted municipal status in 1422, but never developed, and retains to this day the character of a small townlet. It is known for the beautiful Baroque palace of the Leszczyński family (26), erected on the Gothic foundations of the 15th century castle of the Rydzyńskis. The Leszczyńskis palace, built by Pompeo Ferrari in the years 1696–1704 on an "L" shaped ground-plan, was only used for three years, for it was burnt down during the Northern War. At the wish of the next owner, Sułkowski, the palace was rebuilt in the years 1742–1744 by K.M. Frantz. The ground-plan of the palace was then extended to form a rectangle, giving it the form of a fortified residence with corner towers and a rectangular courtyard inside. It was surrounded by a moat, annexes were built and also a winter garden, a chapel, and a large geometrical park was laid out. In 1762, Sułkowski founded a Knights Academy in Rydzyna and, in the event of the family becoming extinct, expressed the wish that the whole estate should be used for educational purposes. His wish was not fulfilled at once. After the death of the last heir in tail, during the time of the partitions of Poland, the Rydzyna estate was seized by the Prussian government. It was only in the inter-war period that the "Sułkowski Foundation" was established and in 1928 a secondary school with dormitories was organized in the palace. Burnt down by the Germans in 1945, the palace was afterwards rebuilt. But it lost its period interior with a wealth of sculptures and paintings.

24

25

Wielkopolska has been known for a long time for its high level of agricultural technique and organization. In particular, the southern part of the Wielkopolska Lowland is among the leading agricultural regions in the country. There are high yields of cereals and sugar beet in this area. Stock breeding (27) and bacon pig breeding is well developed. Privately owned farms of medium size and high commercialization predominate, bringing in good incomes; the percentage of state farms and cooperatives is also considerable. These farms are marked for higher productivity than elsewhere and for good organization. They were set up on the former estates of landowners, utilizing the existing buildings, including the palaces, in most cases in good repair. New farm buildings are being put up round the old ones (28).

27

28

Gostyń, situated between Jarocin and Leszno, is in the area of early settlement. The town received municipal status in 1278. In the 16th century it was a centre of goldsmithery and haberdashery. It declined in the times of the Swedish invasion and Lubomirski's rebellion. In the 19th century it was known for the production of linen and hemp fabrics. Today, it is an industrial centre and provides services for the surrounding districts. It is also known as a service centre of the most developed agricultural area in Poland. A unique feature of Gostyń is the monumental Baroque church of the Philipins in nearby Głogówek, built in the years 1679–1698 (29) by Giovanni and Giorgio Catenaci, and modelled on the church of Santa Maria della Salute in Venice. The dome and the beautiful Baroque-Rococo interior decoration date back to the years 1726–1728 and are the work of Pompeo Ferrari (30).

Leszno is on the borderline of the Lakeless Wielkopolska Lowland and the Wielkopolska Lakeland, in the historical Wschowa Land which is in the border zone between Wielkopolska and Silesia. The princes of both provinces had long disputes about this Land and it was only in 1343 that Casimir the Great established its position as belonging to Wielkopolska. The original settlement was called Leszczno. At the turn of the 14th century, it was the property of the house of knights called Wieniawits, who took the name of Leszczyński from that of the settlement. Leszczno was granted municipal status in 1547. In the middle of the 16th century it became a centre of the Reformation Movement. A follower of the movement, Rafał Leszczyński, brought the Bohemian Brethren there. A Calvinist community was also formed there. After 1620 several hundred Bohemian and Moravian families settled in Leszno. The elementary school of the Bohemian Brethren, founded in 1555, was then turned into a secondary school, the rector of which was Jan Amos Komenský, a Bohemian pedagogue and writer who had fled from persecution. Leszno then became a large cultural and publishing centre. Because of their voluntary act of letting the Swedes into the town, the town was burnt in 1656 by the Polish troops and the Bohemian Brethren were exiled. At the beginning of the 18th century, Leszno belonged to Stanisław Leszczyński, twice elected king of Poland, exiled from the country under pressure from the Russians and Saxons. In 1707, the Saxons set fire to the town. It was rebuilt quite soon after. In the 17th and 18th centuries, the town was known for the production of woollen cloth. However, due to Prussian competition, cloth production declined at the beginning of the 19th century, when the place of the weaving looms was taken by breweries, an earthenware factory, a bell foundry, a coach factory and numerous artisans workshops. In the inter-war period, Leszno was a thriving economic centre of the southern part of Wielkopolska. Today, it is a well developed industrial and trade centre and an important junction of road communication. Since 1975, it has been a voivodship capital.

Although it was destroyed many times, the town has retained its mediaeval layout and several valuable buildings of historical interest. In the Market Place there is a beautiful Baroque Town Hall (31) dating back to 1660, reconstructed after a fire by Pompeo Ferrari in the years 1707–1709. Other historical buildings are, the parish church of St. Nicholas, probably built in the 14th century and remodelled twice in the 17th and 18th centuries in the Baroque style, and the Baroque church of St. John from the 17th century.

30

31

The small town of Buk, near Nowy Tomyśl, boasts of several specimens of old timber buildings, not often met with now in Wielkopolska. The most important of them is the Baroque cemetery church of the Holy Cross, with a dome dated 1760, built on a ground-plan in the shape of a Greek cross (32). Next to the church is a shingle-covered wooden belfry built in 1758.

Some interesting specimens of timber buildings are also to be found at Rakoniewice to the south-west of Buk, near Wolsztyn, namely a wooden Protestant church built in 1662, some 18th century wooden houses with arcades (33) and four 18th century windmills.

Zielona Góra (34), situated in a basin amid the moraine hills of the Zielona Góra elevation, was most probably founded in 1222, and was granted municipal status in 1315. It was the property of the Silesian Piast line of Głogów, later of Żagań. At the end of the 15th century it passed under the direct rule of the Bohemian kings, and in 1742 – together with the whole of Silesia – it was incorporated into Prussia. The basis for the development of the town in the 15th and 16th centuries was cloth and wine making, introduced here in the 13th century by Flemish and German settlers. The production of wine declined in the 17th century, never to recover, although to this day there are some vineyards and small-scale wine production in Zielona Góra and the annual Vintage Festival is an attraction drawing tourists from all over the country. Cloth making continued, however, and was industrialized in the 19th century. Other branches of industry also developed. At the end of the 19th century, the influx of craftsmen and manual workers from Wielkopolska strengthened the Polish element in the town. After the Second World War, Zielona Góra was returned to Poland and within its frontiers gained favourable conditions for development as a voivodship capital and an industrial and cultural centre. In the years 1946–1978, the population of the town increased sixfold to reach about 90,000, that is more than three and a half times the population of 1939.

Łagów is situated on an isthmus between two lakes in a long glacial spillway, amid high moraine hills covered with beech forests (35). The first mention of Łagów in chronicles is from 1299, but the remains of a stronghold indicate much earlier settlement there. At the beginning of the 14th century, Łagów was a fortified settlement of Wielkopolska, and after it was taken by the Brandenburgers became their stronghold from which they made sallies against Poland. In the years 1299–1346 it was a kinghts fief. In 1350, it became the property of the Order of The Knights of St. John of Jerusalem, who built a massive castle there with a 35 metre tower dominating the surrounding countryside. It was enlarged in the 17th century. The Knights (of St. John of Jerusalem) owned Łagów until 1810. There was a small settlement next to the castle, which after a fire was transferred to the present site of the town in 1569 and partially enclosed with a system of defence fortifications. The inhabitants of the settlement were mostly craftsmen who worked to meet the needs of the castle. In 1808, Łagów was granted municipal status. After the Order of the Knights of St. John was dissolved, the town did not have conditions for development and in 1932 it had become little more than a rural settlement. However, its beautiful position and its historical buildings made it a favourite spot for summer holidays and to this day it has retained this character.

32

33

34

35

The development of tourism and also the fact that Wielkopolska is on the route leading from western Europe to Poland and on to the Soviet Union and the countries of east-central Europe, made it necessary to build hotels in the towns and motels along the main transit routes. A speciality of Wielkopolska are the numerous inns built in recent years, which have been given the style of the old Polish inns of bygone days with elements of folk architecture. The photographs show the inn at Gorzyń (37) and the interior of the inn at Kobylec (36).

The northern border of the Wielkopolska Lowland is marked by the wide, peaty valley of the Rivers Noteć and Warta – part of the great Toruń–Eberswalde Pradoline. Here at the place where the Noteć flows into the Warta, there was a powerful stronghold at Santok in the Middle Ages (39), which guarded Wielkopolska from the north and west. According to the chronicle of Gallus Anonymus, it was "the watch-tower and key to the Kingdom". Later it was the seat of castellans and of the church authorities. Lower down, where the small Kłodawka river flows into the Warta, there was a little fortified settlement called Kobyla Góra, which belonged to the defence system of Santok. After the western part of the Santok castellan's territory had been occupied by the Margraves of Brandenburg, they chose this place to build a new stronghold from which they made sallies against Wielkopolska and Western Pomerania.

36

37

A trading settlement grew up by the stronghold, which in 1257 was granted municipal status in 1296, Santok was taken and devastated; later it changed hands several times, until in 1439 it was completely occupied by the Brandenburgers. Poland never recognized the annexation of Santok, maintaining the castellan's function till the partitions of Poland. With the dévelopment of Gorzów, which became one of the chief towns of the New March created by the Brandenburgers, the importance of Santok diminished. Having been granted the privilege of marketing goods, and thus the monopoly on trade with Poland, Gorzów developed well until the Thirty Years' War. The next period of development for the town came in the 18th century, and in the 19th and 20th centuries, Gorzów became a big industrial centre. Badly damaged during the Second World War, Gorzów rallied again to became the economic and cultural centre of the northern part of Zielona Góra voivodship after the war, and in 1975 the capital of a separate voivodship with a population of nearly 100,000 (38). The Synthetic Fibre Factory opened there in 1951 did much to promote the economic enlivenment of Gorzów.

38

39

On the northern verge of the Pradoline, not far from the place where the Gwda flows into the Noteć from the Pomeranian Lakeland, is the town of Piła. It grew out of an old fishing village belonging to the Wielkopolska Opaliński family. It was granted municipal status in 1513. Incorporated into Prussia after the first partition of Poland, Piła was part of the Noteć district where intensive German colonization was carried out. In 1807, it became part of the Duchy of Warsaw and in 1815, having been incorporated into Prussia again, part of the Grand Duchy of Poznań. In the 19th century it developed as an important node of communication. Remaining within the German frontiers after 1918, Piła was the capital of the so-called Border March. Almost completely destroyed during the Second World War, Piła only attained its pre-war population figure after 1970. After its reconstruction it became quite a different town (40). Since 1975, it has been a voivodship capital.

Bydgoszcz, situated on the River Brda at the place where it flows into the Toruń Basin, constituting the eastern part of the Toruń-Eberswalde Pradoline, has its origins in the fortified settlement founded in the times of Bolesław the Brave to guard the dry passage through the swampy pradoline dividing Kujawy from Pomerania. Continous battles were fought against the Pomeranians for this stronghold, with the tide of fortune turning frequently from one side to the other. In the period of feudal divisions, Bydgoszcz belonged to the Kujawian princes. In 1309, it was occupied by the Teutonic Knights, and in 1331 returned to Poland. It was granted municipal status in 1346. The town developed quickly, particularly after Poland regained Gdańsk Pomerania (1466), as an important centre of trade in timber, and salt along the Vistula route.

42

43

A reminder of those days are the large granaries (42), and salt warehouses. Bydgoszcz was badly damaged during the Swedish wars and plagues brought in their wake the depopulation of the town. A change for the better came when – after its incorporation into Prussia – the Bydgoszcz Canal, linking the Vistula and Odra basins was built in the years 1772–1774, making possible the floating of timber from the Polish Kingdom and Galicia. Bydgoszcz them became a big centre of the timber industry. Later the food industry developed there too, in connection with the development of agriculture in the neighbouring, fertile land of Kujawy. The further development of industry brought railroads and made Bydgoszcz an important railway junction. The germanization pressures during the period of Prussian rule after the partitions were very strong and steps were also taken to destroy the historical buildings testifying to the Polish character of the town. The castle there, many old churches and monasteries and even secular buildings were pulled down.

The development of the town in the inter-war period was interrupted by the outbreak of the Second World War. The German occupation began with mass executions, and a considerable part of the population was deported. After the war, Bydgoszcz developed rapidly, above all, due to its industry, and became a voivodship capital. Higher schools of learning, scientific institutes, theatres and libraries were opened. The Bydgoszcz Philharmonia is known for its high artistic level. The central district (41) is being reconstructed and the town is expanding to higher ground and reaching out towards the Vistula. The population has exceeded the pre-war figure twofold and is now nearly 350,000.

The Kujawy Plain is crossed by a strip of finger lakes of which the largest and best known is Lake Gopło (44). There are legends associated with this lake telling of the origins of the Polish state. It was here that the hated Prince Popiel was said to have been eaten by mice, after which Piast, the wheelwright, founder of the first Polish dynasty recorded in history, was acclaimed the new ruler. It is a fact that Kujawy is an area of very early settlement. A written record, called the Bavarian Geographer, from the middle of the 9th century mentions the tribe of Goplanes inhabiting 400 fortified settlements here. In the 10th century, Kruszwica on the shores of Lake Gopło was one of the chief settlements of the Polanes. In the times of Bolesław the Brave it was the seat of the heirs to the throne, and later of a bishopric and castellan. The civil wars of the 11th and 12th centuries led to the decline of the town. It began to develop again in the times of Casimir the Great, who built a brick castle on the site of the former stronghold. Devastated during the Swedish wars, it was dismantled by the Prussians after the first partition of Poland, leaving only an octagonal tower, which is today called Mouse Tower (44). The most valuable historical building in Kruszwica is the Romanesque Collegiate church (45), built in the years 1120–1140 on the site of the former wooden cathedral built by Mieszko I.

There are also buildings of historical interest in the neighbouring towns. In Trzemeszno, which dates back to the 10th century, a stone Romanesque basilica was built by the Benedictine monks. In the years 1782–1791, it was completely remodelled after the design of St. Peter's basilica in Rome (43).

44

45

In Strzelno – which belonged to the Trzemeszno Abbey in the 12th century – there is a church of the Norbertan Nuns, built after 1175 and later remodelled. In 1946, beautifully carved Romanesque columns were discovered between the naves under the Baroque additions (47). Next to it is the rotunda church of St. Procopius, built after 1160, partly reconstructed (46).

46

47

Another natural resource of Kujawy is salt. It has been exploited there since the beginning of the 20th century by the method of washing it out of the salt domes underground. Part of the salt is processed by the soda industry in Inowrocław and part by the new works in Janikowo (49). The saline waters originating from the same salt deposits were known much earlier. They were first exploited in the times of the Congress Kingdom, when two twig towers were built in Ciechocinek. In 1854 a third was built. Like the two preceding ones, it was a three-storey wooden structure filled with blackthorn twigs (48), through which the saline waters passed. At the turn of the 19th century, Ciechocinek developed as a large health resort with baths, pump rooms and sanatoria, and beautifully kept parks were laid out there. After the Second World War, Ciechocinek continued to develop as a health resort.

In the 11th century, Włocławek was one of the most important strongholds of the Piasts, around which a trading settlement grew up. In the years 1215–1793, it belonged to the Kujawy bishops, who had transferred their seat from Kruszwica to Włocławek. In 1261, the town was granted municipal status. Its development as a port and corn trading centre came in the 15th to 17th centuries, after the opening of a waterway leading to the sea. Badly damaged in the 17th and 18th centuries, it only began to recover in the 19th century as a centre of the food, paper, metal and ceramic industries. In 1895, the famous "Celuloza" factory was opened there, as the only one of its kind in Poland at that time. In recent years a big nitrogen works (50) was built near Włocławek. The town now has a population of 95,000. It was not very densely built up in the past and modern residential districts have now been built to house the increased population (51). The most important historical building there is the Gothic cathedral built in the middle of the 14th century.

In Gosławice, to the north of Konin, there is a church with beautiful Gothic vaulting (52) built in the first half of the 15th century. In Poddębice, mentioned in chronicles as a town in 1466, there is a Renaissance palace that belonged to the Grudziński family, built in the years 1610–1617 (53).

It is not certain whether Calisia, mentioned in 142–147 A.D. by Ptolomy, the great geographer of the Ancient World, can be identified with today's Kalisz, for this has not been proved conclusively. It is, however, known that one of the biggest strongholds of the Polanes existed here as early as the 9th–10th centuries. Later, Kalisz became one of the most important political and economic centres of Wielkopolska; in the 13th century it was the capital of a feudal duchy and after the unification of the state – a voivodship capital. It was granted municipal status in the years 1253–1260. Casimir the Great built defence walls round the town. Ruined during the wars of the 17th and 18th century, it began to develop again in the times of the Congress Kingdom. As the capital of a voivodship, and later of a governmental unit, it became one of the most important economic and cultural centres of the Kingdom. Numerous factories were built there at the beginning of the 19th century and the town continued to grow (56). It was a big industrial centre in the inter-war years, after its reconstruction from the devastation caused by the First World War. Incorporated into the Third Reich in 1939, its people suffered persecution and deportation. Today, Kalisz is an important centre of the textile, clothing, metal and food industries. In 1975, Kalisz again became a voivodship capital, with a population of 95,000. The most important historical buildings in Kalisz are the Gothic monastery and church of the Franciscans, the Gothic church of St. Nicholas and also the late Renaissance church of the Jesuits; nearby is the former palace of the Gniezno archbishops, which was remodelled in Classicist style (55), and on the banks of the River Prosna, stands the beautiful W. Bogusławski Theatre (54).

52

53

54 56

55

57

58 Deposits of brown coal occur in many places in Wielkopolska. Mining of brown coal on a large scale started in 1958, first in the vicinity of Konin (57) and then at Turek. Three power stations utilizing the brown coal have been built at Gosławice, Pątnów and Adamów, and also an aluminium plant near Konin. A large new brown coal open cast mine is now under construction at Bełchatów, as well as industrial works to utilize its production.

Situated at the point where Wielkopolska, Małopolska and Mazowsze meet, Piotrków, first mentioned in chronicles in 1217, became a strong centre of trade and handicrafts in later centuries. After the unification of the Kingdom, general assemblies, sessions of the Diet and church councils were frequently held there, and from 1578, it was the seat of the Crown Tribunal. Fires and war damage in the 17th and 18th centuries led to the town's decline. It was only in the 19th century that it became an important economic and cultural centre and from 1867, capital of a governmental unit. Today, Piotrków is a centre of the engineering, glass and textile industries, and since 1975, a voivodship capital. The historical buildings worthy of note in Piotrków are the Gothic and Baroque monasteries, the castle built in 1511 (later reconstructed) and the burghers' houses round the Market Place, which date back to the 18th and 19th centuries. The Voivodship Office is in a sumptuous building in the style characteristic of the fin de siècle (58).

Not far from Piotrków, at Polichno, on the fast motor road from Warsaw to Upper Silesia, there is a new motel (59).

Łódź, although it was granted municipal status in 1423, is a product of the 19th century. The wide-scale programme for the industrialization of the country launched by the government of the Polish Kingdom envisaged the future development of the textile industry in the underdeveloped areas in the watershed of the Vistula and Warta rivers, which had abundant water springs. Numerous settlements were built there and weavers from Bohemia, Silesia and other parts of Germany were brought there. Łódź became the leading settlement of this industrial district. In the years 1835–1837, Ludwik Geyer built the first steam-driven spinning mill there (62). Today it houses the Museum of the History of the Textile Industry. Other industrialists followed his example. The lifting of the customs barrier between the Kingdom and Russia in 1850, opened up absorbant markets for the industry of Łódź, and more and more factories were built: spinning mills, weaving, bleaching and dye works, etc. The transport of goods and products in and out of Łódź was facilitated by the railway lines then being built. During the First World War, the Łódź industries suffered great losses owing to the fact that the Germans removed and took away the machines and installations from the factories. However, Łódź soon recovered after the war. It also became a voivodship capital.

59

60

61

Annexed to the Third Reich in 1939, Łódź went through a period of
persecutions. After its liberation in 1945, the industrial works of the town,
which had not been damaged, quickly started production. Later years brought
the modernization of the textile industry and the development of the
engineering, chemical and clothing industries, as well as other factories. The
town has become an important cultural centre, the seat of the University and
other higher schools of learning, with theatres, a philharmonia, museums and
libraries. Today it has a population of 820,000.

The territorial development of Łódź at first proceeded according to the plans
of R. Rembieliński, in a southerly direction. It was then that Nowe Miasto
(New Town) was built, with the Plac Wolności (Freedom Square) in its centre
(61) and its Town Hall and a Protestant church. Later the town expanded
further south, along the Piotrków route, which is today's Piotrkowska St.
(64). The development of the town was intended to follow a plan of great
clarity that was regarded as a model of good town planning at that time.
Later, however, its development assumed a spontaneous and chaotic
character, with tenement houses, factories, the poor dwellings of the workers
and the sumptuous palaces of the factory owners (63) all jostling each other
and covering ever larger areas. The houses, and even whole urban districts
with no sanitary facilities, defied even the most elementary requirements of
hygiene.

After the Second World War, work was commenced on the restructuring of
Łódź. New, well equipped residential districts are growing up (60). The
central district of the town is being replanned and new public buildings and
blocks of flats are being built there (1).

62

65

66 On the borderline of Wielkopolska and Mazowsze – in the Bzura Valley, which constitutes part of the Great Warsaw–Berlin Pradoline – is the town of Łęczyca. A powerful stronghold existed here as early as the 6th to 8th centuries, the centre of the tribe of Łężycanes, who were included in the state of Mieszko I. From the 12th century, Łęczyca was the capital of a duchy, and later, of a voivodship. The stronghold and the trading settlement next to it, which was later called the Old Town, were situated to the east of the present town on the site of today's village of Tum. After the town was burnt down by the Teutonic Knights in 1331, it was transferred to its present site. Casimir the Great had defence walls erected round the town and built a castle there. Łęczyca was granted municipal status in 1400. In the 15th to 17th centuries, it was a centre of trade and handicrafts, the place of assemblies, sessions of the Diet and church councils. The wars and epidemics of the 17th and 18th centuries brought the decline of the town. In the time of the Congress Kingdom, Łęczyca was chosen as a centre of the textile industry that was being developed. However, owing to the competition from Łódź, the textile industry there declined. Today, Łęczyca is a centre of the engineering and food industries. Nearby the town is an iron ore mine.

The Collegiate church in Tum (65) is an interesting example of Romanesque architecture. It was built in the years 1141–1161 on the site of a Benedictine Abbey that was probably built in the year 997 by St. Adalbert. It is built of stone, with two towers and once had a defence character. It succesfully resisted the attacks of the Lithuanians and of the Teutonic Knights. After a fire in 1473, it was rebuilt and remodelled several times. In 1939, it was bombed and damaged by fire. The reconstruction of the church after the war restored the original Romanesque features. Apart from the general layout, a beautifully carved portal has survived from the original Romanesque Collegiate church. There is an extensive view of the valley of the River Bzura from the windows of the towers (66), which are decorated with Romanesque columns.

The Mazowsze and Podlasie Lowlands

1

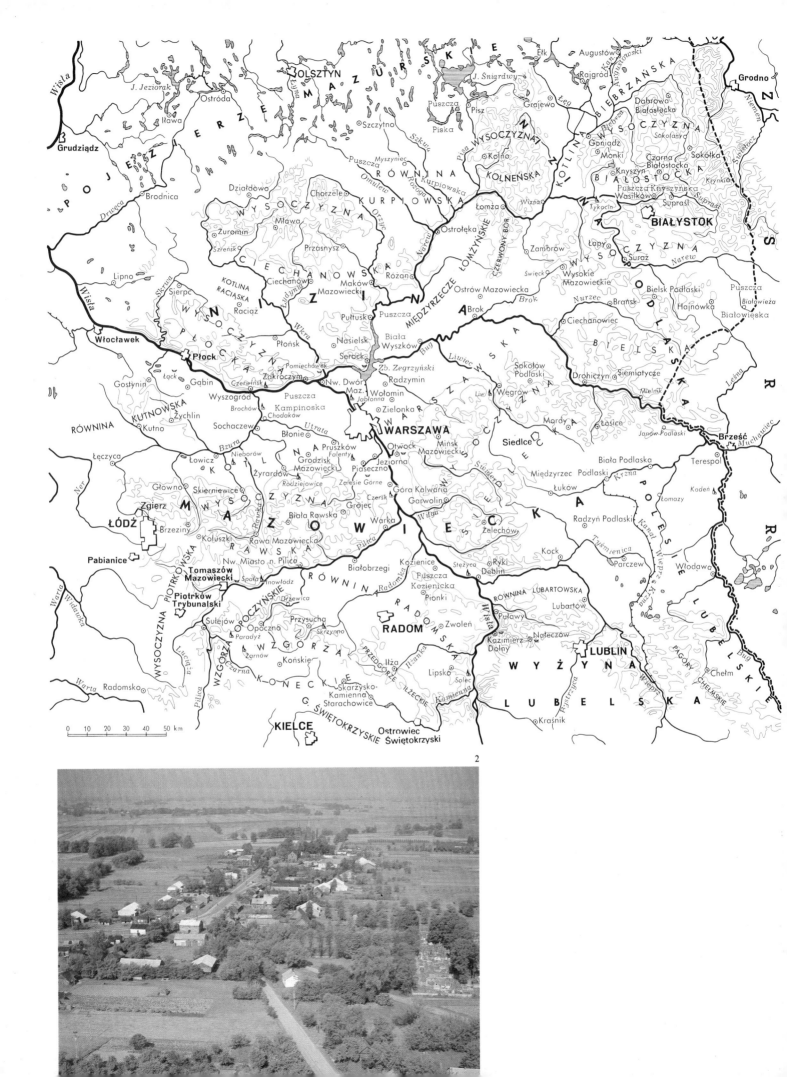

Wisła
Grudziądz
B
POJEZ
ERZE
MAZURSKIE
OLSZTYN
J. Jeziorak
Ostróda
Iława
J. Śniardwy
Ełk
Augustów
Kanał Augustowski
Rajgród
Grodno
Łyna
Szczytno
Puszcza
Piska
Pisz
Grajewo
Łęg
KOTLINA BIEBRZAŃSKA
Dąbrowa
Białostocka
Z
Niemen
Szkwa
Biebrza
Sokolany
WYSOCZYZNA
BIAŁOSTOCKA
Brodnica
Drwęca
Działdowo
Puszcza
Myszyniec
Omulew
Kurpiowska
Rozoga
RÓWNINA
Kolno
WYSOCZYZNA
KOLNEŃSKA
Goniądz
Mońki
Czarna
Białostocka
Sokółka
N
Krynki
Supraśl
Szreńsk
Żuromin
Mława
Przasnysz
WYSOCZYZNA
KURPIOWSKA
Orzyc
Łomża
Wizna
Tykocin
Knyszyn
Wasilków
Supraśl
Lipno
Skrwa
Ciechanowska
Chorzele
Narew
Ostrołęka
Zambrów
Łapy
Suraż
Narew
BIAŁYSTOK
WYSOCZYZNA
Sierpc
KOTLINA
RACIĄSKA
Raciąż
Ciechanów
Maków
Mazowiecki
Różan
MIĘDZYRZECZE ŁOMŻYŃSKIE
CZERWONY BÓR
Święck
Ostrów Mazowiecka
Wysokie
Mazowieckie
Bielsk Podlaski
Puszcza
Białowieża
Włocławek
Wisła
Ludynia
Płońsk
Wkra
Pułtusk
Puszcza
Biała
Wyszków
A
Brok
Brok
Nurzec
Ciechanowiec
Brańsk
Hajnówka
Białowieska
Płock
Zakroczym
Czerwińsk
Nasielsk
Serock
Bug
Liwiec
Sokołów
Podlaski
Drohiczyn
Siemiatycze
Leśna
R
Gostynin
Łąck
Gąbin
Pomiechówek
Nw. Dwór
Maz.
Zb. Zegrzyński
Radzymin
Zielonka
Wołomin
Jabłonna
Mielnik
BIELSKA
Wyszogród
Puszcza
Kampinoska
Brochów
Chodaków
WARSZAWA
Liw
Węgrów
Łosice
Janów Podlaski
Brześć
Muchawiec
KUTNOWSKA
Żychlin
Sochaczew
Błonie
Utrata
Pruszków
Falenty
Otwock
Mińsk
Mazowiecki
Siedlce
Mordy
RÓWNINA
Kutno
Bzura
Łowicz
Nieborów
Grodzisk
Mazowiecki
Jeziorna
Piaseczno
Świder
Biała Podlaska
Międzyrzec Podlaski
Krzna
Terespol
Łęczyca
Ner
Głowno
Skierniewice
Żyrardów
Rawka
Rodziejowice
Zalesie Górne
Góra Kalwaria
Czersk
Garwolin
Wilga
Łuków
Łomazy
Kodeń
Zgierz
Brzeziny
MWYSOCZYZNA
Biała Rawska
Grójec
Warka
Pilica
Żelechów
Radzyń Podlaski
Kanał Wieprz-Krzna
Parczew
POLESIE LUBELSKIE
Włodawa
ŁÓDŹ
Koluszki
Rawa Mazowiecka
Kozienice
Kock
Tyśmienica
R
Pabianice
RAWSKA
Nw. Miasto n. Pilicą
Białobrzegi
Puszcza
Kozienicka
Stężyca
Ryki
Dęblin
RÓWNINA LUBARTOWSKA
Lubartów
Tomaszów
Mazowiecki
Spała
Inowłódz
RÓWNINA
Radomka
Pionki
Wieprz
Wisła
Puławy
Bug
Widawka
Piotrków
Trybunalski
OPOCZYŃSKIE
Drzewica
RADOMSKA
RADOM
Zwoleń
Kazimierz
Dolny
Nałęczów
LUBLIN
PAGORY
CHEŁMSKIE
Chełm
Warta
Sulejów
Opoczno
Skrzynno
Przysucha
Ilża
Iłżanka
Lipsko
Solec
Kamienna
WYŻYNA
WYSOCZYZNA
Paradyż
Żarnów
WZGÓRZA
Końskie
PRZEDGÓRZE
IŁŻECKIE
Wieprz
Rybrzyca
LUBELSKA
Warta
Radomsko
Pilica
Luciąża
Czarna
KONECKIE
Skarżysko-
Kamienna
Starachowice
G. ŚWIĘTOKRZYSKIE
Kraśnik
LUBELSKA
0 10 20 30 40 50 km
KIELCE
ŚWIĘTOKRZYSKIE
Ostrowiec
Świętokrzyski

2

East of the River Vistula, the Baltic Glaciation did not extend so far to the south as it did to the west and the successive stages of this glaciation ended in almost the same place, covering each other. In connection with this, the borderline between the deposits of the Baltic Glaciation (Würm) and of the Central Polish Glaciation (Riss) runs more to the north and is more clearly defined. The whole area of the Mazowsze and Podlasie Lowlands comes within the range of the Central Polish Glaciation. It is an area where the glacial relief has been destroyed, almost without lakes, and comprises three different regions, namely, the Mazowsze Lowland, which is part of the Central European Plain, and the Podlasie Lowland and Lublin-Polesie, which are parts of the East European Plain.

From the historical point of view, the area comprises the provinces of Mazowsze and Podlasie, and in the east very small parts of the former Grand Duchy of Lithuania. Apart from Warsaw and its surroundings, this area is not so industrialized and well developed as other regions of the country.

The Mazowsze Lowland covers the largest area. Its central part is the extensive Warsaw Basin, which is a remnant of a former ice dammed lake of the glacial period, into which numerous river valleys run concentrically. These are either wide pradolines of the peri-glacial period or the narrower river valleys formed in the period when the ice-sheet had already given free access to the Baltic. These valleys link the Warsaw Basin with the rest of the Mazowsze Lowland and the regions surrounding it. Thus the Warsaw Basin is linked in the west by the Bzura Pradoline with the large Warsaw-Berlin Pradoline, and in the north-west by the Vistula Valley with the Toruń Basin and through this basin with the Toruń-Eberswalde Pradoline. In the north-east, the pradoline of the Narew and Biebrza links the Warsaw Basin with the Podlasie Lowland and the River Niemen, and in the east the valley of the River Bug links it with the great Polesie Basin. The Warsaw Basin is also linked directly with Polesie by the valley of the middle Vistula and the pradoline of the Wieprz and Krzna rivers.

The Warsaw Basin divides the Mazowsze Lowland into three parts. They are the northern, southern and eastern Mazowsze Lowlands, each of which comprises smaller units. They are mostly covered by ground moraine deposits, the landforms being considerably levelled by periglacial processes and the action of water. Only here and there is the monotonous landscape relieved by the remains of end moraines.

The Podlasie Lowland, situated to the east of the Mazowsze Lowland, is part of another larger unit, for it is the western end of the Great Byelorussian Elevation, which is part of the East Baltic Plain. It is distinguished by the different direction of the end moraines left by a stage younger than the Warta Stage, of the Central Polish Glaciation (called the Northern Polesie Stage), considered by some researchers to be a trace of a separate glaciation. Within Poland's frontiers, four parts of the Podlasie Lowland can be distinguished, namely, the Kolno Elevation, the Biebrza Basin and the Białystok and Bielsk Elevations.

To the south-east of the Mazowsze Lowland, the western end of the great Polesie Plain, known as Lublin Polesie, extends into Poland. It is characterized by a predominance of accumulation forms, such as large sandy or peatbog plains, from which rise residual humps of glacial origin. This area, like the whole of Polesie, was once covered for a long time by the waters of a great inland lake (probably through the whole of the last inter-glacial period and the Baltic Glaciation). After the lake dried up, an abundance of peat was formed from swamp vegetation. The high level of ground water is responsible for the numerous bogs and shallow silty lakes. To the south there is a cretaceous bedrock, not very deep under the surface.

The deeper substratum of the Mazowsze and Podlasie Lowlands has not been throughly investigated so far. Until recently it was only known that the thick layers of glacial deposits cover Tertiary formations, which, to the east on the Byelorussian Elevation and insularly elsewhere, give way to a cretaceous substratum. Some new information has been obtained from the studies carried out during the last twenty years.

In the west, the bedding of the Mazowsze Lowland is formed by the slopes of the Kujawy-Pomeranian Anticlinorium built of Mesozoic formations. Towards the east, they are covered by thick Cretaceous and Tertiary layers. This area is linked with the West European zone of folded mountains. The areas further east are part of the great crystalline East European Platform, built of igneous rocks, and in connection with this there is the possibility of various minerals occurring there, particularly metal ores. Thus knowledge of the depth of this platform is of great significance. So far it has been ascertained that in the area between Warsaw and Białystok, old crystalline formations go down to a depth of 2,500 metres and form a kind of basin (called the Białystok Depression) while towards the north and south they get shallower, at a depth of 500 to 1,500 metres. The whole platform is covered with thick layers of Cretaceous and Tertiary deposits; towards the south and north east, the Tertiary deposits gradually disappear and Cretaceous deposits are found directly under the Quaternary deposits. Cretaceous deposits in the form of chalk, suitable for writing and drawing, also occur there insularly in several places under Quaternary deposits. They are exploited for industrial purposes. However, the Quaternary deposits are of basic importance. Erratic blocks are used in building, mainly road construction, and the building materials industry uses the gravel and the outwash and alluvial sands. The finer quality sand is used in the glass industry. The various clays and Quaternary loams are basic raw materials for the production of bricks. The most highly valued are the plastic varve loams exploited in the Warsaw Basin, and in the vicinity of Płock and Białystok, for the production of building ceramics. In the past, the bog iron ores found above all in the pradolines were also exploited. The peat occurring over large areas was exploited as fuel and, to a lesser extent, as manure or for industrial purposes. Research and experiments are going on to find ways of utilizing the abundant peat bogs in agriculture. In the smaller peat meadows melioration work has been conducted for a long time. In connection with melioration work the canal linking the Wieprz and the Krzna rivers was built. In recent years, melioration work has been carried out to drain the bogs of Wizna and Kuwasy on the Biebrza. However, the opinion is ever more frequently being voiced that the peat bogs, which are great water reservoirs, should be left untouched in order not to disturb the water and climatic conditions proper to the region. In some swampy areas, the alders and osier thickets that once grew abundantly over the water-logged ground have been preserved in a more or less changed form. Many years ago this was the habitat of the elk, beaver, otter and mink, and also the wood grouse, black cock, and various swamp and water birds. The mink is now extinct, the elk can only be seen now in the nature reserves in the area of the Red Swamp near Rajgród and in the Białowieża and Kampinos Forests, where they have been introduced by man. The beaver now lives in several nature reserves in the valley of the Biebrza and the lake districts. Water birds can still be seen in the marshes and overflow arms of the Narew and Biebrza rivers, whose waters abound in fish, above all sheatfish.

The flora and fauna of these areas have much in common with those further to the north-east. There are many relics of the glacial period, particularly among the peat bog vegetation. In the north-eastern part of the Podlasie Lowland, which has a more continental climate with a longer severe winter, the blue hare has its habitat. Summer all over the whole area of the Mazowsze-Podlasie Lowland is long and hot. The rainfall, which is 500 mm. in the western part (less in some places), increases towards the east, up to 600 mm. an more.

The variations in the vegetation cover are related to the climatic conditions. In the Mazowsze Lowland, dry pine forests on sandy soils predominate, and also in the ice-dammed lake areas of the Warsaw Basin (the Kampinos Forest) and the Kurpie Plain (the Kurpie Forest). In many places the felling of trees in these forests has disturbed the sand dunes, as a result of which sand has encroached upon the surrounding fields and meadows. In the depressions between the sand dunes one often finds raised peat bogs with the vegetation typical of such areas (marsh tea, bog bilberries, cranberries and sundew). Here and there, among the dry pine forests, there are fresh pine or mixed forests growing on patches of more fertile, tighter soils. Most of the better soils have for a long time been cultivated by farmers. Also the heavy, clayey, loamy or silt soils near Ciechanów, Płock, Grójec, Siedlce and Łomża have long been used as arable land. These soils were once grown with hornbeam and oak gronds. Low gronds or even mixed marsh forests also probably grew on the most fertile soils of the Mazowsze Lowland – the black earths covering large areas in the vicinity of Błonie and Sochaczew.

Towards the east the character of the forests in the Mazowsze-Podlasie Lowlands changes. In the fresh pine and mixed forests as well as in gronds, the spruce appears ever more frequently. The mixed pine and oak forests give way to the richer and more humid boreal mixed forests, in which the spruce has a position equal to that of the pine. The moister but more fertile soils are covered with alder-ash ols forests with spruce. The alder-ash ols woods, like the gronds, have lush undergrowth. The Białowieża Forest is the best preserved natural forest complex of the Polish Lowland. At present it covers an area of 1,430 sq.km. (it was once much larger), half of which is in Poland.

The Białowieża National Park (47 sq.km.) is in the centre of it. In the National Park there are almost all the types of forest typical to the eastern part of the Polish Plain, particularly the magnificent oak-hornbeam gronds, boreal mixed forests, alder and ash ols woods, fresh and bog pine forests and osier-thickets. The Białowieża Forest is also the habitat of a rich animal world. Lynx, wolves, deer and roedeer live wild there. The birds living there are grouse, wood cock, hazel grouse, black storks, herons, ruffs, water cranes, owls and eagles. This is the only place where the European bison has survived in its natural surroundings. The elk was introduced there again after the last war.

The earliest traces of man in the Mazowsze Lowland are from the late Palaeolithic Age, approximately 50,000 years ago. A great deal of evidence of the presence of man has been preserved from the close of the glacial period (20–10 thousand years B.C.), when this area was inhabited by hunters and fishermen, who were already using bows. In the middle of the Neolithic Age, agriculture made its appearance in the southern parts of the Mazowsze Lowland and by the Late Neolithic Age (2000–800 B.C.) agriculture had spread all over the Mazowsze Lowland, later embracing the Podlasie Lowland, too. It was the primitive slash and burn agriculture connected with the grazing of pigs, sheep and cattle in the forests and forest clearings. The Lusatian culture embraced the Mazowsze Lowland, where a separate group of this culture was formed, while the Podlasie Lowlands was then inhabited by peoples with a different culture and customs. Traces exist of a late Roman trade route running through Mazowsze (Mazovia) linking the Black Sea with the Baltic.

At the time when the framework of a state organization was being shaped along the Upper Vistula, Odra, Warta and on the shores of Lake Gopło, the sparsely populated Mazowsze region did not play any important role. During the rule of Mieszko I, there were already settlements in the western parts of Mazowsze, probably connected with the movement of settlers from Kujawy and the Łęczyca area, where the powerful stronghold of Łęczyca already existed in the 5th and 6th centuries. The settlers moved in several directions – westwards, along the fertile pradoline of the River Bzura, then to the black earths around Błonie and Sochaczew and to the Grójec and Czersk region, to the Vistula. To the south, they moved into the Piotrków Elevation, where they met settlers from Sieradz coming from the west and settlers from Małoposka coming from the south. The later colonization of the areas to the north of the Holy Cross Mts. was also by settlers from Łęczyca. In the north, settlers from Kujawy moved along the Vistula, crossing it and occupying the areas round Płock, then Wyszogród, then crossing again to the Vistula left bank, they met the settlers from Łęczyca. For a long time, settlement of the Mazowsze region was confined mainly to areas round strongholds and the fields scattered through the forests. In addition to farming, the other occupations of the settlers were hunting and keeping of wild forest bees.

Separatist tendencies were very strong in Mazowsze. Taking advantage of the confusion that resulted from the revolt of the feudal lords against the central authorities and the antifeudal people's uprising, the local potentate Masław set up an independent duchy in Mazowsze in 1037. After this province was regained ten years later by Casimir the Restorer, it passed into the hands of one of the Piast princes, who resided permanently in Płock. By virtue of the last will and testament of Bolesław the Wrymouthed in 1138, which initiated the period of feudal fragmentation in Poland, Mazowsze, together with Kujawy and Sieradz, constituted one province ruled by a prince, which was shortly afterwards divided into several duchies. This was at the same time a period of the most intensive colonization processes, in which the Church played a very important role. Mazovian settlers moved eastwards in the direction of Podlasie along the Narew and Bug rivers and their tributaries. In the northeast they reached the basin of the River Łęg – a tributary of the Biebrza, where their stronghold was Rajgród, captured from the Sudavians. In the south-east they soon met the Ruthenian settlers who were moving from the south along the River Bug and its tributaries. In the 12th and 13th centuries continuous battles were fought over the border strongholds of Drohiczyn, Mielnik and Bielsk. In the north, Mazovian expansion settled the Ciechanów Elevation as far as the territory of the Prussians. The attempts made by the Mazovian princes to incorporate Prussia did not succeed, but brought in their wake Prussian attacks on Mazowsze. In 1226, Prince Conrad of Mazowsze enlisted the help of the Teutonic Knights, who soon occupied Prussia and became a threat not only to Mazowsze, but to the whole of Poland.

In the 13th century and the first half of the 14th century there were continuous battles with the Sudavians and later with the Lithuanians and the Teutonic Knights. The Sudavians were weakened by Polish and Ruthenian expeditions and then destroyed by the Teutonic Knights. The Lithuanian invasions, resulting from the rivalry between Poland and Lithuania for the border zone of Podlasie which was inhabited by Poles and Ruthenians, lasted longer. This long period of constant battles caused a lot of destruction in Mazowsze and Podlasie. Many towns and strongholds were destroyed or went into decline. Threatened by invasion, Mazowsze sought aid from the already united Poland and in 1351 became a Polish vassal land. At this time crossing the Vistula assumed significance, as did Warsaw, which grew up at the end of the 13th century as an intermediary centre in Ruthenian-Teutonic trade. At the end of the 14th century it became the capital of the southern part of Mazowsze. The rapprochement between Poland and Lithuania at the end of the 14th century created more favourable conditions for the development of Mazowsze. Another factor conducive to this was the regaining of Poland's access to the sea (1466). The Vistula became an important communication artery for the transport of agricultural and forest produce from Kujawy and Mazowsze, and later also from Podlasie, Małopolska and even Lithuania and Ruthenian territories, to Toruń and Gdańsk. The towns on the Vistula, Bug and Narew developed. After the last of the Mazovian princes had died the final unification of Mazowsze with Poland took place (1529). The Lublin Union (1569) brought Podlasie to Poland.

In the united state, the central position of Mazowsze assumed special significance. Warsaw became an important junction where routes crossed from Cracow and Wielkopolska to Lithuania and from Wielkopolska and the Prussian towns to Ruthenia. Diets were held there and also the elections of kings. In 1596, King Sigismund III Vasa transferred the capital of the state from Cracow to Warsaw.

In the 16th century and at the beginning of the 17th century, Mazowsze was already densely populated and settlement penetrated ever deeper into the unknown forests. However, the region retained many specific features resulting from its long period of independent development. Intensive development of towns came later there, and so did the development of the estate corvée system. There were not many big magnates estates, but – and this is characteristic of the province – there were settlements of the petty gentry, often running their small farms by themselves. After Poland's union with Lithuania, the petty gentry settled in large numbers in the border zone of Mazowsze and Podlasie, colonizing the Podlasie region and penetrating into Lithuania and Ruthenia. Their political importance increased in the times of the free election of Polish kings, when the votes of the uneducated and fanatic gentry, who were often tools in the hands of the magnates looking after their own selfish interests, were often decisive in determining the future of the country.

A different structure of settlement existed in the Podlasie Lowland, particularly in the area of the Grand Duchy of Lithuania, where there were vast estates belonging to the magnates and to the Crown and it was only in the 16th century, by virtue of a land reform called the "pomiara włóczna", that land regulation and the three-field system was introduced.

The wars of the second half of the 17th century and the beginning of the 18th century and the destruction and epidemics they brought caused the economic decline of the Mazowsze and Podlasie Lowlands. Ninety per cent of the population was lost to the towns, trade and handicrafts slumped. In the rural areas, oppression of the peasants increased, causing resistance and flight. The magnates estates grew larger, particularly in the Podlasie region, and ever more magnificent palaces and parks appeared, built and laid out according to French and English models.

In Warsaw, which was being rebuilt after the wars, new royal and magnates palaces, and also churches and monasteries were erected. The capital lived through a period of greatly accelerated development in the Enlightenment Period. The quick growth of the city is proved by its population, which increased from 30,000 to 120,000 in the second half of the 18th century, placing Warsaw among the first ten biggest cities in Europe. At that time it became a big economic centre. In the city itself and the surroundings, manufactures and banks were set up and the number of shops increased. The Agricultural and Medical Institute was founded at Ujazdów. Cultural and artistic life flourished under the patronage of King Stanisław Augustus Poniatowski. Warsaw was a centre of the struggle for the political and social resurrection of the country, the place where national integration was being forged. Warsaw was the scene of the debates of the Four Year Diet, known as the Great Diet (1788–1792), which passed decisions on a number of progressive changes in Poland's political system, expressed in the Constitution of May 3rd, 1791. Unfortunately these measures were undertaken too late to save the sovereignty of the country. After the second partition (1793), the western part of Mazowsze came under the rule of Prussia, which after the third partition (1795) seized more territories of Mazowsze and Podlasie, situated to the north of the Pilica and Bug rivers. The rest of the Mazowsze and Podlasie Lowlands were taken by Austria. There was a decrease in the population of Warsaw, now deprived of its functions, and economic life declined. In the years 1807–1815, it became for a short time the capital of the Duchy of Warsaw, which comprised the whole of Mazowsze and the southern part of Podlasie. The northern part, as the Białystok district, went to Russia.

After the Congress of Vienna, the whole areas of the Mazowsze and Podlasie Lowlands came under Russian rule. The Białystok district was directly incorporated into the empire and the other territories became part of the Polish Kingdom, linked with Russia by a personal union. Ravaged during the Napoleonic wars, the country gradually began the work of reconstruction. Warsaw, the seat of the autonomous authorities of the Kingdom, also became the site of central economic, educational and scientific institutions. Industry developed, mainly the metal and food industries. The suppression of the November Insurrection (1830–1831) resulted in the withdrawal of the autonomy of the Kingdom. Compulsory contributions and repressions checked its economic development. High customs duties were imposed on Polish goods on the border between the Kingdom and Russia. Seeking possibilities of reaching Russian markets, some of the weaving workshops moved from the Kingdom to Białystok, thus forming the nucleus of a new industrial district. When the customs barrier was lifted in 1850, industry in the Kingdom again began to have access to Russian markets, which created more favourable conditions for development. The home market developed slowly in connection with changes in agriculture. In the western part of Mazowsze there were tendencies towards modernizing the agricultural economy, developing stock breeding and the processing of farm produce. Progress was also made in introducing land renting for the peasants.

The January Insurrection (1863–1864), again plunged the country into the turmoil of war. Mazowsze and Podlasie were the scene of the insurgents' heroic struggle. After the Insurrection had been suppressed there was an increase in repressions and tendencies toward erasing the separate character of the Kingdom and even its name was changed to "Privislinski Kraj" (Vistulan Land).

As regards social and economic growth, the enfranchisement of the peasants in 1864 was a significant move. In the Białystok region this was done in 1861. This paved the way for the development of the capitalist system. There was a rapid growth of industry and Warsaw was one of the industrial districts. Together with the Białystok Industrial District they were the only centres of industry in the Mazowsze and Podlasie Lowlands. Agriculture only showed a definite development in the western part of the Lowland, the rate getting slower and slower towards the east, where the traditional agricultural economy still prevailed, not only in the peasant farms, but also the landed estates. Many big landowners sold some of their land in lots and felled forests (the area of which decreased rapidly) in order to raise funds to pay for hired labour and for improvements on their farms.

During the First World War, the Mazowsze and Podlasie Lowlands suffered considerably from the hostilities, evacuation of the population and the destruction of industrial and other enterprises by the retreating Tsarist army, and afterwards from plundering and deliberate devastation by the German occupational authorities. After independence was regained in 1918, these Lowlands were within the frontiers of the reborn Polish state, but this was an economically neglected area. Only the western part of Mazowsze was better developed. In the Kutno and Płock regions, agriculture was on a higher level.

Warsaw – the capital of the country – was a big centre of industry, trade, culture and science, but it was also a city of great social contrasts. Apart from the central district and the residential districts that were growing up, in which the propertied classes, civil servants and army officers lived, there were poor workers' districts and the densely populated Jewish districts, where small trading enterprises and handicraft workshops were concentrated. There were also contrasts between Warsaw and the area surrounding it, particularly to the north and east, where there were small backward peasant farms and small towns living mainly from excessively developed middleman activities in the trade exchange between the villages and towns. Only in the immediate vicinity of Warsaw, on the left bank of the Vistula was there a developed suburban zone supplying the capital with vegetables, fruit and milk. Along the transport lines several satellite settlements of varying housing standards grew up. The high price of land in Warsaw also led to the location of industrial enterprises in the suburban areas. The Second World War brought terrible destruction. During the September Campaign of 1939, the areas to the west and north of Warsaw and the city itself during its heroic defence, suffered an enormous amount of damage. During the Nazi occupation, the southern part of Mazowsze with Warsaw came within what was known as the General Gouvernement, while the rest of the Lowlands were incorporated directly into the Reich. The policy of terror, national and racial oppression, repressions and persecution and the hard conditions of life, as well as the deliberate destruction of the economic and cultural potential of the country brought enormous losses in material goods and human life, in which the share of Mazowsze and

Podlasie was a very large one. Warsaw was the main centre of the Polish underground resistance movement, so repressions there were particularly cruel. The city was twice the scene of armed risings – in 1943 the rising in the Jewish Ghetto, and in 1944, the Warsaw Uprising. The latter lasted two months (August and September) and was a stubborn battle for every house, every inch of ground. The fighting was followed by the deliberate and systematic blowing up and burning of the remaining buildings by special teams carrying out Hitler's order to completely destroy the city, as a result of which the whole of left-bank Warsaw lay in ruins. Many priceless works of art and relics of the national culture were lost then. Archives, museums, libraries, historical buildings were all destroyed. Eighty five per cent of the buildings of Warsaw became smouldering ruins (nearly 100% in the central district), 90% of Warsaw industry was destroyed, 30% of the water mains and sewers, and 87% of the municipal transport. Human losses are estimated at 600,000 to 800,000 persons. Liberated in January 1945, left bank Warsaw was a desert of stones. Only the districts situated on the right bank of the Vistula, not embraced by the Uprising and liberated several months earlier, remained standing and inhabited by about 120,000 people. Great destruction was also caused by the last phase of the war, outside Warsaw, particularly the areas along the Vistula and Narew, where the front-line fighting lasted longer.

After the Second World War, the country underwent great changes in connection with the new political system and the social and economic reforms that were carried out and gave a new direction and tempo to its development. The first post-war years were devoted, above all, to removing the ravages of the war and occupation. Great importance was attached to the speedy reconstruction of the capital. Like the phoenix, Warsaw rose from the ashes in the course of several years to live again as a modern city, throbbing with life. The clearing of mines and reconstruction of front-line areas that had suffered badly was carried out in a short time. Transport and industry were set in motion and waste land was ploughed. After the period of reconstruction came the time for the planned development of the economy, special attention being paid to the expansion of industry and its restructuring. An important problem that was gradually solved was the activation of the less developed regions of the country, among them large areas of the Mazowsze and Podlasie Lowlands. It takes great efforts to make good the arrears of centuries of retarded development and in spite of the undoubted progress that has been made in this respect, there are still differences between the western part of the Lowlands and the eastern areas.

The biggest concentration of industry in the Mazowsze–Podlasie Lowlands is the Warsaw Industrial District. Apart from Warsaw there are quite large centres of industry in the suburban zone of Warsaw, at Pruszków, Żyrardów and Grodzisk. The speedy rate of post-war reconstruction was connected with changes in the character of industrial production and its concentration in big plants. The dominant position is held by the electrical engineering industry, including the electronic industry, supplying radio valves, oscilloscope tubes and kinescope lamps, radio and TV sets, tape recorders, etc. with works in Warsaw and Piaseczno, the electrotechnical industry, producing high tension apparatus, electric motors and telephone apparatus, cables etc., in Warsaw and Ożarów, and the precision instrument industry in Warsaw and Błonie. The engineering industry has developed well, with the L. Waryński Building Machine Factory in Warsaw and the Machine Tool Factory in Pruszków. Also the industry producing transport vehicles – cars in Warsaw, tractors in Warsaw–Ursus, the Railway Rolling Stock Repair Works in Pruszków and Capital Repair Works in Mińsk Mazowiecki. The "Warszawa" Steel Works producing fine steel and rolled goods has been operating in Warsaw since 1952. The role of the printing industry is growing. It now supplies one third of the national production in this field. The food industry is also developing well. Despite the production growth, the share of the chemical industry represented by pharmaceutical works, factories producing synthetic textile fibre, cosmetics, etc. in the capital, Chodaków and Grodzisk has diminished. There has been a decrease in the role of the light industry, the leading position being held by the linen industry in Żyrardów, the production of pure silk in Milanówek and the expanded clothing industry with its centre in Warsaw. The capital is also an important centre producing and generating power. An extension of the Warsaw Industrial District in the direction of Łódź is Tomaszów Mazowiecki, a centre of the woollen textile industry, the clothing industry and production of synthetic textile fibre.

The next biggest industrial centre after Warsaw in the Mazowsze–Podlasie Lowlands is Radom, which has a well developed engineering industry, leather, ceramic, tobacco and food industries. Near Radom, in Pionki, a big chemical plant has been set in motion, in Kozienice – a big power plant, and in Puławy, a large nitrogen plant. In the north-eastern part of the Lowlands, a quickly growing industrial centre is Płock, known above all for its oil refineries and petrochemical plants, based on crude oil brought by pipeline from the USSR. There is also a growing agricultural machine industry in Płock, as well as a river shipyard and a growing number of food industry factories. The Kutno district is also a centre of the food industry, including sugar factories. In many places in the western part of Mazowsze there are building material factories and glass works.

On the other hand, the eastern part of the Mazowsze and Podlasie Lowlands is still lagging behind as regards development of industry. The only industrial centre here is Białystok and its surroundings, a traditional centre of the textile industry. In other places there are no large industrial plants, only a few small ones. The transport network is rather sparse, too.

Agriculture is also better developed in the western part of the Mazowsze region. Special mention is due to the specialized agricultural production in the Warsaw suburban zone, which has greatly expanded its scope since the war. It supplies fruit, vegetables and flowers not only to the capital, but also to Upper Silesia, Łódź, Szczecin and many other places, and also for export. The vegetable growing area, concentrated mainly to the west of Warsaw, extends quite a way in the direction of Łowicz and to the south. In the vicinity of Grójec and Góra Kalwaria large areas are under orchards. There has been a great expansion of plantations of currant bushes and strawberries.

Agriculture in the north and east of the Mazowsze region, Podlasie and Lublin Polesie has not attained such a high level. The agricultural economy in these areas is still rather traditional and not so productive, the main crops being rye and potatoes. To the east of Warsaw, up the River Bug, there has been a development of pig breeding.

The main urban centre of the Lowlands with an activating influence is 700-year-old Warsaw, which was rebuilt from ruins and maintained as the capital of the country by a decision of the central authorities with the full support of the whole nation. The tempo of its reconstruction is unprecedented in the world. Historical districts, churches, palaces and other buildings that are monuments to Polish culture have been reconstructed with solicitous and painstaking care. The reconstruction of the Royal Castle, started in 1971, is still in progress. Residential districts were quickly rebuilt and new ones erected to meet the needs of the growing population of the city, which now numbers 1.5 million. New thoroughfares and industrial projects have been built. The quick expansion of the city is going on all the time.

Reborn Warsaw is the seat of the central political, administrative and economic institutions of the country. It is also the seat of professional and trade organizations, social organizations, scientific institutes and societies and cultural institutions. There are 13 higher schools in Warsaw attended by 80,000 students and employing 20% of the academic staff of the country.

The largest of them are Warsaw University and the Warsaw Technical University. Warsaw is the seat of the Polish Academy of Sciences and several dozen research institutes, archives and libraries, above all the National Library. Among the numerous museums, the most important are the National Museum and the Polish Military Museum. The Warsaw galleries of modern-art are well known to all. The numerous theatres, some with a very high artistic level known in Europe, the well known Opera House and Philharmonia are among the cultural institutions that count in the world. Warsaw is also the biggest publishing centre in the country and the place where the International Book Fair is held every year. It is also a great industrial and trade centre and central junction.

Apart from its functions as the capital, Warsaw plays an important role as the economic and cultural centre of almost the whole of north-eastern Poland. It is, of course, the main urban centre of the voivodship and the zone directly bordering on it. Apart from those who commute to work in Warsaw every day, there are many people from this zone who travel to Warsaw for shopping, going to the theatre, concerts and shows. The residential settlements outside Warsaw form a great urban complex together with the capital, with a population of over two million.

The second biggest town in the Mazowsze and Podlasie Low-

lands is Białystok (pop. about 215,000), the biggest centre of north-eastern Poland. It is a relatively young town, as it only received the status of a town in the 18th century. It owes its development in the 19th century to the textile industry, which still plays an important role there. During the Second World War, Białystok suffered considerable losses. Eighty per cent of the buildings were destroyed and almost all the industrial plants. After its reconstruction, the town grew very quickly, as the capital of the voivodship and an industrial and cultural centre. Białystok has two higher schools attended by more than 5,000 students. The Białystok Scientific Society is very active. Its inhabitants are proud of its three theatres, symphony orchestra and museum.

Industrial Radom is developing very quickly (pop. 185,000). Before the First World War it was the seat of a governmental unit and since 1975, it is the capital of a new voivodship, also a junction and an ambitious cultural centre of growing significance.

A dynamically growing industrial centre of the Mazowsze region is Płock (pop. 96,000), one of the oldest town of that area which, after a long period of stagnation began to develop quickly in connection with the building of a petrochemical plant there in the Sixties. It has again assumed importance as a social, economic and cultural centre, and since 1975, also as a voivodship capital.

Apart from the above mentioned, there are six more smaller towns fulfilling the function of voivodship centres in the Mazowsze and Podlasie Lowlands. The biggest of these is Siedlce (pop. over 50,000), a centre of the engineering industry and food industry and also of trade. The other voivodship capitals are Skierniewice, Ciechanów, Ostrołęka, Łomża and Biała Podlaska, with a population from 30,000 (Skierniewice) to 35,000 (Biała Podlaska). All of them became voivodship towns two years ago and are just beginning to shape their radius of influence. Apart from their administrative functions, they also have industrial and trade functions and some are junctions. The network of voivodship towns is supplemented by small centres and urban settlements providing services for the surrounding areas. Apart from the Warsaw agglomeration, there are no towns with specialized industrial or recreational functions. Generally speaking, the network of towns in the Mazowsze and Podlasie Lowlands is unevenly developed. The dense, more developed network with larger centres in the west, gets sparser towards the east. The dominant pattern there are small settlements, not very well built, with a predominance of small one-storeyed dwellings, often built of wood. As a matter of fact, the buildings in most of the towns, even, in the western part of Mazowsze, leave much to be desired. In many of them the communal facilities are inadequate. An achievement of the last ten years is the development of educational and cultural facilities in all the urban centres of the Mazowsze and Podlasie Lowlands.

Mazowsze, particularly the northern part of the region, is the biggest area of scattered rural settlement in Poland, namely small hamlets and isolated settlements. This makes it difficult to organize proper services to the rural areas. In the southern part of the region, the predominant type is the street village and in the western part – row villages. Historically, Podlasie is an area with a predominance of line villages built during the "pomiara włóczna" land reform in the 16th century. They often stretch for kilometres in one straight line. In Lublin Polesie, the predominant type are street villages. In the western part of the Lowlands, there is a predominance of brick buildings. In the east most of the buildings are wooden, and one still sees thatched roofs there.

4

5   Warsaw, the capital and heart of Poland (1) is in the centre of the Mazowsze Lowland. Traces of the earliest settlement in the area of today's city date back to the Neolithic Age. In the 10th century, there was a stronghold on the right bank of the Vistula on the site of today's Stare Bródno district, with a trading settlement around it. In the 12th century, villages and trading settlements grew up on both banks of the Vistula. The further development of Warsaw was probably due to the fact that it became a castellan's seat, the residence of the castellan being a stronghold in the place where the Royal Castle stands today. Near the castle, on the steepest part of the Vistula escarpment, a new urban settlement – Old Warsaw – grew up about 1285 (4). At the beginning of the 14th century, it was granted municipal status on the basis of the Chełmno Law. The layout of the town, which has been preserved to this day, has a chequered arrangement of streets (5) and a large Market Place, in which stood a Town Hall that no longer exists today. The town was surrounded with defence walls. Its main functions were connected with the trade carried on along the routes from Wielkopolska and Silesia to Lithuania and Ruthenia. In 1408, Nowe Miasto (New Town) was founded on the area to the north of Old Warsaw, also on the basis of the Chełmno Law.

The importance of Warsaw increased after Prince Janusz I of Mazowsze transferred the capital of his duchy here from Czersk in 1413. In the second half of the 15th century, Warsaw became an important centre of Vistula trade. The inclusion of Mazowsze into the Crown lands (1526) strengthened its ties with other towns of Poland, and its central position in the united Polish-Lithuanian state made it a political and economic centre of national range. From 1564, the general assemblies of the Diet were held in Warsaw, and from 1573 the elections of the kings took place there.

In 1596 Sigismund III Vasa transferred the capital of the state to Warsaw. The 13th century castle was enlarged and remodelled to serve as the royal residence (3). From the middle of the 16th century both towns were enlarged and developed. Handicrafts began to flourish. The Gothic burghers' houses, among others those situated round the Market Place of the Old Town, were enlarged and reconstructed in the Renaissance and Baroque styles (6). The gentry began to move into the town in large numbers and outside its boundaries "iuridicae" (independent settlements) were set up, not subject to the municipal laws, which were the property of secular and ecclesiastical lords. In these settlements, particularly those to the south of the Old Town, new churches and magnates' palaces were built, among others, the palace of the Koniecpolski family, today the building of the Praesidium of the Council Ministers (11), and the Kazimierzowski Palace, today the seat of Warsaw University. A separate town, Praga, grew up on the right bank of the Vistula; in 1573 it was linked with Warsaw by the first permanent bridge across the Vistula. During the Swedish invasion of the years 1655–1657, Warsaw was devastated and looted. Its reconstruction in the second half of the century only embraced the magnates' residences. At the end of the century, new, late Baroque palaces were built, among others, the Pac Palace, famous for its original interiors, executed in the 19th century, for instance, the Mauritanian Room (7). The Northern War at the beginning of the 18th century brought more devastation. Reconstruction work was started after 1716 and in 1724 King Augustus II started the construction of a new royal residence – the Saxon Palace – of which only a part of the colonnade, over the Tomb of the Unknown Soldier (12), remained after the destruction of the last war. In the years 1727–1763, the late Baroque church of the Visitants (10) was built in Krakowskie Przedmieście St. (Cracow Suburb Street). Warsaw went through a period of flourishing development during the reign of King Stanisław Augustus Poniatowski, under whose patronage there was a flowering of art, literature and learning. Trade, manufactures and banks also developed. Beautiful burghers' houses and new palaces were erected, among them the Brühl, Tepper and Blank Palaces. The population of the capital increased to 150,000 in 1744. Warsaw was also a centre of political life and the progressive trends of the Enlightenment Period. It was in Warsaw that state reforms matured, the Constitution of May 3rd was proclaimed and the progressive group known as Kołłątaj's Forge was active. The abolition of the "iuridicae" and the linking of Praga with Warsaw united all the parts of Warsaw into one urban organism. This period of development was interrupted by the second partition of Poland, the Kościuszko Insurrection and the Slaughter of Praga. Warsaw, which was incorporated into Prussia after the third partition, became a provincial town in the border zone. It came to life again in 1807 as the capital of the Duchy of Warsaw, and after 1815 as the seat of the autonomous authorities of the Polish Kingdom. Then came a thriving development of industry, and also of cultural, economic and political life.

6

7

8

9 At that time many monumental buildings in the Classicist style were erected, among them some designed by A. Corazzi, for instance the Staszic Palace, the Bank of Poland, and the Grand Theatre (8); the latter was reconstructed and enlarged after the Second World War and is today the place where the leading Polish theatre and opera companies perform. It is the main feature of the architectural complex around Theatre Square. The Warsaw Nike – a Monument to the Heroes of Warsaw – erected in 1964 near the Grand Theatre (9) is one of the modern symbols of the capital.

After the suppression of the November Insurrection (1830–1831) and the withdrawal of the autonomy of the Polish Kingdom, Warsaw lost its political functions, cultural life came to a standstill and political and national oppression increased. During the January Insurrection (1863–1864), Warsaw was the seat of the National Government. After the insurrection was suppressed, repressions and russification tendencies were intensified. In the second half of the 19th century, the expansion of the railway network made Warsaw an important transport junction and the development of the home market contributed to the economic growth of the city. The clothing, cosmetics and footwear industries, mainly directed towards the Russian market, came into being and the metal and tannery industries were expanded. Modern banks were opened. The bourgeoisie accumulated wealth; the proletariat grew in numbers and social consciousness spread among them. In 1882, Ludwik Waryński organized the first socialist party in Warsaw – the Great Proletariat. In the years 1905–1907, Warsaw was one of the main centres of the revolution.

Cultural life did not develop so well. It was only the revolution of 1905 that brought the legal expansion of private Polish schools and the possibility of organizing Polish social, scientific and artistic associations.

10

The double ring of Russian fortifications surrounding Warsaw checked the territorial growth of the city. As the population was increasing fast, this caused a deterioration of housing and health conditions, particularly the living conditions of the proletariat. A partial improvement of this situation came with the construction of a water supply and sewage system after 1881, the development of the horse-drawn tram service and the opening of a municipal power station (1904) which was followed by electric trams (in 1908). During the First World War, Warsaw was under the rule of occupying forces, with all the oppression and repressions this entailed. In 1916, the administrative boundaries of Warsaw were extended to include the over-populated suburbs which were deprived of basic municipal facilities.

The moment Poland regained independence in 1918, Warsaw again became the capital of the state. In the inter-war years, the city was greatly expanded, new administrative buildings were erected as well as residential districts, schools, theatres, museums, etc. The municipal transport network and industry developed. Numerous scientific, cultural and social societies and institutes were formed and were active in the city. Warsaw was the main centre of political life and was still one of the centres of the workers' movement. The population of the capital increased to 1,290,000 in 1939. The boundaries of the city were extended and new town planning and municipal undertakings were realized. Much was done for Warsaw by its last president (from 1934) Stefan Starzyński, who heroically directed the civil defence of the city in 1939.

The Second World War and the German occupation brought the city tremendous losses in population and material destruction. Warsaw, which was the centre of the Polish resistance movement and underground struggle against the occupant, lost about half of its permanent residents and, together with the population that came to Warsaw from other parts of Poland, human losses amounted to about 800,000 persons. Monuments of national culture, works of art, book collections, archives and museums were destroyed or plundered. Particularly great losses were suffered by the part of the city on the left bank of the Vistula (85%), which was the scene of the Warsaw Uprising. When the city was liberated on January 17th, 1945, only 7% of the buildings were fit for occupation.

Despite this, Warsaw remained the capital of the state by the wish of the nation and by virtue of the decision taken by the government. Warsaw was rebuilt by the common effort of the whole nation on the basis of a physical plan ensuring the rational reconstruction and modernization of the city, improved arterial roads to ease traffic problems and the reconstruction of whole complexes of historical buildings. The next period brought the dynamic growth of the capital befitting its political, economic and cultural role. Warsaw is the seat of the supreme state and political authorities, the national centre of science and culture and a great industrial centre. Its population has already exceeded a million and a half and the area of the city has greatly increased with the building of numerous new residential districts well equipped with service, social and recreational facilities.

11

12

13

14

Warsaw's cultural losses in historical buildings and relics in the years 1939–1945 amounted to 90% of the pre-war figure. In most cases, these losses were the result of a deliberate campaign by the occupant to destroy the monuments of Poland's history and culture. The conception of rebuilding and reconstructing the city after the war was aimed not only at restoring to Warsaw its most valuable buildings or complexes of buildings, but also to reconstruct whole quarters and complexes testifying to the past history of the city and nation, such as the Warsaw Old Town and New Town, Theatre Square, Bank Square (today Dzierżyński Sq.) and Castle Square.

In 1971, the decision was taken to reconstruct the Royal Castle, a symbol of the independence and sovereignty of Poland. Badly damaged during the siege of Warsaw in September 1939, it was demolished by the Nazis after the Warsaw Uprising. With the cooperation of the whole society and the help of Poles living abroad, the castle has been completely reconstructed (3). Work is still progressing on the reconstruction of the interiors, facilitated by the fact that many fragments and elements of the former furnishings and interior decoration were hidden and preserved. The whole of the Royal Way, leading southwards from the Royal Castle, along Krakowskie Przedmieście (Cracow Suburb) Street, Nowy Świat (New World) Street, Plac Trzech Krzyży (Three Crosses Square) and Ujazdowskie Avenue to Belweder Palace (13), which is today the seat of the President of the Council of State, was wholly reconstructed earlier. The present Belweder Palace is as it was after the original small 17th century palace was remodelled to serve as the residence of Constantine, Grand Duke of Russia in the years 1818–1822. Belweder Palace adjoins the Łazienki Park, laid out in Romantic style by Stanisław Augustus round his summer residence. In the park is the 18th century palace complex comprising a number of buildings with various functions. The early Classicist Palace on the Water (14) designed by Merlini, was based on the former 17th century bath pavilion. Burnt down by the occupant, the palace was painstakingly reconstructed after the war, including the interiors (16) and since 1964 has housed a department of the National Museum. Not only were the buildings in the Łazienki Park reconstructed, but also the many free standing sculptures and also the monument to Frederic Chopin, sculpted by W. Szymanowski in 1926 (15), which was reconstructed in 1958.

15

16

The extension of Ujazdowskie Avenue leads southwards to the Wilanów Palace (17). It was originally a manor house, which was purchased in 1677 for King Jan Sobieski and reconstructed by Locci into a magnificent royal summer residence. At present, it houses a department of the National Museum. The palace is surrounded by a park, laid out in the reign of Jan Sobieski and redesigned in the years 1799–1821 in Romantic style.

The main building of the Warsaw Technical University (18) is a rare example in Warsaw of the eclectic type of architecture that prevailed at the turn of the 19th century. It was built in the years 1899–1901 by the architect A. Szyller. A remarkable feature of this building is the huge assembly hall with galleries on each storey rising to the glass roof. The building was partly destroyed by fire in 1944, and was repaired and handed over for use again in 1948.

17

21 In the 19th century, the central district of Warsaw was moved westwards into the area on both sides of Marszałkowska Street and Jerozolimskie Avenue crossing it at right angles. This district of Warsaw was almost completely destroyed during the last war. In the course of reconstruction, the main streets were considerably widened. Marszałkowska Street in particular (1) assumed quite a different appearance. Many new buildings were erected along it, some housing public institutions, others blocks of flats and service premises. At the crossing of Jerozolimskie Avenue and Nowy Świat Street the Party House was built, the seat of the Central Committee of the Polish United Workers' Party. On the west side of Marszałkowska Street, in the huge Parade Square, the Palace of Science and Culture was built in the years 1952–1955, as a gift from the Soviet Union to Poland. It is the highest (234 m.) building in Warsaw (20). It houses the Polish Academy of Sciences, many scientific societies, several theatres and cinemas. Part of it is for the young people (the Youth Palace). It also houses the huge Congress Hall, exhibition halls, sports facilities and restaurants. The new central district of Warsaw has been built round the Palace of Culture and Science. Part of this central district is the East Side of Marszałkowska Street (29) – between Jerozolimskie Avenue and Świętokrzyska Street, a complex built in the years 1962–1970, comprising 23 residential, administrative and service buildings. The design of the East Side is on several planes. Low department store buildings occupy a narrow strip facing Marszałkowska Street. Behind them, parallel to the street, there is a shopping precinct, only for pedestrians, called the Central Passage (21) with shops, restaurants, cafes and other service facilities on the ground floors and mezzanines of the buildings, as well as a panoramic cinema and a theatre. On the secondary plane there are 8 blocks of flats with 11 floors and three with 24 floors. The office buildings include the 14 floor building of Foreign Trade Enterprises "Universal" and the General Savings Bank Rotunda in Jerozolimskie Avenue. The new Central Railway Station (20) built in the years 1973–1976 in Jerozolimskie Avenue between Marchlewskiego and Emilia Plater Streets, is a modern station well equipped to handle heavy traffic. The attractive surface building occupies a relatively small area, but the underground part of the station is very large and, apart from the railway installations, also has various kinds of shops, cafés and other service facilities.

22

Among the new additions to the urban landscape of Warsaw in the Seventies are two super modern hotels, which have increased the city's hotel accomodation by rooms for more than 2,000 persons. They are the "Forum" and "Victoria" hotels. The slim 33-floor building of the "Forum" Hotel is a characteristic feature of the central district (1), at the crossing of Marszałkowska Street and Jerozolimskie Avenue. However, the Varsovians think that the design of the "Victoria" Hotel (22) in Plac Zwycięstwa (Victory Square) is better, for its lower elevation is beautifully composed into the surrounding architectural landscape. The hotel rooms and restaurants (23) are well equipped, modern and attractively furnished, with good air conditioning. Both hotels were built by Swedish firms and belong to the Intercontinental network.

23

24

The post-war development of Warsaw, its territorial growth, and also the increased motor traffic made it necessary to find new solutions to transport and communication problems. Although these problems have been gradually dealt with since the war, they have assumed special importance during the last decade. Important, far-reaching projects to ease traffic problems have been undertaken on a very large scale. One of these projects is the Łazienkowska Thoroughfare for fast traffic, completed in the years 1971–1974, linking the left-bank districts of Ochota, Śródmieście (central district) and Powiśle with the right-bank districts of Saska Kępa and Grochów. The thoroughfare is 14 km. long with fly-over crossings all the way, from Żwirki i Wigury Avenue to Wiatraczna Street. The main engineering projects are the steel, five-span Łazienkowski Bridge over the Vistula (424.2 m. long and 27.5 m. wide), the "Agrykola" viaduct and the viaduct over Paryska Street giving access to the Saska Kępa district, which together with the tunnels have a total length of 2,000 m., as well as 1,700 m. of trestle bridges, about 200 m. of foot-bridges and about 500 m. of subways for pedestrians.

The Łazienkowska Thoroughfare is an engineering feat without precedence in Poland as regards scale and scope. As a modern motor-way with three-lane traffic in both directions, it enables motor vehicles to maintain an even high speed without fear of collisions at crossroads. The capacity of the Thoroughfare is 4,000 to 4,500 vehicles per hour. The clover-leaf junction system linking the thoroughfare with the Wisłostrada motor-way running along the left Vistula embankment and the Praski Boulevard running along the right embankment are economical and functional (26).

The Wisłostrada motor-way, built in a similar way and running along the left bank of the Vistula from Wilanów to beyond Młociny, relieves the rush-hour traffic passing through the central district in the north-south and south-north directions and gives quicker access to the recreational centres in the Kampinos Forest National Park, Modlin, the Kabackie Woods, Skolimów-Konstancin and Góra Kalwaria. A third motor-way is now under construction, which will be called the Toruń motor-way, cutting through the north part of Warsaw from west to east.

In order to meet the growing housing needs of the Warsaw population and improve the standard of housing, many new housing estates and residential districts with shops, services and social facilities have been built. One of the most recently built residential districts is Ursynów in the south of the city, where interesting architectural and town planning solutions have been applied. The differentiated height of the blocks of flats, placed at various angles, the intermingling of the residential buildings with service pavilions, sports grounds, recreational areas and greens, will make Ursynów one of the nicest residential districts in the city (25).

25

26

Warsaw is one of the oldest industrial centres in Poland. In spite of its old traditions, the real development of the factory industry on a large scale only goes back to the 1870s. In 1913, Warsaw's industry employed 66,000 workers, of which 5 factories employing more than 1,000 persons only accounted for 10% of the total number of employed. The metal and engineering industries predominated, employing about 40% of the workers. During the First World War, the industry of Warsaw suffered serious losses. Even so, in 1938, it employed 26% more workers than in 1913. Of this number 52% were employed by the metal and engineering industries and 20% were working in factories employing more than 1,000 persons.

The Second World War almost completely destroyed Warsaw industry. Due to rapid reconstruction, the pre-war employment figures had already been exceeded in 1953, and today the figure is three times that of the pre-war years. The share of the metal and engineering industries has risen to more than 60% of the total number of employed. The electrical engineering and electronics industries have also assumed a more important role. At present, Warsaw has over 40 industrial works employing more than 1,000 persons, which is over 50% of the total number of employed. The largest industrial establishments include: the "Warszawa" Steel Works producing fine steel, which started production in 1957, the Żerań Motor Car Factory (26) and the rapidly developing Tractor Factory at Ursus a suburb recently incorporated into Warsaw.

Warsaw, the chief political, cultural and scientific centre of the Polish nation, was subjected to particularly acute persecution by the Nazi invader and in consequence was one of the most cruelly devastated towns in the country. The first losses came in September 1939 as a result of bombardments and siege, and further losses were caused by the years of occupation. This was a time of terror – round-ups in the streets, arrests, deportations and mass executions. The aim of these measures was to deprive Warsaw of its leading place in the life of the nation, to destroy the Polish intelligentsia, particularly leading political, social and cultural activists. In the woods near Palmiry, on the verge of the Kampinos forest, about 20,000 Poles were executed by shooting in the years 1939–1943. A Mausoleum-Cemetery was put up at the place of these executions in 1948 (28). Suffering Warsaw was liberated during the offensive of the Soviet Army in January 1945. Detachments of the First Polish Army entered Warsaw on January 17th, 1945. About 22,000 Soviet soldiers were killed in the battles fought to liberate the Polish capital. They were laid to rest in a Cemetery-Mausoleum (27).

27
28

Another kind of monument, which is also an expression of protest against war and its horrors, is the Children's Health Centre, a large diagnostic and treatment complex at Międzylesie, near Warsaw. Erected in memory of the child victims of the war, it is a centre which is to restore health, fitness and the joy of life to its little patients. The construction of the Centre was started in 1970. A contribution to the building of the Centre has been made not only by Poles living all over the world, but also by people of other nationalities. Some parts of the Centre are already operating, namely, the out-patients department and the hospital. The Centre will admit children of different nationalities for treatment (29).

Many sports and recreational facilities are being built in Warsaw and the surrounding area to ensure the Varsovians healthy conditions. The biggest recreational complex has been built round the Zegrze Artificial Lake (39), where there are a number of water sports centres, holiday centres built by various institutions, and camping sites. There are also private summer chalets and houses belonging to the people of Warsaw. The artificial lake was created after the construction of a dam on the Bug and Narew confluence in the Sixties.

29

30

In the Warsaw suburbs, there has been a flourishing development of market gardening – vegetables and flowers – both field crops and hotbed and greenhouse cultivation, and also the folio tunnel method. The largest greenhouses are at the state farm in Mysiadło (31).

On the right bank of the River Narew, near the place where it flows into the River Bug, is the town of Pułtusk (32), an old defence stronghold, conferred on the Płock bishops in the 11th century, in whose hands it remained till 1796. A trading settlement developed round the stronghold, which in 1257 was granted municipal status. After it was destroyed by the Lithuanians, the town received another foundation charter on the basis of the Chełmno Law. Pułtusk went through a period of flourishing development after the Union of Poland and Lithuania, when it became an important centre of the corn trade, handling grain sent from the eastern territories to Gdańsk. At this time too, handicrafts developed and cultural life blossomed. In the middle of the 15th century, a school was founded in Pułtusk, run by professors of the Cracow Academy. The main centre of culture and education was the Jesuit College founded in 1567, which was attended by students from all over Poland. After it was devastated and plundered during the Swedish wars, Pułtusk never regained its former significance. At the turn of the years 1944 and 1945, it was in the front line zone and the town was 85% destroyed. Reconstructed after the war, Pułtusk has now become a vital economic and cultural centre with valuable historical monuments, the most important of which are the Bishop's Castle built in 1319 and reconstructed many times, the Collegiate church dating back to 1449, enlarged and remodelled in the 16th and 19th centuries, the former Jesuit College and the Town Hall with its Gothic tower in the middle of the elongated Market Place.

31

32

33

The castle of Ciechanów (33), which was left in ruins by the Swedes in the 16th century, was built by Prince Janusz of Mazowsze to defend the town, harrassed by invasions of the Prussians, then the Lithuanians and later the Teutonic Knights. Ciechanów was already a defence settlement in the 11th century, later the seat of castellans and – from the 15th century – the seat of the "starosts" (heads of the district). It was granted municipal status in the 14th century. The town was known for its trade in horses, cattle and pigs. The decline of Ciechanów was caused by the Swedish wars and fires; finally its fate was sealed by an epidemic of cholera in 1716. It only began to develop again at the end of the 19th century. During the Second World War Ciechanów was incorporated into the German Reich. The German occupant, planning the destruction of the historical quarter of the town, demolished some of the buildings round the original Old Market Square. After the war, the town was reconstructed and enlarged and is now a lively economic and cultural centre. It has been a voivodship capital since 1975.

Ten kilometres to the north of Ciechanów is Opinogóra, which once belonged to the princes of Mazowsze and, from the 17th century passed into the hands of the Krasiński family. In the second quarter of the 19th century, General Wincenty Krasiński built a Neo-Gothic palace there (36), which now houses a Museum of the Romantic Movement. The general's son, the famous Polish Romantic poet Zygmunt Krasiński, spent many years of his life at Opinogóra and it was there that his first poem was written, in which he attributed the name of Opinogóra to the fictional character of Opin, ruler of the Mazowsze plains in pre-historic times. An urn with the ashes of the poet, who died in Paris in 1858, is in the crypt of the Classicist parish church, which was also founded by his father W.Krasiński.

Czerwińsk, situated on the high right bank of the Vistula, today a small settlement, was once a town. The first mention of Czerwińsk, in chronicles from the middle of the 11th century, refer to it as the property of a Benedictine Abbey at Mogilno. At the end of that century it became the property of the Płock bishops. In 1148, Bishop Aleksander brought the Augustinian Regular Canons there and founded an Abbey. The trading settlement which grew up in the 12th century remained the property of the Bishops of Płock, from whom it received a foundation charter based on the Chełmno Law in 1373. The trading settlement that developed round the monastery from the 15th century only received municipal status in 1582. In the 15th century the town which comprised two parts was a place where the debates of the Diet were held. In 1410, on their way to fight the decisive battle against the Teutonic Knights, the Polish forces joined up with the Lithuanian forces here. Czerwińsk prospered from trade on the Vistula until the middle of the 17th century, but declined in the following decades when it was ruined by the Swedes, and later by floods and plagues. In 1896, it lost its municipal status. The only relic of the former splendour of the town is the fortified Abbey (35), with a 12th century Romanesque basilica, a Gothic-Renaissance monastery that was reconstructed several times, and a belftry-gate dating back to 1497. In 1951, the largest group of early 13th century Romanesque frescoes in Poland was uncovered in the church.

34

35

36

Płock, situated on the high bank of the Vistula (36) was an old and important fortified settlement of Mazowsze in the 10th century. In the 11th century it became the seat of castellans and later the centre of a bishopric. It was one of the places of residence of the ruling princes. In 1138 it became the capital of a Mazowsze principality and later of the Duchy of Płock. In the 12th century, a Romanesque cathedral was built in Płock, which was reconstructed several times in later centuries. Archeological excavations on the Cathedral Hill, the site of the original old settlement and later the ducal castle, revealed the remains of 11th and 12th century architecture, including the remnants of a rotunda church and ducal palatine, as well as traces of smelting furnaces from the 12th and 13th centuries. Płock was granted municipal status in 1237. Devastated several times by the Lithuanians and later by the Teutonic Knights. Płock was surrounded by defence walls in the reign of Casimir the Great. At this time too, the castle was enlarged. Incorporated into the Crown lands in 1495, Płock developed well, participating in the trade along the Vistula route. In the middle of the 17th century, the Swedes destroyed the town so thoroughly that hardly a stone was left standing. Its reconstruction was very slow. In 1793 it was incorporated into Prussia. In the times of the Warsaw Duchy (1807–1815), it was the capital of a department and in the Polish kingdom – of a voivodship (1816–1837). In the 19th century, the town began to liven up, trade was revived, small scale industry was started up and there was a development of education and cultural and intellectual life under the sponsorship of the Płock Scientific Society, founded in 1820. In the inter-war years the economic development of the town was weak, but it still continued to be an important cultural centre. The dynamic development of Płock after the Second World War was due to the building of a huge petrochemical plant (37) there in 1964, processing crude oil pumped from the Soviet Union through the "Friendship" pipeline. In the course of less than 20 years, Płock has become a big industrial centre with not only the petrochemical plant but also engineering works, food industry factories and the timber industry. It is also an important river port with its own river shipyard. It is still an important cultural centre. In 1975, it advanced from a district town to became a voivodship capital. The economic development and population growth of the town has brought its spatial development. New industrial and residential districts with well equipped modern buildings (38) have grown up round the old quarter, following the old 14th century spatial layout, with numerous carefully preserved examples of the old architecture. The most valuable of these are the Cathedral, built in the years 1126–1144, and the remains of the castle.

40 In Żelazowa Wola is the house where Frederic Chopin was born on February 22nd, 1810. It was formerly an annex to the palatial residence of the wealthy Skarbek family. Chopin spent the first years of his life there. A small museum has been arranged in the house, in memory of the great artist, in which there are documents, portraits, Chopin's manuscripts, his old piano and period furniture. Sunday concerts of Chopin's works are given in the drawing room of the house by the most outstanding pianists. In the large park round the house, laid out in the Thirties of the present century, there are some interesting specimens of trees and flowers that came from all over Poland as gifts, beautiful shaded walks and quiet nooks where one can rest. The River Utrata, a tributary of the River Bzura, flows through the park. In the western part of the park there is a monument to Chopin, erected in 1894, after the forgotten house at Żelazowa Wola was "disovered" by the Russian M. Balakirev, a great admirer of Chopin.

To the north of Żelazowa Wola, on the edge of the Kampinos Forest, is the village of Brochów, founded in 1113 by the Mazowsze princes. There is a Renaissance church (40) that has survived there from the years 1551–1561 when it was built as a defence church. Frederic Chopin was christened there.

The fertile Łowicz land (41) on the banks of the River Bzura, belonged to the archbishops of Gniezno as far back as the 12th century, and from the 15th century to the primates of Poland, who ruled it as a separate duchy. The capital of this land Łowicz, was one of the oldest fortified settlements in the Poland of the Piast dynasty. Before it passed into the hands of the archbishops, Łowicz was the property of the Mazowsze princes and a castellan's seat. Later it became an administrative and economic centre of the vast church estates. It was granted municipal status in 1350. At the turn of the 14th century, the fortified settlement was turned into a castle fortress, which in later centuries became a magnificent primate's residence. When the Swedes conquered and occupied the town in 1655, they erected strong fortifications there. When they left Łowicz, the Swedes destroyed the castle buildings and the town. Siezed by Prussia in 1795, Łowicz became the property of the government, and in 1807, the Duchy of Łowicz was given to one of Napoleon's marshals, Davout. In 1820 Tsar Alexander I presented it to his brother Constantine. Hence the title of Duchess of Łowicz assumed by Joanna Grudzińska, Constantine's morganic wife. From 1838, the duchy belonged directly to the Tsars. In the inter-war period, Łowicz was a district town in a well developed agricultural region. Badly damaged during the fighting in the Second World War, Łowicz was afterwards rebuilt. Today it is a centre of the food and knitwear industries. The Łowicz Regional Museum in the town has some interesting collections of regional folk art, which is still alive in this region. The colourful regional costumes of the Łowicz people can be seen in all their rich splendour in the Corpus Christi procession held there every year (42).

42

Apart from regional costumes, another manifestation of
the regional individuality of the Łowicz land are its music
and songs, the carved figurines in wayside shrines,
beautiful cut-outs, ceramic ware and also the decorated
cottages, their furnishings and utensils. Łowicz folklore is
richly represented in the villages of Złaków Kościelny
(2 and 43) and Złaków Borowy.

The Baroque palace at Nieborów (44), built by Tylman
van Gameren in the years 1695–1697, was originally the
property of Primate Radziejowski, then it passed first into
the hands of the Ogiński family, then to the Radziwiłłs.
Today it belongs to the National Museum in Warsaw. The
interiors of the palace are richly decorated by Polish,
Italian and Dutch masters. It houses valuable museum and
library collections. In the beautiful park surrounding the
palace there are many buildings, a Classicist annex,
a former 17th century brewery, and various outbuildings,
including a coach house, stables, a former inn and a winter
garden. A unique feature of the park are the sculptured
works of art from various epochs which stand there,
namely, columns, statues, sarcophagi, vases and urns.

Czersk, a fortified settlement of the 11th century and
a custellan's seat, was the capital of a duchy in the years
1262–1429. It was granted municipal status in 1350.
Czersk was known for its cloth and its beer. It also traded
in corn and timber. The changed course of the bed of the
River Vistula and the destruction brought by the Swedish
wars caused the decline of the town. Today it is a small
settlement, whose inhabitants are mainly engaged in fruit
and vegetable growing. High over the settlement rise the
ruins of the castle of the Mazowsze princes (45).

South of Warsaw, in the vicinity of Grójec, is the largest
orchard region of Poland. The apple and cherry orchards
which stretch for many kilometres are a beautiful sight at
blossom time (46).

45

46

Pilica, a left-bank tributary of the Vistula, is one of the most beautiful rivers of the Polish Lowlands. Its source is on the Cracow-Częstochowa Upland. Its lower course flows through a broad valley, widening to 200–300 metres. From the northern verge of the valley, where there are several localities with buildings of historical interest, there is an extensive view over the meadows and pasturelands of the valley and also the forest area to the south.

Radom (48), the chief town of the southern part of the Mazowsze Lowland, is quite a large industrial, cultural and administrative centre. The origins of Radom can be traced back to the 10th century. In the 12th century, it was castellan's seat. It was enlarged and developed in the second half of the 14th century on the basis of the foundation charter granted to it by Casimir the Great. Its development was due to its position on the trade route leading from Wielkopolska and Silesia to Lithuania and Ruthenia. In the 15th century it also became a cloth-making centre. It was the place of many assemblies of the gentry, and in the 17th and 18th century, the seat of the Treasury Tribunal of the Polish Republic. The speedy development of industry in Radom in the 19th century came after a railway line was built linking it with the Dąbrowa Basin and Warsaw, and indirectly, with Russia.

47

48

Puławy was a centre of magnate estates at least from the 15th century. Its real development came when it passed into the hands of the Czartoryski family. Prince Adam K. Czartoryski and his wife Isabella made this residence a centre of intellectual and political thought, one of the most important cultural centres of the Enlightenment Period. The palace, remodelled in Neo-classical style about 1800, was visited by the most eminent artists and politicians of those times. In the surrounding park, designed by Isabella Czartoryska and remarkable for its fine composition, there are Romantic style buildings, among others, the Gothic House and Sybil's Temple (50). They housed the original art collections which later became the nucleus of the collections of the Czartoryski Museum in Cracow. After the November Insurrection, the palace, which was confiscated by the Tsarist authorities, was used as a school for "young gentlewomen" and in 1862 as the Polytechnical Institute of Agriculture and Forestry. Today, the palace houses a number of agricultural research institutes. In the years 1962–1967, a giant nitrogen compounds plant (49) was built near Puławy, which contributed greatly to the development of the town.

A fine example of late Renaissance architecture in Podlasie is the parish church at Radzyń Podlaski (51), built in 1641.

49

50   51

Polesie extends into Poland across the middle reaches of the River Bug in the area between the confluences of the rivers Krzna and Wełnianka and is known as Lublin Polesie. It is a flat plain, and thus the outflow of water is made difficult. The ground water is near the surface and in the depressions left by former lakes peat bogs have formed. In the western part of Lublin Polesie, the lakes have remained, forming the group known as the Łęczna–Włodawa Lakes. They are small – only seven of the whole 67 lakes cover an area of more than 100 ha. Most of them are shallow and overgrown with reeds at the edges. Some of the lakes are surrounded by bogs and are thus not accessible.

Siedlce, the chief town and cultural centre of Podlasie, was late in its development. The village of Siedlce belonged to the Gniewosz family, who took the name of Siedlecki in the 15th century. In 1549, King Sigismund Augustus granted municipal status to the part of the village called Nowe (New) Siedlce. About 1670, the town passed into the hands of the Czartoryski family. It was in the 18th century, when the town belonged to Chancellor Michał Czartoryski, and later to his son-in-law Hetman Ogiński, that Siedlce reached its prime. It is from this period that the most valuable historical buildings date, such as the palace of Aleksandra Ogińska, née Czartoryska (53) – now a bishop's palace – remodelled from an old manor house, the Town Hall and the Baroque parish church with presbytery. In 1809, Siedlce became the capital of a department, in 1815 – of the Podlasie voivodship. Since 1975, Siedlce has been a voivodship capital.

Liw was a fortified settlement, the seat of castellans. A defence castle, at first built of timber, then at the turn of the 14th century, of brick (54) was put up here by the Mazowsze princes. A trading settlement grew up under its protection, which was later called Stary (Old) Liw, and which was granted municipal status in 1350. In 1446, Nowy (New) Liw was granted a foundation charter and until 1789 had separate municipal authorities. Both centres developed from trade in corn and both of them declined during the wars of the 17th and 18th centuries and also due to competition from Węgrów. Today, Liw is a small market town. The remains of its 15th century Gothic castle were conserved and in the years 1956–1961, it was partially restored and used as a regional museum. The castle was built on a hill made by heaping earth on the swampy area in the valley of the River Liwiec. Due to the wide sandy beaches and the shallow, still pure waters, the has become a place of recreation, particularly for children (55).

54

55

58

59

The chief river of Podlasie, the Narew (56), with its right-bank tributary the Biebrza, was once the only means of communication through the dense forests, untrodden by man, along which the inhabitants of Mazowsze moved into Podlasie and the lands of the Prussians. Flowing through the Kurpie Forest, the Narew divides it into the Green Forest (northern part) and the White Forest (in the south).

Today the forest in this area, particularly around Ostrołęka, is not nearly so dense, having been cleared to make way for cultivated fields and meadows (57). The inhabitants of the Kurpie forest area are most probably the descendents of the people of Mazowsze who in the Middle Ages sought refuge here from the Sudavians, Lithuanians and Ruthenians. Later it became a refuge for peasants escaping from the corvée system and even members of the gentry escaping from the threat of punishment. The Kurpie people, who had no corvée system and were free subjects of the king, governed themselves by the case-law of the keepers of wild bees, which only became written law in the year 1559. They were ruled by a "starost" (head of a district) elected from among the wild bee keepers. They earned their livelihood from bee-keeping, hunting, fishing, making pitch, charcoal burning and distillation of potash, and also from digging and processing amber. To this day, the Kurpie women make linen cloth and woollen rugs. Cut off from the rest of the world, they preserved their specific regional character in their buildings (58), customs and costumes (59).

Łomża developed from a 10th–11th century stronghold guarding a crossing of the River Narew. It was granted municipal status in 1418, and grew into one of the biggest towns of Mazowsze with well developed handicrafts and flourishing trade with Gdańsk, Prussia and Lithuania. The 17th century saw a decline of the town, from which it only began to recover in the 19th century, as capital of a government unit. The fighting in 1944 brought the destruction of 70% of the buildings of the town. Post-war reconstruction also included the buildings of historical interest (60). In the last 30 years, Łomża has developed rapidly; new industrial plants and residential districts have been built there, and since 1975 it has been a voivodship capital. The population has increased to two and a half times the previous figure.

The extensive, swampy Biebrza Basin (61) dividing Mazowsze from Podlasie, is a paradise for water and marsh fowl in the spring thaw. The not very productive sedge meadows are mown in summer and the hay stacked to be taken away in the winter when the ground freezes.

Tykocin, a border stronghold of Mazowsze, was most probably a fortified settlement of the Sudavians earlier on. It was granted municipal status in 1425. Incorporated into Lithuania in 1426, it was granted to the Gasztołds. In 1542, it became the property of the king. As a trading centre it developed favourably. A big castle was built there, which was destroyed during the Swedish wars. In 1661, the Diet presented Tykocin to Hetman S. Czarniecki for his services in the war against the Swedes. As the dowry of his daughter Aleksandra, it passed into the possession of the Branicki family in 1663. It was in this period that the most valuable historical buildings were erected in the town, namely, the late Baroque Monastery of the Missionary Fathers with a church from the years 1742–1749 (62), and the earlier synagogue and free school. Tykocin, already devastated during the Swedish wars, declined in the 19th century due to competition from Białystok.

64 Białystok, the main industrial and cultural centre of north-eastern Poland, was most probably founded by the Grand Duke of Lithuania Gedymin about 1320. It was incorporated into the Crown lands together with the whole of Podlasie in 1564. As part of the Tykocin "starost's" district it passed into the hands of the Branicki family, and became the administrative centre of their estates. Tylman van Gameren built a Baroque palace for them here in 1697. Hetman Jan Klemens Branicki obtained municipal status for Białystok in 1749. In the years 1728–1758, the palace was enlarged and remodelled into a magnificent magnate's residence (63), which was called the "Podlasie Versailles". The Hetman had a military garrison in Białystok and founded schools: a military college, a school for administrators of estates and a school for young men. He also built a hospital and a theatre and encouraged the development of handicrafts and manufactures. The town continued to grow. The 19th century development of the town was connected above all with the importance of the Białystok Textile Industry District. After the First World War, Białystok was a voivodship capital with a well developed textile industry, but apart from the central district, most of its buildings were wooden and there were not many public facilities. At this time the church of St. Roch (64) was built. Designed by O. Sosnowski, it is one of the most interesting examples of the sacral architecture of the inter-war period. The Second World War and Nazi occupation brought the extermination of a large number of the inhabitants of Białystok (55%) and big material losses (80% of the buildings and almost all the industrial establishments). The central district of the town was almost completely destroyed. The post-war development of Białystok has been due to the speedy reconstruction and expansion of its industry and the location of many administrative, economic, scientific and cultural institutions there.

65

66

67

Reconstructed and modernized, Białystok is now an up-to-date, well equipped town. New residential districts and housing estates have been built, some of which have been located amid the old wooden buildings which are fast disappearing from the urban landscape (65). The most interesting historical buildings have also been reconstructed, including the Branicki palace, which today houses a Medical Academy.

Together with economic growth, a new kind of building can be seen in the rural areas, mostly brick-built, better equipped but at the same time rather standardized; it is replacing the old regional type building, mostly of timber. In order to save these old houses and farm buildings from destruction, the Skansen type of museum is being developed in Poland. Interesting old rural buildings are also being moved to other ethnographic museums. In the Agricultural Museum that was opened in 1963 in Ciechanowiec on the River Nurzec, at the residence of Father Krzysztof Kluk, an eminent natural scientist of the Enlightenment Period and the father of Polish agricurural science, more than 2,000 exhibits have been accumulated, including old timber buildings of historical interest from the north-eastern part of Poland. There one can see several peasant cottages, windmills, cowsheds, a barn with a horse-driven mill, a threshing shed, and an 18th century granary that once belonged to a manor house. The photograph shows a small rural granary, which is a typical example of the architecture of the north-eastern areas of Poland (66).

To the north of the place where the River Krzna flows into the River Bug, the Bug leaves the Polish Plain and cuts a deep valley through higher ground. In this part of its course, it divides the Siedlce Elevation, belonging to the Mazowsze Lowland, from the Drohiczyn Elevation, which is part of the Podlasie Elevation. It was along this valley, on the right bank of the River Bug, that Ruthenian settlement moved north in the 9th to 11th centuries, marking its progress by the strongholds of Mielnik, Drohiczyn and Bielsk, and the numerous barrows found there. The Byelorussian population inhabiting some areas of the southern part of the Białystok voivodship are the descendents of these settlers. In the 13th century, the area was a bone of contention between Mazowsze and Lithuania, and finally came into the possession of the Polish Crown, together with the whole of Podlasie in 1569. From the barrow on the high bank of the River Bug near Drohiczyn, there is an extensive view of the Bug valley and the area on its left bank.

The origins of Drohiczyn can be traced back to the times of early Ruthenian settlement. Later it was in the hands of the Sudavians for a time. In the 12th century, Drohiczyn was the capital of the Ruthenian Duchy of Drohiczyn. At the beginning of the 13th century it belonged to Prince Conrad of Mazowsze, who in 1237 brought the Knights Order of the Dobrzyński Brethren there. They were shortly afterwards banished by Daniel Romanowicz, prince of Włodzimierz and Halicz. Conquered by the Lithuanians in 1280, it remained in their hands for nearly 300 years. The Lublin Union (1569) brought it into the Crown lands as the capital of the Podlasie voivodship. The 15th and 16th centuries marked the period of the most flourishing development of Drohiczyn, which was granted municipal status in 1498 and was then an important political and economic centre. War damage and natural disasters in the years 1657–1662 caused the economic decline of the town. After the fire of 1803, the situation of the town went from bad to worse and the left-bank part of it became little more than a village. Today it is a small centre of trade and handicrafts serving agriculture, but proud of its relics of the past, such as the Baroque monastery and church of the Franciscans dating back to the 17th century, the monastery and church of the Benedictine monks from the 18th century, the college and church of the Jesuits (later the Piarists), which dates back to the turn of the 17th century, the Orthodox Church from the end of the 18 th century and several houses and manors of historical interest.

The Lithuanian princes often brought back prisoners from their expeditions against the Tatars, settling them in various parts of the Grand Duchy of Lithuania. As the years passed these people forgot their own language, but they kept their Muslim religion and different customs. They were more than loyal to their new motherland, a proof of which was their participation in Polish wars and insurrections, sometimes as separate Tatar formations. Within the frontiers of today's Poland, in the extreme east of the Białystok voivodship, in an area that once belonged to Lithuania, there are still two Tatar villages – Bohoniki, a Tatar settlement from the 15th century, and Kruszyniany, which was given to captain of the Tatar Company, Kryczyński, by King Jan Sobieski, as a reward for saving his life after the Vienna campaign in the battle of Parkany. The wooden two-tower mosque in Kruszyniany (69) dates back to the 18th century. There is also an old Tatar cemetery in the village, with tombstones on which there are inscriptions in the Latin and Arabic alphabets.

68

69

In the Middle Ages, the border zone of Mazowsze, Lithuania and Ruthenia was grown with dense forests. The remains of these forests in today's Poland are the Augustów, Knyszyn and Białowieża forests. Situated on the Baltic-Black Sea Divide, far from the main transport routes, the Białowieża Forest has to a great extent retained its primaeval character. From the 15th to the 18th centuries it belonged to the kings, who had the exclusive right to hunt there. Before setting off to fight the Battle of Grunwald, King Władysław Jagiełło hunted here to provide meat for his army. He also organized a special forest guard to protect the animals from poachers and the trees from felling. After 1815, Białowieża Forest became the property of the Russian Tsars. They set up a game park in which they kept the native animals and also animals brought from other countries. The excessive number of animals kept in such a small area led to the devastation of the vegetation. During the First World War, the German occupants conducted a plunder economy in the Forest. As a result of poaching and hostilities a large number of the animals were lost. The bison and elk became extinct there. After the war, in 1921, the Białowieża National Park was created on an area of about 5,000 ha, to protect the best preserved part of the Forest between Narewka and Hwożna (71). Hornbeam-oak gronds predominate there, and a large area is covered with boreal mixed forests with spruce trees (70). Along the banks of the rivers and streams there are alder-ash-ols forests.

70

71

72

73

75

74

A campaign was undertaken to restore the bison to the Forest. At that time there were only about 40 of these animals in the world in various game parks and zoological gardens, of which three were in Poland, in the Pszczyna Forest, from where they were brought to Białowieża in 1865. These bison, with three purchased from Sweden, were to repopulate the Forest with bison (75). In 1938, there were 30 bison in Poland, of which 13 were in Białowieża Forest. Fifteen bison survived the Second World War. Today, there are more than 500 bison in Poland, living in various nature reserves (300 in Białowieża). Some of them live wild in natural conditions. The elk has also been restored to the Forest (72), and even the grey squirrel. There are also wood grouse, black grouse, hazel grouse and Scolopax rusticola in the Białowieża Forest.

The Coastal and Lakeland Belt

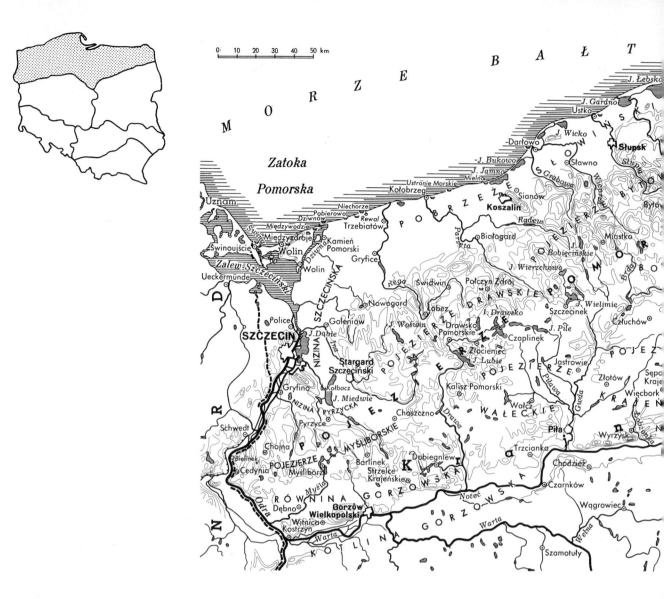

1

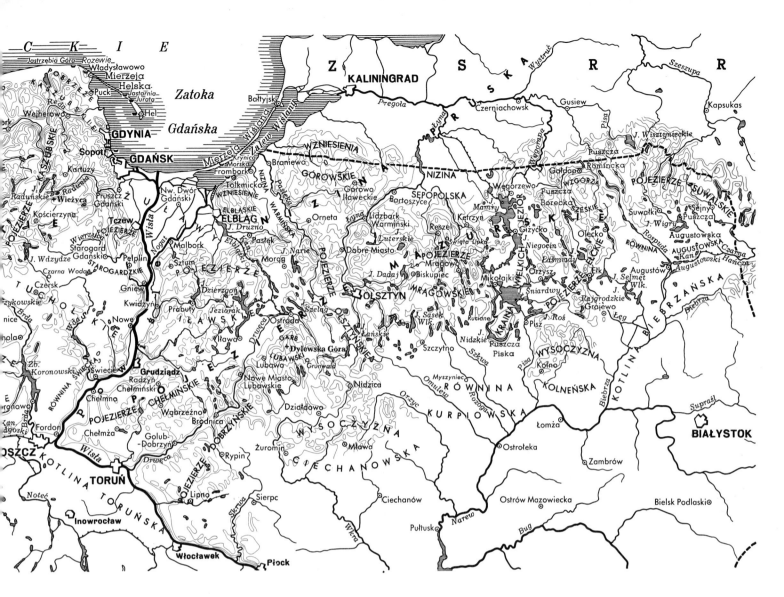

North of the lowland belt, the cover of glacial deposits gets thicker, with rising ridges of end moraines and in their foreground stretch vast outwash plains. Everywhere there are innumerable lakes of all shapes and sizes. This area, the relief of which was shaped by the last phase of the Baltic (Würm) Glaciation, spread out in a wide belt from the Jutland Peninsula in Denmark, along the lower reaches of the Odra, Vistula and Niemen, right up to the north-east, and is known as Pojezierza (Lakeland).

In the lakeland belt, the glacial landforms have been preserved best. Erratic blocks, brought there by glaciers from the Scandinavian mountains, have not crumbled yet and the mixture of clays, sand, gravel and stones deposited by glaciers, known as boulder clay, has not been leached out or washed away by water, retaining its original chemical composition and structure almost entirely. On the undulating areas of ground moraines, there are still ellipsoidal hills, known as drumlins and long narrow ridges of sand and gravel, known as eskers. The young and well preserved glacial relief is the reason for the waters collecting in the depressions (the outflow often not yet established) forming lakes. Immediately after the withdrawal of the ice-sheet, the lakes occupied an area several times greater than today. During the centuries, due to outflow of water, drying up, filling up by alluvial deposits, or the encroachment of vegetation, and also due to the activity of man, many of the lakes have disappeared. Their former existence is indicated by lake deposits, marls, gyttja and peat found in many depressions.

North of the Lakeland belt, the terrain gets lower and levels out, turning into the belt of coastal lowlands running round the southern coastline of the Baltic Sea (called Pobrzeże in Polish). In addition to the glacial deposits and landforms, its structure and relief was also shaped by river and sea deposits, brought there after the withdrawal of the ice-sheet. With the changing history of the Baltic, there have been changes in the coastline and the shaping of the coast. The action of the sea has undermined the capes and cliffs jutting out into the sea and carried the material swept away, together with sand brought by rivers, to other places on the coast. As a result, the sea has claimed the land in some places, leaving cliffs, while in other places the land has moved out into the sea in the form of low sand bars, or spits, cutting off former bays and transforming them into shallow lagoon lakes or lagoons. Dunes have formed from the sand accumulating on the spits. Thus the once rugged Pomeranian coastline has been levelled out.

In view of the differences in climate, soil and vegetation, the western and middle part of the Coastal Belt and Lakeland is included in the Central European Plain, and the eastern part – in the Eastern Baltic Plain.

The Vistula divides the Lakeland and Coastal Belt into two parts – the Pomeranian Lake District and the Pomeranian Coastal Belt, between the Lower Odra and Lower Vistula, and the Mazurian Lake District and the Prussian Plain between the Vistula and the Niemen.

The axis of the Pomeranian Lake District is a ridge of terminal moraines, winding from the Odra to Kartuzy. This ridge, with an altitude not exceeding 150 m. in the west, rises as it nears the Baltic; the highest point is Wieżyca, where the altitude is 329 m. in the extreme east. Also the eastern part of the ridge has more varied landforms. Fast flowing rivers have created deep valleys over which rise hills divided by glacial drainage channels occupied by lakes.

The ridge of end moraines is a barrier to the prevailing north-westerly winds and due to this the northern slopes of this ridge have an abundant rainfall (more than 750 mm. annually). The temperature is lower here than in the adjoining areas, the winters are longer and colder, the summers shorter and cooler. The watershed of a number of rivers, small but with abundant waters runs alongside the Pomeranian moraine ridge. These rivers flow into the sea or are tributaries of the rivers Odra, Noteć and Vistula. All along the moraine ridge there are lakes, mostly finger lakes, the biggest and deepest being Lake Drawsko (area 18.6 sq.km., depth 83 m.).

South of the moraine ridge the terrain gets lower and the landforms are not so varied. There are large areas of outwash plain sands here, from under which hillocks and small areas of undulating country rise; they are built of moraine clays and low ridges of end moraines left by the earlier stages of the Baltic Glaciation. The climate here is warmer and dryer, rainfall diminishes towards the south, dropping to less than 550 mm. annually. The lakes are not so numerous here and the finger lakes are not found so frequently. Most of them are shallow and round. The largest lakes of this area are Wielimie, Wdzydze and Charzykowskie.

The Pomeranian Lake District comprises the West Pomeranian, East Pomeranian and South Pomeranian Lakes, and also Lower Powiśle, which is the area round the lower Vistula.

The Pomeranian Coastal Belt adjoins the Pomeranian Lake District in the north and extends from the Isle of Rugen to Cape Rozewie. In Polish territory, the western part of the Coastal Belt is the Szczecin Lowland, around the Odra Estuary and gradually widening to the north Szczecin Lagoon. One arm of the Odra – the Western Odra – flows directly into the Lagoon, the other – the Eastern Odra, also known as the Regalica – is linked with the Lagoon by the large, but shallow delta lake, Dąbie, which is the remains of the once much larger Lagoon. There is another deep lake farther inland, the bottom of which is lower than sea level, which was also once part of the Lagoon, namely Lake Miedwie. The low-lying land round today's Lagoon is covered with alluvial sands and peat, and the higher land with loams (the Pyrzyce Plain). The Szczecin Lagoon is large and shallow and is connected with the sea by three narrow straits – the Piana, Świna and Dziwna. The middle and eastern part of the Pomeranian Coastal Belt is a ground moraine plain, varied by the remains of end moraines, with the wide peat covered valleys of the lower reaches of rivers flowing into the Baltic from the Lakeland. This is the Słowiński Coastal Belt. Owing to the action of the sea, the coastline in the western part of the Pomeranian Coastal Belt is gradually receding (about

1 m. annually), while in the eastern part the land is gradually moving out into the sea.

The climate of the Coastal Belt is influenced by the masses of polar-maritime air coming from the Atlantic. The winters are short and mild, the summers cool and the autumns long. The influence of the maritime climate is evident in the vegetation and soils of the Pomeranian Coastal Belt, and also the Pomeranian Lake District. In the past the moraine clays were the site of beech forests, while mixed pine and beech forests grew on the more gravelly and stony soils, so these soils are not very podsolized and brown soils are often found. The black-earths created on the glacialcurhine clays round Pyrzyce are among the most fertile in the country. The peat covered river valleys, where alder woods once grew, are today mostly meliorated meadowland giving a hay harvest or arable land. The sandy spits of the coast, the numerous raised peat fields and the less fertile sandy soils where dry pine forests grow cannot be used for farming. There are large areas of pine forests on the outwash plains, the largest being the Tucholskie Forest. Quite large areas of the old beech forests have survived on the Island of Wolin (made into a National Park), near Szczecin (The Beech Forest), and near Drawsko, Wejherowo and Kartuzy.

The influence of the maritime climate is particularly evident in the Pomeranian Coastal Belt, where there are species of flora peculiar to north-western Europe, such as the climbing evergreens ivy and Pomeranian honeysuckle found in the deciduous forests, and also the Swedish rowan, and on wetter soils, the black crowberry, Erica heather and such orchidaceous plants as Listera (ovata) and Goodyera (repens). The peat-bogs are also of an Atlantic character. There is halophyte vegetation in the marshy coastal meadows. Separate mention is due to the unique reserve at Bielinek on the Odra, with the only pubescent oak forest of Mediterranean type in Poland and specific herbaceous plants.

To the east, the Pomeranian Lake District and Coastal Belt end at the Vistula valley and the area round its delta. Seven thousand years ago, the mouth of the Vistula was much higher than it is today and the sea bay occupied the whole of its present delta area and the Vistula Lagoon. The whole of the area was gradually covered with alluvial deposits. In the course of several centuries, the delta area, today covering 174,000 ha – of which 47,000 ha is below sea level and is known as the Żuławy-Fens – has been drained and developed. The shallow Lake Druzno, which is gradually being overgrown, was once part of the Lagoon.

The Gdańsk Bay is enclosed on the western side by the Kaszuby Coastal Belt, consisting of steeply sloping promontories interspersed by wide post-glacial valleys. The 34 kilometre spit known as the Hel Peninsula, formed of sands carried there by the sea, starts at the Swarzewo Promontory and runs in a south-easterly direction. It is five to six metres above sea level and narrow (in some places only 200 to 500 metres wide), the end of it being club-shaped. Dry pine forests grow there, most of them planted by man to stabilize the sands.

To the east of the Vistula delta the Coastal Belt gets wider, turning into an extensive plain of ground moraines, known as the Prussian Lowland, which is crossed by low ridges of end moraines, and is part of the East-Baltic Plain. This area is covered with boulder clay. In some places there are heavy clays on the basis of which slightly podsolized, brown soils and even black earths have been formed. Only the extreme southern part of the Prussian Plain belongs to Poland; it is separated from the open sea by the shallow Vistula Lagoon, almost completely closed in by the 50 km. long Vistula Spit.

To the south of the Prussian Lowland, between the Vistula and the Niemen, is the wide belt of the Mazurian Lake District. It is characterized by intricate intersections of end moraines originating in various stages of the Baltic Glaciation, ground moraine plains and belts of outwash plain. In the north moraine clays predominate and in the south, outwash plain sands, but the dividing line between these two zones is not so evident as in the Pomeranian Lake District. The elevations of the Mazurian Lake District, the highest of which are Dylewska Hill (alt. 312 m.) in the west and the Szeskie Hills (alt. 309 m.) in the east, constitute a water node, from which rivers flow in all directions. Only a few of them flow into the sea, or rather the Vistula Lagoon. Most of them flow either directly into the Vistula or its tributaries: the Bug, Narew and Biebrza rivers, or into the Niemen or Pregoła. These rivers are linked by a number of canals, passing through numerous lakes. The most important are the Elbląg and Augustów canals. The Mazurian Lake District has fewer lakes (about 2,500) than the Pomeranian Lake District (about 4,000), but most of them are bigger and taken together cover a larger area (about 1,400 sq.km.), constituting 45% of the area of all the lakes in Poland. Most of them are rather shallow moraine lakes.

The climate of the Mazurian Lake District, and also of the Prussian Lowland, is more continental than that of Pomerania. The summers are hotter with more sun, spring comes late and is cool, and the winters are long and – going further east – more frosty. The eastern part of the Mazurian Lake District has some of the coldest weather in Poland. Snow lies a long time there, the summers are short and the rainfall considerable (550 to 700 mm. annually), although there is less rain than in the Pomeranian Lake District.

The Mazurian Lake District can be divided into four parts. The Iława Lakes and Dobrzyń-Chełmno Lakes in the west are included by some authors in the Pomeranian Lake District, and thus in the Central European Plain. On the other hand, the centrally situated Mazurian Lake District proper and the Suwałki Lake District in the east (the latter being part of the Lithuanian Lakeland) are included in the East Baltic Plain.

The Mazurian Lake District proper has many lakes. The biggest of them are Lake Śniardwy (106 sq. km. and 25 m. deep) and Lake Mamry (102 sq. km. and 44 m. deep), and also Lake Niegocin, Jagodne, Ryńskie, Tałty, Bełdany, Nidzkie and Roś. Together with the smaller lakes they are situated in a wide depression stretching from north to south and form the complex called The Great Mazurian Lakes.

Fine forests once grew in the Mazurian Lake District, dry pine forests in the south and fresh pine or mixed forests in the north. Beech trees are still found in the western part, mainly in mixed forests. Towards the east, the beech trees gradually disappear, giving way to spruce trees, which are usually found in fresh pine forests and mixed forests. The largest forest complex is the Pisz Forest, which grows mostly on the outwash plain to the south of the Great Mazurian Lakes and is composed mainly of fresh and dry pine woods. Raised or transitory peat bogs are quite common in the forests: they are overgrown with dwarf pines and peat bog vegetation among which are some relics of glacial flora. Large areas of river valleys and depressions left by lakes, where alder woods once grew, are today cultivated meadows. The Suwalski Lake District is in the extreme east. This is an area of high relief with beautiful glacial landforms (eskers and drumlins). There are deep glacial channels through which flow rivers linking the lakes, which are not generally large, but deep. It is here that Poland's deepest lake is situated, namely, Lake Hańcza (area 2,9 sq. km., depth 108 m.). Another very deep lake, but larger is Lake Wigry (area 21.7 sq. km., depth 73 m.), partly situated on the outwash sands of the Augustów Plain, where there are many finger lakes, often very deep, stretching in a latitudinal direction (Lakes Necko, Białe, Studzieniczne and others). The mixed forests and spruce forests which once grew all over the Suwalski Lake District have almost all been felled. The southern part of the area is largely covered by the Augustów Forest, where dry and fresh pine woods predominate with quite a large percentage of spruce. There are also quite a lot of alder woods there, and on the transitory peat bogs there are bog pine forests with quite a large percentage of pubescent birch and willow trees. The Augustów Forest is rich in forest berries, mushrooms and game. Many water and marsh fowl live there, the wood, black and hazel grouse nest there and it is also the habitat of the blue hare. Beavers live in some places is special reserves.

The waters of the Lakeland Belt and the coastal lakes and lagoons are rich in biotic life. In the deep, well oxygenated waters of the oligotrophic lakes there are valuable species of fish, such as the laveret, white-fish, smelt and others. In the lakes with more organic compounds (eutrophic lakes), and less oxygenated, there is a predominance of bream, accompanied by pike, roach, tench, bleak, perch and others. The crucian carp is found in the shallow peaty, dystrophic lakes. The transitional environment between the fresh waters of the lakes and the salt waters of the Baltic are the Szczecin and Vistula Lagoons. The number of fish species found in both lagoons is smaller than in the fresh water lakes or the sea. On the other hand, those species that find the lagoons a good habitat have plenty of nutrition and are numerously represented. These are maritime species that do not need very salty waters or fresh-water fish that are not harmed by some salt in the water. Sea fish (herring, cod and flounder) are found in small numbers. There are more of the species typical of estuary waters, namely, shad, thwaite and smelt, and migrant fish like the eel and the now comparatively rare salmon and bulltrout, but fresh-water fish are predominant.

The lakes and lagoons also abound in water fowl. Wild duck, wild geese, coot, waterhen, grebe, heron, gulls and sea swallows live here in large numbers. In some places swans and cormorants live in protected bird sanctuaries. In the migratory seasons, many northern birds are seen, many of which spend the winter here.

The Quaternary formations covering the Lakeland and Coastal Belt areas and the Tertiary deposits beneath them do not indicate possibilities of valuable mineral resources being found here. In various periods man has shown an interest in the cretaceous limestones brought there by the ice-sheet, the Tertiary Toruń loams, valuable in brick production, and the brown coal deposits, Amber, petrified resin probably derived from the Eocenic coniferous forests, is another of the Tertiary deposits. The majority of the amber deposits are in the sea and are washed up on the shore by the waves, most frequently in the vicinity of the Gdańsk Bay. There was once a lively trade in amber. Today it is used to make jewellery and ornaments, most of which are exported. But out of the Quaternary deposits the most utilized by man are the clays. The glacial deposits supply large quantities of sand and gravel for the building industry. The peat is also exploited, and sometimes the lake deposits, for instance, the meadow marls used for liming soils and for the production of lime and even cement. Bog ores were also extracted at one time.

Man settled late in the Lakeland and Coastal Belt because the ice-sheet was later in withdrawing there than in other parts of Poland. The earliest traces of man's presence date back to the early Mesolithic Age. In the Neolithic Age, the primitive slash and burn agriculture appeared, penetrating there from the south along the Odra and Vistula banks and gradually moving to the Szczecin Lowland, the lower reaches of the Vistula, the Chełmno Lakes and Mazurian Lake District up to the River Pregoła. At the beginning of the Bronze Age, when Pomerania was within the range of the Lusatian culture, different cultures – probably pre-Baltic – prevailed in the Mazurian Lake District.

At the beginning of the Iron Age (700–500 B.C.), the poorer Pomeranian culture separated itself from the Lusatian culture. In the la Tène Age (150 B.C. to the beginning of our era), Pomerania was known for the high quality of its iron products, particularly weapons. On the other hand, the Baltic cultures of the Mazurian Lake District, the Lithuanian Lakeland, and the Prussian Lowland developed more slowly. The Stone Age lasted about 500 years longer in these areas.

The growth of trade with Rome along the Amber Route leading to the Bay of Gdańsk, brought the first mention of the people inhabiting these parts, whom the Romans called the Venedi or Veneti. About the 1st century A.D., the Scandinavian Goths appeared here, and not long after them, the Gepids came for a short period.

Not much is known about the history of these parts in the period of the Great Migration. In the early Middle Ages, the areas round the mouths of the rivers Odra and Vistula and some parts of the Słowiński Coastal Belt were already densely populated by Slavonic Pomeranians. In the 9th and 10th centuries, Wolin and Kołobrzeg were known as big trading centres. On a 10th century archaeological site in Wolin, Persian coins and Egyptian beads were discovered. Wolin then had a population of 5 to 10 thousand and competed with the biggest Baltic ports. The local artisans had mastered the art of smelting glass, working iron, goldsmithery, weaving and shipbuilding, Kołobrzeg was known as a centre of shipbuilding and salt works. In the 12th and 13th century Szczecin took the leading place. It was a town with a stronghold and had a population of 5,000, and was also a centre of Slavonic cults, which resisted Christianization for a long time. As time went on Szczecin became a wealthy town, a trade centre and capital of the most important of the Pomeranian principalities.

In Eastern Pomerania, the fortified settlement of Truso was already known in the early 9th century. It was situated on a bay which then cut deep into the land and was probably a trading post of the Vikings. But the biggest fortified town and trading centre of the area was Gdańsk. The earliest mention of Gdańsk in written sources comes from the 10th century, but archaeological finds indicate that it existed much earlier. The above mentioned centres and the densely populated areas surrounding them were separated from the rest of the Polish territories by impenetrable forests. Only along the courses of the Odra and Vistula were contacts easier and this was the route taken by the war expeditions of the Polanes into the land of the Pomeranians and of the Pomeranians into the land of the Polanes, and it was along the banks of these rivers that the main wave of settlement moved. Settlers from Wielkopolska, moving along the banks of the River Brda had occupied the Krajna land. Settlers from the densely populated Kujawy made their homes in the Chełmno Lakeland and then moved along the valley of the River Drwęca to the Lubawa Ridge. Settlers from Wielkopolska, moving along the lower reaches of the Vistula, met Pomeranian settlers who had come from the north and whose outposts were the towns of Gniew and Tczew. Prussian settlers moved into the area from the east.

Already in the year 967, the Polanes had gained ascendency in the rich and populous part of Pomerania along the banks of the River Odra as far as Wolin and Kołobrzeg and later penetrated Vistulan Pomerania. The first Polish ruler, Mieszko I settled his son Świątopełk in Pomerania. Bolesław the Brave founded a bishopric in Kołobrzeg in the year 1000. After his death, Pomerania broke away and became independent. In the following centuries, Polish rulers made repeated attempts to gain control of Pomerania, and though they managed to link Vistulan Pomerania more closely with Poland for a longer period, all attempts were ineffective as regards Western Pomerania, which retained its independence. Gradually it got divided into several duchies, whose relations with Poland were varied. Some of the Pomeranian towns also gained a considerable degree of independence. In the 13th century, many of them had their own self-government based on Magdeburg or Lubeck Law and constituted a sort of municipal republic under the patriciate of merchants, often of foreign origin. The merchants were followed by German craftsmen, who gained superiority over the Slav population, first in the economic sense and then in numbers. The Pomeranian towns had close ties with the Hanseatic League. In the rural areas, the Slav population was in the majority and this state of affairs lasted for several centuries, despite the steady progress of German colonization, conducted mainly by the monasteries. More and more German knights settled in Pomerania. Towards the east, the number of German settlers dropped.

The territories to the east of the Vistula were inhabited by Prussian tribes. The expansion of Polish influences in this area was the aim of the mission of Bishop Adalbert, who was sent there by Bolesław the Brave in 997. The bishop lost his life and the whole undertaking ended in failure. Polish and Ruthenian expeditions raided the territory of the Sudavians beyond the River Biebrza, and in turn, the Sudavians made incursions into Mazowsze and Podlasie.

The Mazovian princes were particularly interested in expansion into Prussian territories and as they were not strong enough to do this by themselves, Conrad of Mazowsze invited the Order of the Teutonic Knights to Poland in 1226 (Order founded by German Crusaders in 1190, changed into an Order of knights in 1198, expelled from Hungary in 1225). The Teutonic Knights undertook to defend the frontier with Prussia and bring Christianity to the heathen Prussians. They received the Chełmno Land as fief, this concession being confirmed by the Emperor and the Pope and extended to include all the Prussian lands conquered by the Order. The "conversion" of the Prussians took half a century and ended with their extermination or germanization. The former local population was replaced by German settlers. In 1308, the Teutonic Knights occupied Gdańsk by strategem, and then Gdańsk Pomerania (1309) and Kujawy (1332). This started the period of Poland's struggles with the Teutonic Knights. The expansion of the Order became a threat to Żmudź (Samogitia), and then to the whole of Lithuania, and this led to the Polish-Lithuanian Union. The Polish-Lithuanian victory over the Teutonic Knights at Grunwald in 1410 put an end to their expansion. Then came the Thirteen Years War, ended with the Peace of Toruń (1466), which restored Gdańsk Pomerania and the Chełmno Land to Poland and also gave the Poles part of Prussia with Malbork and Warmia, known from then on as Royal Prussia. The rest of the state of the Teutonic Knights became fief to the Polish Crown, and in 1525, with the agreement of the King, became a secular state (known as Ducal Prussia) under the hereditary rule of the last Grand Master of the Order Albrecht Hohenzollern. In the years that followed, numerous settlers from nearby Mazowsze went to live there; hence their name – the Mazurians. In the course of the 16th century, the southern part of Prussia, with the exception of the towns, became ethnically Polish.

The restoration of Gdańsk Pomerania to Poland initiated a period of flourishing development of Baltic trade. The export of corn and other Polish products to Western Europe through Gdańsk grew rapidly attaining a very high figure. Gdańsk had a population of 75,000 and became the biggest and most prosperous town of the Polish Respublica and one of the most wealthy towns in Europe. Other towns in the Lower Powiśle area, particularly Elbląg and Toruń, developed and grew richer. In addition to trade, handicrafts developed in the towns, their capital accumulated and science and art flourished. Nicolaus Copernicus was the son of a Toruń burgher and Hevelius, another astronomer, came from Gdańsk. The Flemish school, and the influence of the Italian Renaissance, superimposed on the old, austere Gothic style, created the characteristic "Gdańsk style".

As far back as the days of the Teutonic Knights, the inhabitants of Gdańsk had brought settlers with a knowledge of melioration from the West, mainly from the Netherlands, to do drainage work on the Żuławy (Fens). They transformed the low-lying marshy wilderness into highly productive agricultural land. The example of Gdańsk was followed by big landowners, who organized "olęderskie" (Dutch) settlements in various localities along the banks of the Vistula.

The towns of Western Pomerania also developed, particularly Szczecin. It was through Szczecin that the agricultural products of Wielkopolska, and linen and woollen fabrics from Silesia, were exported to the West, and through Szczecin that cloth from Flanders, French and Brabant linen, herrings and salt were imported to Poland. However, Brandenburg was making this trade ever more difficult. In the middle of the 13th century, Brandenburg siezed the Lubusz Land and became a threat to Western Pomerania. The Brandenburgian expansion to the east and the expansion of the Teutonic Order to the west, which coincided with it, led to Western Pomerania being cut off from Poland for a certain time. The growing threat lead to a partial unification of the Pomeranian lands in the middle of the 15th century, during the rule of Prince Bogusław X. There were also tendencies towards a union with Poland, which did not however take place. In 1521, Pomerania recognized its allegiance to the Emperor. From that time onwards, the ties of Pomerania with Poland became weaker and weaker. Brandenburgian influences became all the greater in the 17th century when, with Poland's consent, the Prussian fief was settled on Brandenburg Hohenzollerns (1618), who tried to free Ducal Prussia from its dependence as a fief. An opportunity presented itself for this during the long Polish-Swedish wars. In 1621, the Swedes landed and seized the Pomeranian coastal area, with the exception of Gdańsk. Forced to withdraw from Royal Prussia after four years of war, they kept the Prussian ports (except Gdańsk, Puck and Królewiec) for several years. During the Thirty Years War, the Swedes occupied Western Pomerania and in 1637 Bogusław XIV, the last prince of Pomerania, died. The Peace of Westphalia (1648) divided Western Pomerania between Sweden and Brandenburg. In 1655, the Swedes again invaded Poland ("The Swedish deluge"). Forced to withdraw after five years of fighting, they left ruined towns and villages behind them. This difficult time for the Polish Respublica was taken adventage of by the Hohenzollerns, who succeeded in getting Ducal Prussia freed from Polish suzerainty. In 1701, the Kingdom of Prussia was founded, comprising Brandenburg and Prussia, and in 1720 the Hohenzollerns extended their kingdom to include Szczecin and the surrounding areas. In 1763, Prussia seized Silesia and then, as a result of the partitions of Poland, Royal Prussia, too.

In the second half of the 19th century, when the speedy industrialization of Germany and the development of its home market created good conditions for the development of agriculture, Pomerania and East Prussia became food suppliers to the Reich. Agriculture, still mostly in the hands of the big landowners, despite the generally rather poor soils, attained a high level of productivity. The numerous small towns were being stimulated. But the traditional, large urban centres like Szczecin, Gdańsk, Toruń and Elbląg were losing their importance in view of the fact that the centres of German economic life were moving westward. The rural population was also emigrating to the west, particularly from Western Pomerania and East Prussia. The Polish element in Pomerania retreated before the germanization pressure. However the people of Kaszuby and the Kociewiaks in Eastern Pomerania resisted germanization and the Chełmno and Krajna lands also retained their Polish character. Despite the enlivenment of the national movement at the end of the 19th century and the preservation of the Polish language, a large percentage of the Lutheran Prussian Mazurians were germanized. Thus the result of the plecisite organized in the southern part of East Prussia after the First World War was unfavourable for Poland and only a very small part of the area went back to Poland. On the other hand, the area formerly known as Royal Prussia was restored to Poland, but without Elbląg and Gdańsk. The latter, with the surrounding area, was made into a Free City under the protection of the League of Nations. The narrow access to the sea gained by Poland was the object of hostile German propaganda, aimed at liquidating the so-called Polish corridor, separating East Prussia from the other territories of the Reich.

The parts of Pomerania regained after the war, which with the other parts then formed the Pomeranian Voivodship, with Toruń as its capital, played an important role in the Polish state of the inter-war years. They were among the best developed areas of the country and were "a window looking out on the world", making possible the development of maritime trade. As Gdańsk did not guarantee secure access to the sea, a new port, Gdynia, was built. Gdynia, which in 1924 was a small fishing village, soon became the leading port on the Baltic. A merchant fleet and navy was then built, which during the Second World War proved its worth.

Polish Pomerania, open to the attacks of the enemy on all sides, was occupied by the Nazis, despite the heroic fight of its inhabitants, symbolized by the famous defence of Westerplatte in the first days of September 1939. Liberation came with the Soviet offensive in the winter of 1945.

Both lake districts and 500 kilometres of the Coastal Belt, from the Isle of Uznam to the Vistula Spit and the mouth of the River Pasłęka, were included in the reborn Polish state in 1945. The last phase of the war brought enormous losses to this area, the communication network, industrial works, port installations and system of melioration were all seriously damaged. The fertile Żuławy (Fens) were flooded and numerous farms and villages ruined. The towns were a scene of destruction, particularly the large ones like Gdańsk, Szczecin, Elbląg, Stargard. Kołobrzeg, for which a stubborn battle was fought, was razed to the ground. As the German forces retreated, population from the neighbouring Polish territories immediately began to move in, later followed by settlers from other parts of the country and repatriates from the USSR. The newcomers, together with the small number of Polish inhabitants who had survived the occupation in the territories belonging to Poland in the interwar years and the autochtons, went to work to rebuild and develop the regained territories.

The Coastal and Lakeland Belt is today an integral part of Poland. A considerable part of Poland's foreign trade goes through this area, above all, the steadily growing turnover with overseas countries. The main centres of the maritime economy are the port complexes of Gdańsk-Gdynia and Szczecin-Świnoujście, linked by land transport routes with the hinterland. Kołobrzeg has again become a trading port. The cargo handled in the Polish ports was 69 million tons in 1978. This was mainly coal, crude oil, ores and grain. Gdańsk has now become the leading Baltic port thanks to its expansion and the modernization of the port installations and warehouses, and above all, due to the Northern Port built after 1971. The Szczecin-Świnoujście port complex, which is also a transit port for the countries on the Danube, has also been modernized and expanded. Gdynia is the biggest general cargo handling port, adapted to handle container cargo. Ships from several dozen foreign countries call at the Polish ports and the Polish maritime ships have their base there. The Polish Merchant Fleet, numbering 323 ships (about 3 million BRT) transported nearly 42 million tons of cargo in 1978. They sail to the most distant ports of the world.

The fishing fleet has also developed vigorously. The total tonnage of its trawlers, cutters, mother-ship and fish collecting and transport units is more than 342,000 BRT. The fishing grounds, which before the war were limited to the Baltic, have now been extended to distant oceans. In 1978, catches totalled nearly 570,000 tons of sea fish. A large percentage of the catches are processed at sea by factory ships or on land by the fishery factories along the coast. Much smaller catches from the lakes, amounting to about 8,500 tons of fresh-water fish annually are supplied by inland fishermen. The merchant ships and fishing vessels are built by the shipyards in Gdańsk, Gdynia and Szczecin. These shipyards, greatly expanded since the Second World War, place Poland among the biggest shipbuilders of the world. About 70% of their production is exported. Polish fishing units in particular have won world fame.

The shipbuilding industry is not the only industry of the coastal belt. Gdańsk is also an important centre of the electrotechnical, metal, chemical, textile, timber and food industries. Among the largest industrial establishments in Gdańsk are the radio factory, the phosphorous fertlizer plant and the recently built oil refinery. The food industry has developed in Gdynia and the engineering industry in Elbląg. Important industrial works are in Tczew, Lębork and Wejherowo. In Szczecin, apart from enterprises connected with the maritime economy, there are many food processing, clothing, chemical, electrical engineering and metallurgical works, including the "Szczecin Foundry", the only iron foundry in the coastal belt. Other important industrial plants are the Szczecin Building Machine Factory, producing mainly for export, the Motor Mechanism Factory and the Fertilizer Plant in nearby Police.

In the Lakeland Belt, industry is not very developed as efforts to industrialize the area on a larger scale were only started after these lands were restored to Poland. Large industrial enterprises have been set up in several medium sized towns on the banks of the lower Vistula. Grudziądz is a centre of the engineering, rubber, building materials and food industries. Toruń is a centre of the chemical and food processing industry and Starogard has the "Polfa" Pharmaceutical Works, a factory making ships furniture and a footwear factory. In Tczew there is a gas metre factory, a car gear factory and a river port and shipyard. In Świecie there is the biggest cellulose and paper mill in Poland. Another one is being built at Kwidzyń.

The biggest industrial centre in the Mazurian Lake District is Olsztyn, which has a car tyre factory, a plastics plant, an engineering works, a building materials factory and also food industry and timber industry enterprises. There are food processing factories in quite a number of places. However, the timber industry is the most numerously represented, mostly by saw-mills. The biggest timber industry enterprises are in Ruciane, Pisz and Augustów.

A characteristic feature of agriculture in the Lakeland and Coastal Belt is the high percentage of state farms. Owing to the extensive meadow and pasture lands, cattle breeding plays an important part here. On the fertile soils of Lower Powiśle, the Pyrzyce region and round Kętrzyn the cultivation of wheat and sugar beet is developing, and also of barley and rape. In view of the high commodity value of agriculture in this area, it supplies large quantities of milk and dairy products and also beef cattle.

The forests covering large areas of the Lakeland and Coastal Belt have made forestry an important sector of the economy here, which means supplies of large quantities of timber processed in the numerous timber industry enterprises, and also forest fruits, a large percentage of which are exported.

The network of smaller towns, mostly well built and well equipped, is dense enough, but the larger urban centres are rather unevenly distributed. The biggest town is Gdańsk (pop. about 445,000), the capital of Gdańsk voivodship. Together with Gdynia (pop. over 225,000) and Sopot (pop. over 50,000) it forms an urban agglomeration of three sister towns (Trójmiasto), fulfilling important administrative, scientific and cultural functions. The Trójmiasto complex has 7 higher schools of learning, many scientific institutes, archives, libraries, museums and theatres. The magnificent historical buildings in the Gdańsk style which have been painstakingly reconstructed are a big tourist attraction.

275

The urbanized Powiśle area has other smaller but important urban centres. First comes Toruń (pop. about 165,000), capital of the Toruń voivodship, a university town with cultural facilities and industry. Elbląg is also a voivodship capital (pop. 103,000). It has lost its former importance as a port, but has become an industrial town. Mention is also due to historical Grudziądz, which is now an industrial town, and Malbork, the old capital of the Teutonic Knights, with the great castle of the Grand Masters of the Order, a unique building of historical interest, which has been rebuilt. There are also many historical buildings in the smaller towns of Powiśle.

The further away from the lower reaches of the Vistula, the smaller the towns get and their network is not so dense. In the eastern part of the Lakeland Belt the largest town is Olsztyn (pop. about 130,000), the capital of Olsztyn voivodship, with two higher schools of learning and a number of cultural institutions. It also has a developing industry. The new voivodship town of Suwałki (pop. 35,000) is much smaller. To the west of the Vistula, two voivodship towns Słupsk (pop. about 85,000) once the capital of a duchy, and the newer town of Koszalin (pop. 82,500) are of medium size. But the main economic and cultural centre of the whole of Western Pomerania, and the second biggest town of the whole of Pomerania, is Szczecin (pop. 380,000), which is an important Baltic port and capital of Szczecin voivodship. Szczecin has 5 higher schools of learning, numerous scientific and cultural institutions and industrial enterprises. Among the historical buildings testifying to the rich past of Szczecin, the most magnificent is the great Renaissance castle of the Pomeranian princes. Nearby Stargard, once the capital of the Pomeranian princes, also has many historical buildings.

Most of the towns of the Lakeland and Coastal Belt supply services to surrounding areas of varying size, as well as being administrative centres of various levels. They also have cultural and educational functions, some of them being industrial towns or junctions. There are also specialized settlements, namely the holiday resorts mostly along the coast, and small ports, most of them fishing harbours.

In the rural areas, most of the settlements are on what used to be the big landed estates of the junkers. Most of them have been turned into state farms. In the Mazurian Lake District, the villages are usually scattered, though one does come across nucleated ones, mostly street villages. There are also some which do not follow any particular layout. In Pomerania, the villages are not so scattered. In the Coastal Belt, the dominating type is the cluster village while further inland street and row villages predominate. Some green villages are also met with.

The rebuilt and developed areas of the Coastal Belt and Lakeland have many attractive places for holiday-makers and tourists. The numerous seaside resorts draw millions of holiday-makers every year. The biggest tourist traffic is in the Gdańsk area. Sopot, the resorts on the Hel peninsula, Krynica Morska, above all, face real invasions of holiday-makers in the summer season. The seaside towns of the western part of the Coastal Belt, particularly Międzyzdroje and Świnoujście, have also become very fashionable resorts. Many of the holiday-makers are from Scandinavia, as there is a ferry service between Poland and Sweden. There are some beautiful seaside resorts in the Słowińskie coastal area, the most popular of them being Kołobrzeg and Łeba.

The lake districts offer different tourist and holiday attractions. The varied scenery, numerous lakes and rivers, the riches of the forests, which abound in game, give the Lakeland a special, unique beauty. The most popular is the chain of Great Mazurian Lakes. The main tourist centres here are Giżycko, Mikołajki and Ruciane. However, there are many who prefer to go to the Suwałki Lakeland, especially the very attractive group of lakes round Augustów. On the western side of the Vistula, the most popular area is the Kaszuby Lake District, where the main centres are Kartuzy and Kościerzyna. Another lakeland tourist centre is the Drawsko Lake District, where in addition to the many lakes there are mineral springs and rich deposits of therapeutic mud. The most well known spa in this area is Połczyn-Zdrój. However, generally speaking there is not so much tourist traffic in Western Pomerania as in Mazury and Warmia.

4

The northern part of Poland is a land of a thousand lakes, scattered among hills, forests, meadows and peat bogs. The most easterly part of the Lakeland Belt is the Suwałki Lake District. It is an area of moraine ridges, piled high upon each other, often strewn with boulders brought there by the ice-sheet from Scandinavia. Cattle graze in the meadows and pastures of the hills. Owing to the difficulties in cultivating this type of country, arable land is of secondary importance here.

In deep depressions, singly or in groups, the lakes here are mostly small, but very picturesque. The highest and most beautiful part of this lakeland area is embraced by the Suwałki Scenic Park (7) including the deepest lake in Poland (108 m.) Hańcza (4), with a beach wreathed in boulders. Due to its depth and the purity of its waters, reminiscent of mountain lakes, it is counted among the oligotrophic lakes. The Smolnickie Lakes, in a deep depression (to 100 m.), particularly Lake Jaczno (3), and also the nearby Kleszczowskie group of lakes (7) are very picturesque too. This area constitutes a water node from which numerous streems flow through the rivers Rospuda, Netta, Biebrza and Narew towards the Vistula and through the rivers Czarna Hańcza, Marycha and Szeszupa, to the Niemen and through the rivers Błydzianka and Pisa northwards to the River Pregoła.

The most beautiful view of the Scenic Park is from Cisowa Hill. Although it is not the highest of the Suwałki hills (alt. 258 m.), its cone-shaped peak is visible from afar (7). Krzemieniucha Hill (alt. 289 m.) north of Suwałki and Rowelska Hill (alt. 298 m.) in the extreme north near Wiżajny are higher. This beautiful area, sunny in summer time and snow-covered in winter, has excellent conditions for tourism, which have not been fully exploited.

Originally, the whole of the area between the Great Mazurian Lakes on the one side and the Niemen and Biebrza rivers on the other was inhabited by the Sudavians, a Baltic people closely related to the Prussians and Lithuanians. They often made sorties into the neighbouring Polish and Ruthenian lands. During the 13th century they were greatly weakened by retaliating attacks by the Poles and Ruthenians, and later by the Teutonic Knights. The last blow was struck at the Sudavians by the Teutonic Knights in 1283, when they siezed their lands, including the western part of former Sudavia, resettling the surviving inhabitants in the vicinity of Pasłęk and also on the Sambia peninsula, where they preserved their language and customs till the 16th century. The rest of the Sudavians escaped to Lithuania, where they were quickly assimilated with the native population. After the Sudavians had ceased to exist as a nation, and all that remained of them were numerous strongholds and place names, their land was overgrown with forests, and was the object of continuous wars between the Teutonic Knights and the Lithuanians. The meadows, the wild forest bees and the lakes, which were well stocked with fish, attracted Lithuanian, Ruthenian and later Polish population from the surrounding areas to the forests.

The Lithuanian princes hunted big game there and had a hunting lodge on the site of the former Sudavian settlement on an island in Lake Wigry. In the 16th century, the Polish kings granted some lakes and parts of the forest to Lithuanian and Ruthenian lords. In the forest areas still belonging to the Polish kings, Queen Bona introduced a rational forest economy and encouraged settlement there. People came to settle there from Lithuania, Podlasie and Mazowsze. In the second half of the 17th century, the monasteries of the Dominicans and Cameldolites undertook the colonization of the forests.

In 1602, the Domincans took over the former estates of the Wiśniowiecki and Sapieha families from the successive owner Jerzy Grodziński, who had founded a town there, and called it Juriewo. In the years 1610–1619 they built a monastery and church in late Renaissance style (6). During the Swedish wars, the town of Sejny (for this was the name it took from the river) was burnt down. It did not recover again till the end of the 18th century.

In 1667, king Jan Casimir granted part of the royal forests to the Cameldolites, consenting to their settlement on the royal island called Wigry. In the years 1699–1745, they built a church and monastery there. The Cameldolites started tree felling, pitch production and smelted iron from bog ore; they also engaged in fishing and agriculture, the produce of which they processed in the mills, distilleries and breweries belonging to the monastery, becoming very wealthy. In the years 1682–1690, the Cameldolites founded a village, Suwałki, by the crossing of the River Czarna Hańcza. Suwałki was granted municipal status in 1715. In the third partition of Poland, the Suwałki area went to the Prussians, who confiscated the estates of the monastery. In 1807, the Suwałki area was incorporated into the Duchy of Warsaw, and in 1815 became part of the Polish

Kingdom. The administrative status of the area was rather complicated and underwent frequent changes. Before the partitions of Poland it was part of the Troki voivodship of the Grand Duchy of Lithuania. Under the Prussians, the Wigry district was set up, but the district seat was Suwałki. In the times of the Duchy of Warsaw, the district seat was transferred to Sejny. After the creation of the Polish Kingdom, the Augustów voivodship was set up; in 1834 it was renamed a governmental unit with its seat in Suwałki. From 1866, it was known as the Suwałki government unit comprising the four districts of: Augustów, Suwałki, Sejny and Mariampol. After Poland regained independence in 1918, the Suwałki area became part of Białystok voivodship. The district of Sejny, through which the Polish-Lithuanian frontier ran, was liquidated. It came into being again in 1956. Then in 1975, when the Suwałki voivodship was set up, like all the other districts of the area, it ceased to exist. During 5 years of Nazi occupation (from 1939–1945), the Suwałki area was incorporated into East Prussia. After the liberation of the country, it was one of the less developed areas of Poland. Its more rapid development has only taken place in the recent decade.

8

9   Lake Wigry is considered the most beautiful in Poland. It has an area of more than 20 sq. km. and is 73 m. deep. The shape of the lake is like the letter "S" and its lenght along its axis is up to 20 km. It is composed of three parts called "plosos". The most varied as regards scenery is the western "ploso" with a high shoreline in the south from which there is a magnificent view of the inlets, spits and islands of the lake. The northern shore of this "ploso" is lower with thick forests; there are many small lakes in the forest. Three of them are linked with Lake Wigry, namely Okrągłe (Round Lake), Długie (Long Lake), and Muliste (Muddy Lake), each of them being different from the others. The central "ploso" has low, forest-grown shores and some deep inlets. The northern "ploso" has many villages on its shores. At the northern end is the Wigry church (8), rising high above the water. Destroyed twice, during both world wars, it has been twice rebuilt. The ruined buildings of the monastery, comprising the so-called Royal Court and about a dozen hermitages, have recently been reconstructed on the initiative of the Ministry of Culture and Art and handed over to be used as a holiday hotel. On the other side of the lake is the village of Stary Folwark. A well known hydrobiological station operated here in the inter-war years. Nearby, where the River Czarna Hańcza flows into Lake Wigry, there is a beaver sanctuary (9). Thanks to man's care, the number of beavers, which had gone down to only a few after the war, has now risen to nearly a thousand. They live in sanctuaries, mostly in Suwałki voivodship. Lake Wigry is the only one in Poland where the Coregonus lavaretus has survived in natural conditions; here it is a different endemic variety.

South of Lake Wigry is an extensive outwash plain area on which the Augustów Forest grows. Fresh pine forests predominate here, the pines being very tall and straight. There are large areas of dry pine forest; mixed forests with spruce are not so frequently found. In the damper areas there are alder-ols woods covering quite large areas in the lower, southern part of the forest. The plunder economy during the Nazi occupation and later tree felling are responsible for the fact that today most of the forests are young. Apart from timber, the Augustów Forest supplies considerable quantities of resin, blueberries and mushrooms. There are also many animals in the forest. Wild bear and deer live there in large numbers and in the southern part one may see the elk or the blue hare (Lepus timidus). In the spring mating season, the forest is the habitat of the black grouse, wood grouse and Scolopa rusticola. The animals are taken care of by the foresters and given extra food in winter in special feeding places (10). The River Czarna Hańcza (11) flows through the Augustów Forest and this part of it is a well known canoe route, leading through numerous lakes and along the Augustów Canal to the main holiday centre of the Suwałki area – Augustów.

When, as a result of the partitions of Poland, the mouth of the Vistula was in Prussia, the idea was born of building a waterway by-passing Prussia in the east. It was to link the Vistula with the rivers Czarna Hańcza and Niemen through the rivers Narew, Biebrza and Netta. The plans for the construction of the canal were drawn up by Ignacy Prądzyński. Building work was started in 1825, but was interrupted by the November Insurrection. It was later resumed by the Bank Polski and completed in 1839.

10

11

The canal is 101 km. long and was made utilizing the canalized River Netta, the Augustów lakes and the River Czarna Hańcza. It had 18 locks, which raised the water level from the River Biebrza to Augustów by 15 metres and from the River Niemen to Augustów by 41 metres. There was a lot of traffic along the canal for 20 years. Later, as no further link-ups were built and because of the railway competition, it lost its importance. Today, the canal is mainly used for tourist purposes (13). Excursions by river boats are organized for the numerous tourists coming to the Augustów lakes. The canal is also used for floating timber from the Augustów Forest to the sawmills on the shore of Lake Białe in Lipowiec and to the railway station in Augustów. Timber is best kept in the water (12).

The central part of the Mazurian Lake District and also its main tourist area is the Land of the Great Mazurian Lakes, a wide depression going in a meridional direction. The lakes along its axis, linked by canals, form a levelled water system 116 m. above mean sea level, its waters going south through the River Pisa to the River Narew, and north through the River Węgorapa to the River Pregoła. The lakes cover 20% of the area here. The most southerly of the Great Mazurian Lakes is Lake Nidzkie (14), surrounded on all sides by the Pisz Forest. It is shaped like the letter "C" and its length along its axis is nearly 23 km. There are several holiday places on the shores of the lake, the biggest is Ruciane at its northern end.

Lake Nidzkie is linked up through several smaller lakes to Lake Bełdany, into which the River Krutynia flows (15). This is a popular canoe route about 90 km. long, passing through several lakes.

18   19

Lake Bełdany fills the southern part of a long post-glacial depression extending as far as the town of Ryn. The central part of this depression is filled by Lake Mikołajskie and the northern part by lakes Tałty and Ryńskie. Lake Mikołajskie links up with Lake Śniardwy (16), the biggest of the Polish lakes. It covers an area of nearly 114 sq. km., but it is not deep (10 m. on an average). In the north-west, Lake Śniardwy links up with the small Lake Łuknajno, where there is a wild swan sanctuary. Lakes Śniardwy and Łuknajno, with a considerable part of the Pisz Forest, many lakes and the lower reaches of the River Krutynia were recently made into a scenic park. At the narrow neck between lakes Mikołajskie and Tałty, is the little town of Mikołajki (17) once a Mazurian village. Tourist traffic started to develop there at the end of the 19th century. Situated in the heart of the Land of the Great Mazurian Lakes, it is one of its main holiday centres.

The finger lakes of the Mikołajskie group are linked up with Lake Niegocin through the canal joining the lakes Tałty and Jagodne. Lake Niegocin is wide and not very deep and is a favourite place for yachting. Many holiday centres have grown up round the lake, the biggest of which is Giżycko. Situated on the isthmus between lakes Niegocin and Mamry, it grew up round a castle built there by the Teutonic Knights in the 14th century. The name of the town was derived from the name of a priest, Gizevius, who was an untiring propagator of the Polish character of the Mazurian Lake District. To the north of Giżycko is the second largest Polish lake, Mamry, covering an area of nearly 105 sq. km. Very irregular in shape, it comprises several parts bearing different names. The most southerly part, called Kisajno, is very picturesque with many islets and merges with the south-western part known as Dobskie. This is where the famous Island of Cormorants (19), where these birds nest, is situated. On the shore of the northern part, that is, Mamry proper, is the town of Węgorzewo, the fourth biggest holiday centre in the Land of the Great Mazurian Lakes. Apart from the Great Lakes, there are innumerable small lakes, some of them really delightful, for instance, Lake Stoczek (18), not far from Orzysz, with its luxuriant growth of water plants.

To the west of Lake Mamry, near Kętrzyn, the main headquarters of the German armed forces in the Second World War was set up in the forest, surrounded on three sides by the waters of Lake Gierłoż. It was here that the unsuccessful attempt to assassinate Hitler was made on July 20th, 1944. When the German troops were retreating in 1945, the headquarters was blown up. All that has remained of it are the huge concrete blocks (20) of which the underground shelters were built (resistant to all kinds of bombardment), the remains of various buildings and also the camouflaged wire fence with metal leaves that enclosed it. The low lying country to the north of Kętrzyn is part of the Prussian Lowland, the most south-westerly part of the East Baltic Coast. It is covered with loam deposits, the remains of the lakes that formed when the tongue of the glacier was withdrawing. On the loam deposits, under the cover of deciduous and mixed forests, fertile brown soils were created. In the early Middle Ages this area was settled by the Prussian tribe of Barts, an indication of which are the remains of a score or so strongholds. This tribe resisted the Teutonic Knights the longest, till the 16th century, and retained its language and customs. In the years 1424–1448, Barcia was the centre of a great uprising of the Prussians, thus the rule of the Teutonic Knights was particularly cruel here. To keep the conquered people in order, the Teutonic Knights built castles, around which towns grew up. The names of these towns are derived from the name of the tribe, like Bartoszyce or Barciany or, as in the case of Sępopol, Rastenburg and Drengfurth, stem from Prussian words. The names of the last two towns were changed after the last war to Kętrzyn (in memory of the well known historian Wojciech Kętrzyński, a son of that land) and Srokowo (in memory of the outstanding geographer Stanisław Srokowski, the author of studies on this area). In the inter-war period, this was an area of huge Prussian junkers' estates. After the war, these were turned into state farms. A huge agricultural-industrial complex has been operating in the Kętrzyn area for the last few years, the biggest of its kind in Poland, with a modern, highly mechanized agricultural economy based on cultivation of wheat and sugar beet and on cattle breeding.

20

21

In a small Mazurian village called Święta Lipka, near the border with Warmia, there is a church which is one of the finest examples of Baroque architecture in Poland. As early as 1400, there was a shrine here with a statue of the Holy Virgin, who was said to have appeared there amid the branches of a huge linden tree. Pilgrimages were made to the statue from Warmia, Mazury and even from Mazowsze. The shrine and the statue were destroyed by Protestants from Kętrzyn, but the cult continued. In the years 1687–1692, the big new church and monastery of the Jesuits was built there (22).

The former capital of the Warmia bishopric, Lidzbark, is situated on the River Łyna on the site of a previous Prussian settlement that existed round a stronghold that was conquered in 1241 by the Teutonic Knights. In 1251, they granted the settlement to the bishops of Warmia, who in 1308 gave it municipal status. In 1350, Jan of Meissen, Bishop of Warmia, had his residence transfered there from Orneta. In 1357, Lidzbark became the capital of Warmia. In the years 1350–1400 a magnificent castle was built there (23). Trade and handicrafts developed in the town. In the second half of the 14th century it already had defence walls, a Town Hall and a wooden water-supply system. The town was a member of the Prussian Alliance aimed against the Teutonic Knights. In 1466, by virtue of the decisions of the Toruń Peace, Lidzbark with the whole of Warmia came under the rule of the Polish king. In the years 1503–1510, Nicolaus Copernicus lived in Lidzbark castle as the physician and adviser of his uncle Bishop Łukasz Watzenrode. After its incorporation into Poland, Lidzbark gained great political, economic and cultural importance. Such eminent humanists as Jan Dantyszek, Stanisław Hozjusz, Marcin Kromer, and later the poet and writer of fables Ignacy Krasicki, were all bishops of Warmia. In 1749, the Chronicle of Gallus Anonymous was discovered in the library of the bishopric and issued in print. After the first partition of Poland (1772), Warmia was incorporated into Prussia and lost its importance. A large military garrison was located there. In the last stage of the Second World War, Lidzbark was badly damaged but already by 1958 the population of the town had surpassed the pre-war figure. As regards buildings of historical interest, apart from the castle with its courtyards surrounded by beautiful arcaded galleries, there is also the 15th century late Gothic castle approach with fortifications from the end of the 16th century, a winter garden, which was enlarged about 1770 by Bishop Ignacy Krasicki, and in the town itself, the Gothic parish church and the remains of the defence walls of the town with the High Gate built in 1532.

22

23

Orneta, situated west of Lidzbark, was first mentioned in chronicles in 1308, but already in 1313 it was granted municipal status by the bishop of Warmia and became the seat of the bailiffs of the bishopric. In 1440, the town joined the Prussian Alliance; in 1466 it was incorporated into Poland. The following period brought prosperity to the town, which was developed and enlarged in Renaissance style, and later in Baroque style. After it came under Prussian rule in 1772, the town declined, only recovering in the second half of the 19th century.

The most beautiful historical building in Orneta is the Gothic basilica built before 1379. The interior decoration dates from the 15th to 18th centuries (24). The only preserved 15th century Gothic Town Hall in Warmia can also be seen in Orneta. Burghers' houses were built round it in the 17th and 18th centuries.

The origins of Olsztyn, picturesquely situated amid hills and lakes, go back to 1334, when in this weakly populated forest-grown area, the Warmia Chapter built a castle. A settlement grew up round the castle, first mentioned in chronicles in 1348; in 1353 it was granted municipal status. In 1440, Olsztyn took part in the activities of the Prussian Alliance, and in 1454, its population, rising against the bishop who favoured the Teutonic Knights, took control of the town and placed it under the rule of the Polish king. The period when the town belonged to Poland was one of flourishing development, both economic and cultural. Many buildings, secular and sacral, were put up at that time and the town was surrounded with defence walls. In the years 1516–1521, Nicolaus Copernicus was the administrator of the town on behalf of the Warmia Chapter. In 1520, he commanded the defence of the town against the Teutonic Knights. A reminder of the presence of Copernicus in the town is the sundial in the castle, which he made himself. The incorporation of the town into Prussia in 1772 caused its decline. The castle was turned into a warehouse at that time. Olsztyn revived to flourish again when it became a railway junction and a large military garrison was located there. As from 1911, it was a regency capital. The population increased quickly, from 4,800 in 1864 to 38,000 in 1914 and 50,000 in 1939. Despite strong germanization pressure, Olsztyn was a centre of the Polish national movement all through this period. Polish societies, schools and banks were active and Polish newspapers appeared there. In 1921, Olsztyn became the seat of the Union of Poles in Germany. After Hitler came to power, this movement was suppressed and the Polish activists were imprisoned or executed. Olsztyn was very badly damaged in the last phase of the Second World War. After the war, it became the capital of a large voivodship and industry developed there. In 1967, a large factory producing motor car tyres was started up in Olsztyn (27). The town has been rebuilt and its cultural functions have increased. In 1950, the Kortowo Higher School of Agricultural Economy was opened there (26) and has since been greatly enlarged. The town has its theatres, and scientific centres, one of which is named after W. Kętrzyński. The pre-war population of Olsztyn was surpassed as early as 1953, and in 1978, the figure was more than 130,000 inhabitants. Olsztyn's historical buildings include the castle, which now houses the Mazurian Museum, a late Gothic parish church, now a cathedral church, which was built before 1445, and the remains of the old town defence walls with the High Gate built in the 15th century (25). In the centre of the town is the Town Hall built in the years 1912–1917 in Dutch Renaissance style (25).

26

27

The "great war" between Poland and the Order of the Teutonic Knights was started by the Knights when they invaded the area called Dobrzyń Land.

The winter of 1409–1410 was spent by both sides preparing for the final encounter. Polish towns contributed money for the campaign, the princes of Mazowsze joined in the preparations for armed conflict, and knights from Silesia and Bohemia came to fight. On June 30th, 1410, the Polish forces crossed the Vistula over the bridge near Czerwińsk and joined up with the forces of Witold, Grand Duke of Lithuania, made up of Lithuanian and Ruthenian companies and also relief brigades of Tatars and Valachians. The forces of the Teutonic Knights, strengthened by many knights who had come from western Europe, were concentrated near Chełmno nad Świecie. The battle was fought on July 15th, 1410, between the villages of Grunwald and Stębark. Both sides had strong forces; the Teutonic Knights' army was smaller but much better equipped, particularly in comparison with the Lithuanian forces. The army of the Teutonic Knights was commanded by the Grand Master of the Order himself, Ulrich von Jungingen. The first to strike were the light cavalry companies of the Lithuanians and Tatars. They scattered the mercenary infantry detachments and caused confusion in the artillery positions set up by the Teutonic Knights, drawing strong enemy forces into battle with them. Under the pressure of the heavy cavalry charge of the Teutonic Knights, some of the Lithuanian detachments had to withdraw. At the same time heavy fighting was going on in the other sectors, both sides throwing new companies into action. The attack of 16 of the best companies of the Teutonic Knights, led by the Grand Master himself, did not succeed in turning the tide of the battle. They were cut down by the Polish forces and the Grand Master was killed. The best knights of the Order fell in battle and many were taken prisoner. The battle ended with the capture of the fortified camp of the Teutonic Knights. It was one of the biggest battles fought in the Middle Ages. The scattered survivors of the Teutonic Knights' army withdraw as far as Malbork. Their castles and towns fell one after another. Finally Jagiełło grouped his forces for an attack on Malbork, but did not succeed in taking the castle. Peace was then concluded.

Although this was a great military success, it did not bring any great change. But it raised the prestige of the Polish-Lithuanian monarchy and remained alive for ever in the memories of the Poles. So on the 550th anniversary of that great victory a monument (28) was raised on the fields of regained Grunwald. It consists of three elements: a granite obelisk on which the heads of knights are carved, 30-metre masts with the flags of the Polish and Lithuanian armies and an amphitheatre, in front of which is a relief map of the battlefield. In the beautifully arranged interior of the amphitheatre (29) there are exhibits connected with the battle. The whole monument area has been suitably laid out and the site of the battle of Grunwald is now a place where various ceremonial events are held. It is visited by numerous excursions from all over Poland and from abroad.

In Nidzica, in the former land of the Prussian tribe of the Sasins, near the boundary with Mazowsze, the Teutonic Knights built a castle in 1310, which later, in the years 1381–1404 was considerably enlarged. The town was founded in 1381 and surrounded with defence walls. In 1410, it was captured by Jagiełło's army. In 1444, it joined the Prussian Alliance, but after the Peace of Toruń, it was again incorporated into Prussia. The area surrounding Nidzica was a place of lively Mazovian colonization in the 14th and 15th centuries. In the 18th century there was a Polish school there, noted for its high level of teaching. The town was ruined in both world wars. Today, after reconstruction, it is a centre of production and services for a small agricultural area.

Rising above the town is the castle of the Teutonic Knights (30), which was restored after the last war. Today it houses a tourist centre and cultural institutions.

The Chełmno Land, granted to the Teutonic Knights in 1228 by prince Conrad of Mazowsze, was used by them as a base from which they conquered Prussia and also for sorties against Poland. In 1293, the Teutonic Knights built a castle at Golub on the River Drwęca, which was the seat of the Commanders of the Order of the Teutonic Knights.

28

29

WIELKA WOJNA
Z ZAKONEM KRZYŻACKIM
W LATACH 1409–1411

After the Peace of Toruń, Golub was returned to Poland together with the whole of the Chełmno Land and developed as a centre of trade and handicrafts. In the years 1611–1625, it was the place of residence of Anna Vasa, sister of Sigismund III Vasa, who bestowed upon her the "starostwo" of the district of Brodnica. She enlarged and remodelled the castle in Renaissance style (31). The frontier between the parts of partitioned Poland ruled by Prussia and Russia separated Golub from its former suburb of Dobrzyń, which then developed as an independent town. In 1950, Golub and Dobrzyń were merged and became the administrative centre of a new district and this accelerated their development. The beautiful Golub castle, which is now a cultural and tourist centre, is used for various ceremonial events.

Toruń is situated on the Vistula not far from its confluence with the River Drwęca. After they had been granted the Chełmno Land, the Teutonic Knights built a small wooden stronghold there. A trading settlement grew up around it, which was granted municipal status in 1233. In the years 1250–1280, defence walls were built round the town.

32

33

Toruń developed quickly and became a member of the
Hanseatic League. At the end of the 13th century the Teutonic
Knights built a castle east of Toruń; they enlarged it in the
years 1384–1392 and founded Nowe Miasto (New Town) on
the far side, which was to compete with the old town. The
limitation of the freedoms of Toruń by the Teutonic Knights
checked its growth. So in 1440, it took the lead in the Prussian
Alliance. The revolt of the town in 1454 against the Teutonic
Knights, who were driven out, marked the beginning of the
Thirteen Years' War. The people of the town destroyed the
castle and joined Nowe Miasto to Toruń. After it was returned
to Poland and granted many freedoms and privileges, Toruń
developed well as an economic and cultural centre. Nicolaus
Copernicus was born there in 1473 and spent his childhood in
the town. The wars of the 17th and 18th centuries brought the
decline of the town. After the second partition of Poland, the
Prussians built a fortress there and turned Toruń into a frontier
garrison town. At that time many of the relics of Toruń's
former splendour were destroyed. The town began to revive
again in the second half of the 19th century. In 1918, when it
was returned to Poland again, Toruń became the capital of the
Pomeranian voivodship and its population was doubled. After
the Second World War, the Nicolaus Copernicus University
was opened in Toruń and industry developed there. From
1975, Toruń has again become a voivodship town and its
population is now over 160,000.

Situated on the high bank of the Vistula, Toruń is one of
Poland's most beautiful towns (2). Part of the defence walls
with gates and turrets on the bank of the Vistula have been
preserved. In the Market Place is the large Town Hall built in
1393 and remodelled in the Renaissance period (32). Round
the Market Place and in the streets running into it there are
many Gothic (34), Renaissance and Baroque (35) houses.
Other buildings of historical interest include the Gothic
churches of St. John (32), dating back to the 13th–14th
centuries and St. Mary's Church (33), also from the same
period.

New residential districts have grown up round the Old Town
quarter since the last war (2, 33), along with a University
quarter of interesting architecture (36).

35

34

36

Chełmno existed as a stronghold as early as the 10th century, later becoming the seat of Piast castellans. In 1215, it was the seat of a missionary bishopric, set up to bring Christianity to the Prussians. In 1228, it was granted to the Teutonic Knights and from 1332 it became for a time their main seat. A year later it received municipal status on the basis of a modification of the Magdeburg Law. At the turn of the 13th century, Chełmno was a thriving centre of trade belonging to the Hanseatic League. It was badly damaged during the Thirteen Years' War and, after the Peace of Toruń, was returned to Poland, becoming a voivodship capital. In the 16th–18th centuries, a branch of the Cracow Academy existed there. Incorporated into Prussia in 1772, Chełmno continued to be a lively centre of the Polish national movement.

Chełmno is one of the few Polish towns where the mediaeval defence walls, with 17 towers and the Grudziądz Gate, still stand today. Within the defence walls the original mediaeval layout of the streets and Market Place with the Town Hall (37) and 5 churches has been preserved.

Lower down the Vistula from Chełmno is the town of Grudziądz. About 1218, it was the seat of a missionary bishopric for Prussia and in 1228 it was granted to the Teutonic Knights. A castle was built here after 1250, in which the Commander of the Order resided. Grudziądz received municipal status in 1291. In 1388, undermined by flood waters, the town collapsed into the River Vistula. In 1440, the town joined the Prussian Alliance and in 1454, the Grudziądz citizens forced the Teutonic Knights manning the castle to capitulate. Grudziądz was returned to Poland in 1466. The Meetings of the Diet of Royal Prussia were held there. The Swedish wars brought ruin to the town. After it was incorporated into Prussia, a fortress was built there, which was one of the most powerful in Europe. Industry began to develop in Grudziądz in the second half of the 19th century. After the First World War, the town became an important centre of trade and industry. The biggest rubber factory in Poland was opened in Grudziądz in 1924.

37

38

During the Second World War, the town suffered heavy losses, but was quickly rebuilt. Industry developed well and Grudziądz also became a lively cultural centre. The granaries, which were built onto the defence walls on the banks of the Vistula in the 17th and 18th centuries, still stand today. The massive tower of the 14th century Gothic cathedral (38) rises over the town as a dominating feature. Further north, in the land of the Prussian Pomezans, on an island in the Vistula once called Quidin, the Teutonic Knights built a base for attacks on the Prussians. It was destroyed many times by the Prussians, and also by the Pomezans. In 1250, Kwidzyń (Quidin) passed into the hands of the Pomezan bishops, and in 1285 it became the seat of a Chapter. In the years 1320–1347, a castle with arcaded galleries and a large "dansker" (39) and next to it a three-nave cathedral, were built there. After the Battle of Grunwald, the Pomezan bishop paid homage to Władysław II Jagiełło. In 1440, Kwidzyń joined the Prussian Alliance, but after the Peace of Toruń, remained with the Teutonic Knights. In the 16th century, the town went through a period of favourable development and in 1772 became a regency seat. In 1945, Kwidzyń was very badly damaged. Today, it is a thriving industrial centre and a large cellulose industry plant is now under construction.

Gniew, situated on the left bank of the Vistula, was an old Pomeranian stronghold. In 1229, the Gniew Land was granted to the Cistercian Order of Oliwa and in 1276, under the last will and testament of the Pomeranian prince Sambor I, passed into the hands of the Teutonic Knights, becoming their first bridgehead on the left bank of the Vistula. In 1282, they built a castle there, which was used as the seat of a Commander of the Order. The settlement which grew up round the castle was granted municipal status in 1297 and in the 14th century it was surrounded with defence walls. After its return to Poland in 1466, Gniew developed well from trade in corn and timber. It was the seat of a royal "starostwo", which in the years 1667–1699 was in the hands of the Sobieskis. Jan III Sobieski often stayed at the castle and built a Baroque palace in the castle approach area. Later the town lost its importance. Its mediaeval layout has been preserved with the remains of the defence walls; there is a Gothic parish church in the Market Place. On the verge of the Vistula valley is the castle, which was burnt down in 1922 and partly rebuilt after the Second World War (40).

39

40

41

42 Further to the north, on the right bank of the River Nogat the
Teutonic Knights started building a castle in 1274 and in 1276
granted municipal status to the settlement round it.
In connection with the transfer of the main seat of the Grand
Masters of the Order from Venice to Malbork, the castle was
greatly enlarged. The original castle, from then on called the
Upper Castle, was extended. Then the Middle Castle with
a large refectory and the Lower Castle were built on the site of
the old approaches to the castle.
In the years 1330–1350 a second ring of defence walls was
built round the castle and granaries were put up on the bank of
the River Nogat. At the end of the 14th century, a magnificent
palace was built for the Grand Master between the Upper and
Middle Castles. As a result Malbork became one of the most
powerful fortress-castles of those times (41). In 1410, when the
Teutonic Knights were preparing to defend the town, they set
fire to it. The castle was captured by Polish forces in 1456.
After it was incorporated into Poland in 1466, Malbork
became a voivodship capital. When it was incorporated into
Prussia in 1772, the castle was used as barracks, warehouses
and workshops for the army. Only a few of the interiors
escaped devastation then. After 1817, the reconstruction of the
castle was started. It !asted until 1921. In 1945, the castle and
the town suffered great damage. Today, following
reconstruction work, the chambers of the castle (42) have been
turned into a museum. The castle is a big attraction for tourists.

43

44

45

Frombork was founded in 1278. In 1310 it received municipal status and for several centuries belonged to the Warmia Chapter. In 1466, together with the whole of Warmia, it came under Polish rule. Nicolaus Copernicus lived and worked in Frombork from 1510 with only short periods of absence until his death in 1543. It was here that he wrote his immortal work "De revolutionibus orbium coelestium". The buildings of historical interest in Frombork are the magnificent Gothic cathedral (43), built in the years 1329–1388, and also the tower dating back to the second half of the 14th century with the rooms where Copernicus lived and worked. In 1973, on the 500th anniversary of the birth of Copernicus, a monument to his memory was unveiled in front of the cathedral. Its historical buildings and its position on the shore of the Vistula Lagoon have made Frombork an attractive tourist centre. Various facilities to accommodate tourist traffic have been built there (44). The Vistula Lagoon is linked with the River Drwęca through the River Elbląžka and Lake Druzno by the Elbląg Canal, which is 178 km. long. Today the canal is mainly used by tourists. The difference in water level over a sector 92 km. long (which amounts to 99 metres) is overcome with the help of five inclined planes, over which the river boats are lifted on steel cables by machines driven by water-power (45).

The Vistula Spit, a fifty kilometre long sand bar, created by the action of winds and waves over centuries, separates the Vistula Lagoon from the open sea. It is covered with pine woods planted by man to stabilize the dunes. There are fine beaches on both sides of the Spit, so it is a favourite haunt of those who like sea bathing and sunbathing. To the west, the Vistula Spit separates the Gdańsk Bay from the delta area of the Vistula – the Żuławy Fens. The building up of the Spit and the accumulation of alluvial deposits from the Vistula in the Gdańsk Bay made it ever shallower and it receded northwards. In the 13th century, the Vistula Lagoon occupied a much larger area than today, reaching a lot farther south and linking up with Lake Druzno. There were also lagoon lakes stretching to the south-east from Gdańsk. The Vistula Spit was not always a continuous sand bar, the water breaking through it in many places, so that the Lagoon and lake linked up directly with the sea. Up to the 14th century, the Vistula forked out into two arms, namely the Wisła Elbląska (Elbląg Vistula), which was the main arm, and the Wisła Gdańska (Gdańsk Vistula). The Nogat was an idependent river. During the flood of 1371, the River Nogat joined the Vistula and the Vistula waters flowed partly into the Nogat. It was then that the Gdańsk Vistula became the main arm. In 1840, when ice floes dammed the river 14 kilometres from the old mouth of the Vistula, it broke through to the sea, shortening and changing its course, bringing most of its waters into a new river bed called Wisła Śmiała (Bold Vistula). In order to straighten the course of the river even more, the Vistula Spit was cut through near Świbno in 1895. The old arms of the Vistula, namely the Gdańska (now the Vistula Backwater) and Elbląska (Szkarpawa) were closed by locks and changed into canals. The same was done with the River Nogat. The River Motława, having its source in the Kaszuby Coastal Belt, with the River Radunia, also flow into the Gdańsk Vistula. In the delta area, under the cover of luxuriant marsh forests, fertile soils were created from the alluvial deposits of the Vistula, which began to attract settlers quite early. In the 12th and 13th centuries, the higher ground amid the marshes of the delta was already inhabited by settlers. In the 14th century, the Teutonic Knights started draining the Żuławy Fens from the eastern side, bringing settlers from northern Germany, Friesland and the Netherlands to do this work. They were people experienced in draining and drying land. The river banks were regulated, embankments, canals and ditches were built, as well as windmills which worked the pumps. The fens were divided into polders which were cultivated.

47   48

46

In the 16th century, the Żuławy Fens were already known for their high level of agriculture. They supplied food to Gdańsk, Elbląg, Malbork and more distant areas, too. In the 19th century the old dippers and pumps driven by windmills were replaced by steam pumps, and in the 20th century these, in turn, were replaced by electric pumps. As a result of many centuries of man's activity in the delta, the whole area (174,000 ha, of which 47,000 ha was low-lying land 1.8 m. below sea level) was drained. Just before the end of the Second World War, the retreating German troops blew up the embankments, causing 40,000 ha of farm land to be flooded and 32,000 ha water-logged. The bogs that formed as a result of this were covered with a "forest" of reeds growing to a height of three metres and the rest of the land was overgrown with weeds. The Żuławy Fens at that time were more like they had been six centuries before than the agricultural area of not so long ago. Despite the many difficulties that had to be overcome, the Żuławy Fens had been drained again by 1949, and the drainage installations were modernized at the same time. Many state farms were set up in the area. Today, the Żuławy Fens are a land where wheat, sugar beet and rape-seed are cultivated, and also of meadows and pastures where cattle graze (49). A large number of the old buildings have survived in the Fens. They are windmills of the Dutch type (47) and half-timbered churches and houses, many of them with arcades (48).

49

The origins of Gdańsk go back to very distant times. According to references made of it in "The Life of St. Aldalbert", there was already a large settlement there in the year 997, around a stronghold at the confluence of the rivers Radunia and Motława. It consisted of two parts – a settlement at the foot of the stronghold on the bank of the Motława where it bends towards the Vistula and a settlement of fishermen and craftsmen at the confluence of the Radunia and Motława, on the site of the Old Town of today. As regards the political aspect, Gdańsk belonged to the Polish state as far back as the times of Mieszko I. In 1148, there was already a well organized port there with considerable shipping traffic. In the period of feudal divisions, Gdańsk was the capital of an independent duchy ruled by Pomeranian princes. Prince Świętopełk (1220–1266) did a great deal to promote the development of the town and in 1225 granted it municipal status. He founded the churches of St. Catherine and St. Nicholas and encouraged sea trade. The town was surrounded by earth and timber ramparts and at that time extended beyond the later Old Town to the south, as far as the Church of St. Nicholas. In 1242, Prince Świętopełk in alliance with the Prussians, who were rising in revolt, dealt many heavy blows at the Teutonic Knights, but in the end was forced to surrender and gave up Gniew to the Order. The last of the Pomeranian princes Mszczuj II, bequeathed Gdańsk and the whole of the Duchy of Wielkopolska to Prince Przemysław II, who took possession of it after Prince Mszczuj's death in 1294. The murder of Przemysław II, in 1296, just after he had been crowned king of Poland, marked the beginning of the battles fought over Gdańsk Pomerania. The powerful Święca family of nobles, who ruled in Gdańsk Pomerania after the death of Mszczuj II, surrendered the duchy to the margraves of Brandenburg after the death of Wacław II, king of Poland and Bohemia. In 1308, the Brandenburgers laid siege to Gdańsk but could not conquer the stronghold defended by Polish knights. The commander of the Polish knights, Bogusza, turned to the Teutonic Knights for help. The Teutonic Knights came to the aid of the Polish knights, drove out the Brandenburgers, but by a treacherous move got the Polish knights to leave their stronghold and in the night made an unexpected attack on the town, murdering its people and setting fire to the buildings. Shortly afterwards, despite the resistance of the knights and towns of Pomerania, they occupied the whole of Gdańsk Pomerania. After capturing Gdańsk, the Teutonic Knights enlarged and remodelled the former castle of the Pomeranian princes as a residence of the Commander of the Order. During the 14th century, four independent urban organisms grew up round the castle. In 1312, the Teutonic Knights granted separate urban rights to the settlement of Osiek by the castle, which was inhabited by the fishermen and craftsmen from the town ruined in 1308. In 1343, to the south of the Old Town, they founded the Main Town on the River Motława, which became the central district of the future Gdańsk.
The town developed and gained power rapidly and soon became a member of the Hanseatic League. From 1374, there is again mention of the Old Town, rebuilt on the site of the former ruined town. In 1380, the Teutonic Knights founded the New Town to the north of the castle on the bank of the River Leniwka, nearer to the sea and rivalling with the original town.

After the victory at Grunwald, Gdańsk paid homage to the Polish king and in 1440 joined the Prussian Alliance. In 1454, the people of Gdańsk revolted against the Teutonic Order, destroyed the Commander's castle and got control of the town. In the same year, by virtue of a special privilege granted by Casimir IV Jagiellończyk, the town was incorporated into Poland. In the years that followed, Gdańsk participated in the war against the Teutonic Order, supplying the king with money and armed forces.

In 1455, the Main Town Council, with the consent of the king, issued a decision to destroy the New Town, resettling the population on its own territory. By a royal privilege of 1457 the separate administration of the Gdańsk towns was annulled and it became one urban organism. In the course of the following centuries Gdańsk was granted many privileges and considerable independence and went through a period of all-round development, becoming a great economic and cultural centre. The town expanded, particularly to the east and south. A storage district grew up on the other bank of the River Motława – the Island of Granaries – and further east, on the other side of the Nowa Motława river, the Lower Town was built. To the south of the Main Town the Old Suburb developed. In the last of the wars against the Teutonic Order (1519–1521) Gdańsk again fought on the Polish side. In the following decades, Reformation trends became more and more evident in Gdańsk. In the years 1525–1577, the Gdańsk burghers rebelled against the Polish authorities a number of times, but the kings dealt with them by strict rule, punishing the offenders and withdrawing privileges for a certain time. The greatest economic and cultural development of Gdańsk was at the beginning of the 17th century. At that time most of the foreign trade of the Polish Respublica was concentrated in Gdańsk, which exported the corn, timber and other rural products that were brought by the Vistula waterway from all over Poland and was the main importer of goods from western Europe, such as English and Flemish cloth, spices, wines, etc. At the same time, Gdańsk became a big production centre, making cloth, furniture, metal goods, paper and arms.

52

53

The population of the town increased from 25,000 in the 15th century to 77,000 in the middle of the 17th century. Gdańsk was the biggest and most prosperous town in Poland. Art and learning flourished, and Gdańsk was famed for its Academic Grammar School. The wealthy burghers accumulated collections of books and works of art. Many scholars, natural scientists, historians, physicians were active in Gdańsk at that time, among them, the eminent astronomer Jan Heweliusz (Hevelius). Outstanding architects, sculptors and painters worked in Gdańsk and it is thanks to them that the finest Renaissance and Baroque buildings in Gdańsk were created. Numerous poets lived there, writing in Latin, Polish and German. The printing houses attained a high level of perfection. Many works by Polish writers were published there.

In the middle of the 17th century, the town walls could no longer contain the rapidly growing town and they were replaced by more modern, massive defence walls with bastions.

54

55

56

During the Swedish wars, despite the obvious trading losses suffered by the town, Gdańsk remained loyal to the Polish Respublica, both in the years 1626–1629, when the people of Gdańsk decisively rejected the Swedish proposals, and in the years 1655–1657, when almost the whole of the country was occupied by the Swedish army. This loyalty, exceptional in those times, was rewarded in 1658 by an official act of gratitude in the form of a special constitution passed by the Diet. In the years 1733–1734, Gdańsk again defended the Polish king Stanisław Leszczyński to the last, withstanding a long siege by Russian and Saxon forces. When news came of the preparations for the partitions of Poland, Gdańsk did everything possible to remain with Poland, even at the price of being territorially cut off from the motherland. In 1793, at the news of the entry of the Prussian army, the people of the town took up arms.

57

58

In 1797, there was a united revolt of Poles and Germans against Prussian rule. This led to severe Prussian repressions in Gdańsk. In 1807, after a long siege, Gdańsk was taken by Napoleon's French and Polish forces. The Free City of Gdańsk was then set up; it experienced an economic slump due to England's continental blockade and the burdens of war. Incorporated into Prussia again in 1815, the town lost many of its privileges. Then came years of stagnation, from which Gdańsk was only to recover in the second half of the 19th century, when the port was enlarged and the shipbuilding industry developed there. In 1879, Gdańsk was the seat of the authorities of the province of West Prussia. Despite germanization pressures, the Polish national movement continued to exist in Gdańsk.

In 1919, by virtue of the decisions of the Treaty of Versailles, Gdańsk was proclaimed a free city together with its surroundings and almost the whole of the Żuławy Fens along the River Vistula. The Free City of Gdańsk was governed by a Senate under the protectorate of the League of Nations and a High Commissioner appointed by the League was in residence there. Poland was represented in Gdańsk by a Commissioner General of the Polish Respublica, who looked after the interests of the Polish institutions there. The port of Gdańsk remained under the authority of the Port Council, of which half the members were Gdańsk directors and half Polish. Gdańsk had a customs union with Poland. During the inter-war years the port of Gdańsk was modernized and the town grew in size. There were Polish schools, social and scientific organizations there, as well as associations of Poles affiliating almost the whole of the Polish population. Polish-Gdańsk relations, which at first were formal and correct, began to deteriorate considerably after Hitler came to power in Germany in 1933.

At dawn on September 1st, 1939, the first shots of the Second World War were fired in Gdańsk. They came from the guns of the German battleship "Schleswig-Holstein", which had just arrived in Gdańsk on an official visit. A heroic resistance was put up by the defenders of the Polish Post Office and the small force at the trans-shipping depot on the sand bar called Westerplatte, formed in the 17th century, resisted the attacks of the enemy for seven days.

During the fighting in March 1945, Gdańsk suffered great devastation. The historical central district was particularly badly hit. Work was started to rebuild the town immediately after it was regained and went on till 1960. The port of Gdańsk was soon working again despite the considerable damage it had suffered. In July 1945, the first ship entered the port after the war and in December the same year Gdańsk was already handling cargo from ocean line ships. In the Seventies, the construction was started of the Northern Port. The cargo handled in Gdańsk increased from 5 million tons in 1948 to more than 25 million tons in 1977.

As regards trans-shipment, Gdańsk has risen to the first place among the Baltic ports. Most of the goods handled are bulk cargo, such as coal, ores, grain, etc. The Gdańsk shipyards were also rebuilt and enlarged. Various branches of industry have developed there, to mention the engineering, chemical and food industries. In 1972, the construction of an oil refining plant was started near Gdańsk.

The town has also become a centre of science and culture. Shortly after liberation, the Gdańsk Technical University was opened, to be followed by the Medical Academy, the Teachers' College and the Higher School of Economics. The two last mentioned higher schools created conditions for the opening of the University of Gdańsk in 1970. Today, there are seven higher schools in Gdańsk, as well as numerous scientific institutes and societies, archives and museums. Gdańsk has its theatres, an opera house and philharmonic orchestra. The beautiful beaches and holiday facilities attract large number of tourists. The population of Gdańsk, which was 250,000 in 1939 and only 118,000 in 1946, is now about 450,000.

Among the buildings of historical interest in the Old Town mention is due, above all, to the Great Mill on the bank of the River Radunia, built in the second half of the 14th century (50), the Gothic Church of St. Catherine next to it, dating back to the same period (50) and the late Renaissance Town Hall. The most magnificent buildings are in the Main Town (1). The 14th century defence walls surrounding it, with turrets and towers, have been partly preserved. The Royal Way leads through the Renaissance Golden Gate (53), next to which is the late Gothic building that was once the seat of the Brothers of St. George, to Długa Street and Długi Targ (Long Market Place) (52). On both sides of the Royal Way there are Renaissance and Baroque burghers' houses, which have been reconstructed from the war ruins. Długa Street ends at the Main Town Hall, built in the years 1378–1382, enlarged in the 15th and 16th centuries; it has a slender tower (52), crowned with a cupola on which there is a guilded statue of king Sigismund Augustus.

Next to the Town Hall is the Court of Artus, dating back to the end of the 15th century, originally Gothic and remodelled in the years 1616–1617 in late Renaissance style (54), with beautiful interior decoration (55); this was once the place where the wealthy burghers held their assemblies. In front of the Court is the Neptune Fountain dating back to the 17th–18th centuries, with the White Eagle symbolizing the links of Old Gdańsk with Poland (56). The Royal Way ends at the Green Gate, a Renaissance palace on the bank of the River Motława, which was built as a residence of the Polish kings. The Main Town has retained its regular mediaeval layout with 9 streets running at right angles to the River Motława and ending in what were called Water Gates, where goods were loaded and unloaded.

In the centre of the Main Town stands the massive Church of St. Mary (52), from the years 1343–1502. It was burnt down in 1945, but has been reconstructed. The old houses surrounding the church have also been rebuilt. On the bank of the River Motława there is an old wharf crane dating back to the middle of the 15th century (58). It now houses a Maritime Museum.

There were once 200 granaries on the island on the other side of the River Motława. Only a few

of them have survived. In the 17th century the construction was started of the New Port near the mouth of the River Leniwka, which later handled almost all the cargo and passengers coming to Gdańsk. This port was enlarged when it was being rebuilt after the war. On the sand bar of Westerplatte, the other side of the River Leniwka, a monument has been erected to the memory of the heroic defenders of the Westerplatte depot (57).

The Gdańsk shipyards are on the River Motława where it flows into the Vistula Backwater. Completely destroyed in 1945, the shipyards have been reconstructed and considerably enlarged. Various types of ships are built there, both merchant and fishing vessels (59) for the Polish shipping companies and for export. The Shipyards have their own Design Office (60). In 1972, the construction was started of the Northern Port to the east of the mouth of the River Leniwka; it is a very large modern port, part of which is already in operation (61). Many modern residential districts have grown up round the old quarters of Gdańsk in recent decades. The one known as the Przymorze District is worth special mention due to its position and interesting architecture (62).

61

63 North of Old Gdańsk are Wrzeszcz and Oliwa, formerly independent
settlements, which were incorporated into Gdańsk in the inter-war years.
In 1186, Prince Sambor I of Pomerania brought the Cistercians to
Western Pomerania. They built a monastery which they called Oliwa.
About 1200, the monastery church was built, which was most probably
the first brick-built Romanesque church in Pomerania. It was destroyed
in the years 1224–1234 by the Prussians and the Teutonic Knights and
was rebuilt at the end of the 13th century in Gothic style. Burnt down
and rebuilt several times it was given a Rococo style façade in 1771 (63).
Inside the church there is a magnificent Rococo organ built in 1750, on
which concerts are given. In 1660, the Oliwa Monastery was the scene of
the signing of the peace treaty which put an end to the Polish-Swedish
wars. In the years 1740–1782, a beautiful park was laid out round the
monastery. In 1772, the Prussian government confiscated the property of
the monastery and in 1831 the Order was dissolved and the church
handed over as a parish church. In the 19th century, Oliwa became
a well known summer holiday resort. In 1874 it was granted municipal
status and in 1925 was incorporated into Gdańsk as one of its districts.
After the Second World War, Oliwa was an independent town for a few
years, after which it again became a district of Gdańsk (in 1947).
The north of Gdańsk is Sopot, which from the middle of the 16th century
became a favourite summer holiday resort for the people of Gdańsk, and
later a famous seaside resort known for its curative baths. Its long pier,
extending 512 metres out to sea, is very popular with holiday-makers
(64).
The first mention of Gdynia was in 1224, as a village granted to the
Cistercian monks of Oliwa. It remained a village until 1926. In 1922, as
Gdańsk was outside the frontiers of Poland, it was decided to build a new
sea port there on the site of Gdynia. The place chosen for the future port
was at the outlet of the southern arm of the wide and swampy Reda
Pradoline into the Gdańsk Bay. The port comprised two parts: the inner
part formed by excavating the peat from the floor of the pradoline, and
the outer part formed by building jetties extending out into the sea. Then
docks, canals and quays were built and next to them the shipyards, cold
storage plants, a rice-husking mill, an oil mill and other plants connected
with the port.

In the course of little more than a dozen years, Gdynia became the biggest port on the Baltic as regards the amount of cargo handled, the figure in 1937 reaching 9 million tons. The town developed on the slopes of the hills above the port and in 1939 already had a population of 120,000. The port of Gdynia was badly damaged during the spring offensive of 1945. But in July of the same year the first ship entered the port after the war.

In the years that followed, Gdynia was expanded and modernized, specializing in the handling of general cargo. The amount of cargo handled grew from 5.7 million tons in 1949 to 13.5 million tons in 1977, coal only accounting for 3.8 million tons. Gdynia is also a passenger port (65). It is the home port of the liner "Stefan Batory", which services the north American line. Its industry has grown rapidly. The former rather small shipyard has been greatly expanded and industry servicing the port and fisheries has been developed. Gdynia has also become an important centre of science and culture and the quickly growing town now has a population of 240,000.

The most northerly point of Poland is Cape Rozewie, on which the first Polish lighthouse was built as early as the 16th century. The lighthouse of today dates back to the year 1771; it was enlarged in 1910 and it has recently been made higher so that it can be seen over the tops of the trees growing round it (66).

From the Swarzewo Promontory, which is part of Cape Rozewie, the spit called the Hel Peninsula extends in a south-easterly direction for 34 km. Only 200 m. wide at its base, the Hel Peninsula widens out to three kilometres at its end, where it is also higher. Pine woods grow on it, which are cultivated to stabilize the sands. The side facing the open sea has a rather monotonous landscape and the beaches are narrower (69), while on the Puck Bay side the shoreline is more varied and the beaches are wider, though more muddy. In the 17th century, the spit consisted of five islands, on which there were Polish fortifications and – at least from the 14th century – fishing villages were located there. As time went by the islands joined up to form the Hel Peninsula of today. In the inter-war period, particularly after a railway line had been built linking Gdynia with Hel, the fishing villages there grew into well known seaside resorts. Their popularity has increased still more since the war due to the construction of a road leading to Hel.

66

67

The best known seaside resort is Jastarnia, which was already mentioned as early as 1378. In the years between the two world wars, various facilities for tourists were built there, and a luxury holiday resort – Jurata – was built nearby. After the war, the fishing and yachting ports were enlarged and holiday homes were built (68).

The first written records of the town of Hel are from 1351, referring to municipal authorities. But the first foundation charter was not granted till 1378. The inhabitants of Hel lived from fishing herrings and the export of fish to Pomerania and inland to other parts of Poland. When the shoals of herring disappeared from this part of the Baltic, the town declined. At the beginning of the 15th century the town of Nowy Hel (New Hel) was founded two kilometres away from old Hel. In 1454, Hel and part of the peninsula were granted to Gdańsk by Casimir IV Jagiellończyk.

However, the town did not develop very well and in 1872 it lost its municipal status. At the beginning of the 20th century, the settlement that had so far only been inhabited by fishermen gradually turned into a seaside resort and developed considerably during the inter-war period. In September 1939, Hel put up a heroic defence against the Nazi troops, holding out for more than a month. After the war, the harbour and fishing base were enlarged and in 1963 Hel again received municipal status. In the Protestant church dating back to the 15th century there is now a Museum of Fishing. In the main street, the old half-timbered fishermen's cottages with gables facing the street still stand (67). They were built in the middle of the 19th century.

68

69

The most easterly part of the Pomeranian Lakeland is the Kaszuby Lake District. It is also the highest, rising in the middle to an altitude of 328 m. The high moraine hills are divided by deep glacial channels either filled by finger lakes or marshes and peat bogs left by former lakes, or by deep river valleys. The River Radunia flows in a deep valley cutting through the hills, carrying the water from the longest glacial channel in this Lake District, in which there are ten lakes. The largest of them is Lake Raduńskie, covering an area of 8.8 sq. km. and 40 m. deep. It is surrounded by farm land (72). Further to the south, near Wieżyca, is Lake Ostrzyckie (73), surrounded by beautiful beech woods. This is a well known tourist area with good facilities for recreation and water sports (73). Many holiday makers spend their holidays in the well built Kaszuby villages. Going southwards, in the vicinity of Kościerzyna (74), the soils get more sandy and large areas are covered with pine forests. In the depressions there are often peat bogs.

70

71

72

73

South of Kościerzyna is the large irregularly shaped Lake **74**
Wdzydze, covering an area of 14.2 sq. km. Its maximum
depth is 55 m. There is an old Kaszuby village, Wdzydze
Kiszewskie, on the shore of the lake, which is a well
known holiday place and also an important centre of
Kaszuby folk culture. A large Ethnographic Park with
a Skansen type museum has been set up in the village with
a number of old buildings that are examples of the rural
architecture of the Kaszuby people (75).

Further south is a large area of outwash plain on which the Tucholskie Forest grows. It is crossed by the rivers Wda (77) and Brda. Here, near the village of Odry, there are stone rings that were probably once used in old pagan rites. They are made of large erratic blocks (76) arranged in several rings with a diameter of 16–24 m. Both the River Wda and River Brda are popular tourist routes. Timber is also floated down the Brda (77).

75

76

Most of the towns of Eastern Pomerania were founded in the 14th century. Two former district towns were founded much later; one of them, Wejherowo, was founded in 1643 by the wealthy Wejher family on the borderline of the Reda Pradoline and the hills of the Kaszuby Lake District. It received municipal status in 1650. The Market Place was laid out (70) at that time and houses were built round it; on two sides of it there are churches. The town did not develop very well. Its real development only came in the second half of the 19th century, when a railway line facilitated access to it. From its return to Poland in 1920 until 1975 it was a district town. Today, many of its inhabitants commute to work in Gdynia.

In the central, high part of the Kaszuby Lake District on an isthmus between two lakes, the Carthusian monks who had been brought from Prague built a church in the years 1380–1405 and also several hermitages round it. As time passed the Order became very wealthy, but the wars and plagues of the 15th to 17th centuries caused the monastery and the settlement round it to decline. After the first partition of Poland, the Prussian government confiscated the monastery's property and after the dissolution of the Order there in 1826, destroyed most of the buildings. In 1818 Kartuzy became a district town and from that time on gradually began to assume an urban character. However, it was not granted municipal status until 1923. Kartuzy has been a centre of the Kaszuby regional movement for a long time. The most beautiful building in the town is the Gothic church with a roof of unique shape, rather like a coffin. It was built in the years 1731–1733 (71). Next to the church are a refectory and the only surviving hermitage.

77

78

79

80

Bytów, in the western part of the Pomeranian Lakeland, was already a Slav stronghold in the 9th and 10th centuries. In the 14th century, Bytów changed hands many times between the princes of Gdańsk, the Brandenburgers and the Teutonic Knights, and later also the princes of Western Pomerania. In the years 1390–1405, the Teutonic Knights built a massive castle there (79). After the death of the last of the Pomeranian princes in 1635, Bytów returned to Poland, but not for long. In 1657, by virtue of the treaty of Wielawa and Bydgoszcz, it was handed over to the Elector of Brandenburg as a fief in return for his aid to Poland in the war with the Swedes.

By virtue of the same treaty, Stare Drawsko also came under the rule of Brandenburg. It was a former settlement on the border between Wielkopolska and Pomerania, which as early as the 13th century had been conquered by the Brandenburgers. In 1368, it was incorporated into Poland by Casimir the Great, who built the massive Drahim castle there, of which today only ruins remain (82). Picturesquely situated on an isthmus between lakes Drawsko and Żerdno, Stare Drawsko is now a favourite place for summer holidays.

In the Słowińskie Coastal Belt, near Łeba, a National Park has been set up to protect the shifting sand dunes on the coast (81) as well as the lagoon lakes: Łebsko, Gardno and Sarbsko, the Scared Hill of the Pomeranians, Rowokół, and the Słowińskie villages where the old language, customs and traditional building style have been preserved the longest.

On the right bank of the River Słupia there was a stronghold as far back as the middle of the 10th century. In the 13th century, the town of Słupsk grew up from the settlement round the stronghold. It belonged to the princes of Gdańsk till the end of that century. Next it changed hands, successively going to the Brandenburgers, the Teutonic Knights and the princes of Western Pomerania. In 1310, the Brandenburgers founded a new town on the left bank of the River Słupia. Słupsk developed in the 14th to 16th centuries. It was the capital of an independent duchy and an important trading centre. In 1653, it again came under the rule of the Brandenburgers. In 1945, the town was badly damaged. After it was rebuilt it became an important economic and cultural centre. Since 1975 it has been the capital of a voivodship.

81

82

Above the mouth of the River Wieprza, on Darłowo Hill, there was an old Pomeranian stronghold in the 11th century. At its foot there was a trading settlement belonging to the princes of Gdańsk in 1205. In 1270, Darłowo was taken by Prince Wisław II of Rugen, who built a castle there and granted municipal status to the settlement. In 1316, the town passed into the hands of the Western Pomeranian princes who often resided in Darłowo.

In the 14th and 15th centuries Darłowo developed well and joined the Hanseatic League. After the death of the last of the Pomeranian princes in 1637, the whole of Western Pomerania came under the rule of the Brandenburgers by virtue of the Peace of Westphalia; later it went to the Prussians.

Today, Darłowo is one of the fishing ports of the Polish coast (83) and nearby Darłówko is a seaside resort.

Koszalin, situated about 10 km. from the sea, near the lagoon lake of Jamno, was first mentioned in chronicles in 1214. In 1248, it became the property of the bishop of Kamień who granted it municipal status in 1266.

87 In the 13th and 14th centuries, Koszalin became a trading centre and belonged to the Hanseatic League. When the Reformation Movement achieved victory, the town came under the rule of the princes of Western Pomerania; after the Thirty Years' War, in 1648, it came under the rule of Brandenburg and later – under Prussian rule. The wars, fires and plagues of the 17th and 18th centuries caused the town to decline. It only started developing again in the 19th century when it became a regency seat and due to the building of railway lines linking it with Gdańsk and Szczecin. In 1939, Koszalin had a population of about 33,500. The Second World War brought great losses to the town. After the war, particularly from 1950 when it became a voivodship capital, Koszalin was rapidly rebuilt and now has a population of 85,000. The central district of the town, which was destroyed during the war, has been reconstructed and a new Town Hall has been erected in the Market Place (84).

The beginnings of Kołobrzeg as a trading centre go back to the 7th century. There was a salt-works there, guarded by a stronghold, around which a trading settlement grew up. At the turn of the 10th century, Kołobrzeg belonged to the monarchy of the first Piast rulers. In 1000, Bolesław the Brave founded the first bishopric there. In the 10th to 12th century, Kołobrzeg was the main stronghold of Western Pomerania. Danish and Swedish ships called at Kołobrzeg to take cargoes of salt and Kołobrzeg had trade contacts with such distant lands as Byzantium and the Arab countries. In 1248, it became the property of the bishops of Kamień. In the middle of the 13th century a settlement of German colonists was founded between the stronghold and the salt works, which in 1255 was granted municipal status and became a member of the Hanseatic League. After the Reformation Movement had achieved supremacy, Kołobrzeg freed itself from the rule of the bishops, but as a result of the Thirty Years' War, during which the town was occupied and plundered by the Swedes, it passed under the rule of the Brandenburgers.

Later, it was ruled by Prussia.

The development of Kołobrzeg went in a new direction after the building of the first twig tower there in 1710. The second was built in 1718 and two more had been built by the end of the 19th century. Gradually, Kołobrzeg became an important spa. On the other hand, the importance of Kołobrzeg as a port has diminished.

In March, 1945, after ten days of stubborn fighting, detachments of the First Polish Army and Soviet troops took Kołobrzeg. The town was 90% destroyed and its population was reduced to 2,800. The reconstruction of the town took many years. Today it has a population of more than 55,000. The Kołobrzeg port was opened in 1960. With its excellent beaches (86), Kołobrzeg has become a very popular seaside resort, also visited by Swedish tourists. The spa facilities in the town have also been developed. New sanatoria (85) and hotels have been built for those coming to Kołobrzeg for a cure. A monument (86) has been erected there in the place where, in 1945, Polish soldiers confirmed Poland's access to the sea by taking a ceremonial oath.

The high cliffs of the coast in the western part of Pomerania are constantly threatened by the undermining action of the waves. In the 13th century, the centre of the village of Trzęsacz, situated to the west of Kołobrzeg, where a Gothic church was built later (in the 15th c.), was 1.8 km. from the sea. In 1750, it was 58 m. from the sea, and in 1820 – only 13 m. In 1874 the church was closed and in 1884 it stood on the very edge of the cliffs. In 1901, part of the church collapsed into the sea. Only a small part of the church remains today (87).

In the 10th century, there was a stronghold on an islet in the boggy valley of the River Ina, mentioned in chronicles from the year 1124 as Stary Gród. It was given the name of Stargard in references dating back to 1140, when it was mentioned as a castellan's seat. It was granted municipal status in 1253 by the Pomeranian prince Barnim I. The foundation charter embraced the Lower Town on the islet and the Higher Town on the left bank of the River Ina. After the feudal divisions of Western Pomerania in 1292, it was incorporated into the Duchy of Szczecin. Due to its position on the boundary of the fertile Pyrzyce Land, Stargard became an important centre trading in corn, which was transported along the River Ina to the Szczecin Lagoon. It was then one of the biggest towns in Pomerania, enjoying many freedoms. As a result of competition with Szczecin, disputes arose quite frequently, sometimes settled by taking up arms. During the Thirty Years' War, the Swedes captured the mouth of the River Ina and blocked the corn trading. In 1653, the town came under the rule of the Brandenburgers and until 1720, that is till Szczecin was taken, it was the seat of the authorities governing Western Pomerania. At the end of the 18th century industry was developed in Stargard. In 1939 it had a population of nearly 40,000.
During the fighting in the spring of 1945, Stargard was badly damaged. Since it was rebuilt, the town has become an important centre of industry and services, with a population of more than 55,000.
Stargard's historical buildings include the Gothic Church of St. Mary built at the end of the 13th century, later enlarged and after the war partly reconstructed (88). Next to it is the late Gothic Town Hall built in 1569, remodelled in 1638 in late Renaissance style (89). Parts of the old defence walls with turrets and gates dating back to the 15th–17th centuries and the later fortifications with bastions from the 16th and 17th centuries have been preserved, too.

88

89

91 To the south of Stargard is the Pyrzyce Plain, known for its fertile black earths formed on lake deposits of loam. Settlement was early here and it was mentioned in the Bavarian Geographer in the 9th century as the land of the Pyrzyczanie tribe.

As "pyro" in the pre-Slav language meant wheat, the area must have been known already then as a wheat growing area. The early settlement of the Pyrzyce Land by Germans led to its speedy germanization. An important part in this process was played by the Cistercian monastery in Kołbacz, founded in 1174 by Prince Bogusław I, who granted large estates to the Cistercians. In 1276, the Brandenburgers entered the Pyrzyce Land, transferring it from the Poznań church administration to the Kamień bishopric and later to the Lubusz bishopric. Nevertheless, the Pyrzyce Land remained in the hands of the Szczecin princes and the huge estates of the monastery also passed into their hands after secularization.

After the Thirty Years' War, the Pyrzyce Land was ruled by the Brandenburgers, then by the Prussians. Today, the Pyrzyce Land is an area of modern, mechanized agriculture, growing wheat and sugar beet. State farms play an important role in this area (90).

There was a small stronghold on the high bank of the Odra, guarding a river crossing, as early as the 9th century. At the end of the 10th century it was enlarged by Mieszko I into a mighty fortress guarding the western frontier of Poland. Here, on June 24th, 972, the famous battle of Cedynia was fought, as a result of which Mieszko I and his brother Czcibor defeated the forces of Margraves Hodo and Siegfried who led an expedition against Poland. In the 11th century Cedynia was a castellan's seat and later it belonged to the Pomeranian princes. In 1252, it was incorporated into Brandenburg.

Cedynia became known again at the end of the Second World War, as the place from which the great offensive of the Soviet forces and the First Polish Army heading for Berlin was started on April 16th, 1945. A monument (91) has been erected at Cedynia to commemorate this event.

Szczecin grew up on the high left bank of the River Odra, not far from where it flows into the Szczecin Lagoon. As early as the 9th century there was already a large stronghold fortified with earth and timber ramparts 12 m. wide and a deep moat on the site of the present Castle Hill. Higher up the River Odra from the stronghold there was a trading and handicrafts settlement. It developed quickly and already in the 10th century had the attributes of a town. It had extensive contacts with the Scandinavian countries and Western Europe. In 987, Mieszko I captured Szczecin and together with the whole of Pomerania incorporated it into Poland. After the death of Bolesław the Brave, the town regained its independence, but nearly 100 years later, in 1121, it was taken by Bolesław the Wrymouthed. In 1124 a Polish mission baptized the inhabitants of the town. In the 11th century, Szczecin was an independent merchants "republic" trading in corn, salt and fish. In the second half of the 12th century, it lost its independent position, coming under the rule of the Pomeranian princes and the stronghold became a castellan's seat. A German settlement began to develop higher up the Odra than the existing Slav one.

92
93

95 In the years 1237–1243, Prince Barnim I granted Szczecin municipal status and by 1278, at the latest, it had become a member of the Hanseatic League and had a population of 5–9 thousand. In the 13th and 14th centuries defence walls were built round the town. In the middle of the 14th century, Prince Barnim II started to build the castle. In the 15th century shipping developed on the rivers Odra and Warta and most of the trade from Wielkopolska went through Szczecin. At the end of the 15th century, Prince Bogusław X transferred the capital of the Duchy of Western Pomerania to Szczecin and built a large Renaissance castle in the place of the previous modest residence. The obstacles placed in the way of shipping on the rivers Odra and Warta by the Brandenburgers slowed down the growth of Szczecin and at the turn of the 16th century the Baltic ports, particularly Gdańsk, had got ahead of Szczecin, which at that time had a population of 18,000. The Thirty Years' War brought great damage and losses to Szczecin. In 1630, the town was occupied by the Swedes. The year 1637 brought the death of the last of the Pomeranian princes, Bogusław XIV. By virtue of the Peace of Westphalia in 1648 Szczecin together with the mouth of the Odra remained with Sweden.

As a result of the Northern War, which brought further damage and losses to the town, Szczecin came under Prussian rule. The population at that time was only 10,000.

Linked up with the rest of Pomerania, Szczecin became the capital of the Pomeranian province and the Szczecin regency. Maritime trade developed again and the first manufactures were opened in the town. At the turn of the 18th century, numerous historical buildings from the time of the independent Duchy of Pomerania were either pulled down or remodelled.

The second half of the 19th century saw a great development of Szczecin. The town still only had 21,000 inhabitants in 1816; in 1850 it already had a population of 40,000 and by 1914 the figure had jumped to 250,000. Trade and shipping flourished and the port was enlarged. At the beginning of the 20th century Szczecin was the biggest port on the Baltic handling 6.2 million tons of cargo annually.

At the same time, the town was undergoing development. To the west of the Old Town a new central district grew up. The war and then the Great Depression of the years 1929–1932 brought a slump and many of the industrial establishments and shipping lines were closed down. During the Second World War, Szczecin was bombed several times when the Allies made their massive air raids. About half of the buildings of the town were destroyed, the heaviest losses being in the central district with the Old Town quarter, and also in the port and the industrial plants near it. The reconstruction and modernization of the port was started in 1946; since then the amount of cargo handled has been growing quickly. In 1950 the port was already handling 5 million tons and by 1977 the figure had risen to 16.5 million tons (not counting Świnoujście).

Szczecin handles cargo in transit from the German Democratic Republic, Czechoslovakia and Hungary. The shipyards have been rebuilt and enlarged (93) and at Police, by the Szczecin Lagoon, a huge chemical plant has been built.

Szczecin has become an important centre of science and culture with higher schools, scientific institutes, museums, archives, its own philharmonia, theatres and libraries.

Rebuilt from ruins, the town is still developing. High on the Wały Chrobrego (The Rampart of Bolesław the Brave) looking over the River Odra, are the magnificent buildings of the Voivodship People's Council and the Maritime Museum, as well as the Maritime Station. In the Gothic-Renaissance castle of the Pomeranian Princes, rebuilt and partly reconstructed (95) there are now museums, theatres and other cultural institutions. Near the castle is the 12th century Tower of the Seven Coats (95) which has been preserved.

The central district, with its characteristic star-plan layout of squares and streets (94), has also been reconstructed. Today, Szczecin has a population of 380,000.

The Szczecin Lagoon is what has remained of a sea bay that once occupied a much larger area. Today the area of the Lagoon is 968 sq.km., of which 479 sq.km. are within Poland's frontiers. It is shallow (5 – 7 m.) (97). The Szczecin Lagoon is linked with the sea by three straits called Piana (which is in the GDR), Dziwna and Świna. They were once much wider than today, but have been narrowed by the formation of sand bars. These processes were intensified by the islands of Wolin and Uznam situated between the Lagoon and the Baltic, which consist of a higher part built of moraine clays and a lower part built of sand carried there by the waves and wind. A large part of the Island of Wolin is covered with luxuriant beech forests. Wolin is also a haven for rare species of birds, of which mention is due to the white eagle (Haliaetus albicilla) (98). A National Park has been set up on the island.

In the 9th century, both islands were the territory of the tribe of Wolinians, whose main centre was the stronghold of Wolin. The settlements that grew up round it were known in the 10th century as a thriving trade centre and merchants' "republic". Wolin had extensive trade contacts with the Scandinavian countries, north Germany, Prussian Sambia and Russian Novogrod. It was ruined several times in the 11th and 12th centuries by the Danes. Although it was granted municipal status in 1278 by Prince Barnim I, the town did not develop.

98

99

Świnoujście on the island of Uznam was already known in the 12th century, but it did not develop until the 17th century when work was started on the construction of a port there. It was granted municipal status in 1765. After 1825, the town became a health resort. In the inter-war years it was renowned for its tourist attractions as a seaside health resort. In 1948, work was started on the construction of a large base for fishing vessels going to distant fishing grounds, with fish processing plants on the spot. In the Sixties the Świnoujście port was enlarged to service big ships that cannot enter Szczecin because of the shallow waters of the Lagoon. In 1977, 8.2 million tons of cargo were handled here, mostly bulk cargo. Świnoujście does not neglect its functions as a holiday and health resort. There is a tourists' ferry service from Świnoujście to Sweden and also the recently started service to England (99).

Index
of Geographical Names

Compiled by Izabela Chabowska

The index gives the names of contemporary geographical units and of important geographical-historical units that are wholly or partly within the frontiers of present-day Poland. The index also gives the names of reserves and national parks. The following abbreviations have been used in the index:

Str. – straits
Mt. Mts. – mount, mountains
Cv. – cave
L. – lake
Pen. – peninsula
P. – pass
C. – cape
Res. – reserve
Riv. – river
Is. – island
Wf. – waterfall

Index
of Photographers

Contents